SURFS UP

http://www.cengagesurfsup.co.nz

T0358032

SEARCH

SURFS UP

HOME   PRODUCT   SHOP   CONTACT US

NEW PIHA SURFBOARD

NCEA
Accounting
A BEGINNING
LEVEL ONE

Lilian Viitakangas with **Alastair Campbell**

NELSON
CENGAGE Learning™

Australia • Brazil • Japan • Korea • Mexico • Singapore • Spain • United Kingdom • United States

NELSON
CENGAGE Learning

NCEA Accounting – A Beginning
Level 1 Student Book
3rd Edition
Lilian Viitakangas
Alistair Campbell

Cover design: Cheryl Rowe
Illustrations: Brenda Cantell
Production controller: Jess Lovell

Any URLs contained in this publication were checked for currency during the production process. Note, however, that the publisher cannot vouch for the ongoing currency of URLs.

First edition published 1995.
Second edition published 1998.

For product information and technology assistance,
in Australia call **1300 790 853;**
in New Zealand call **0508 635 766**

For permission to use material from this text or product,
please email **aust.permissions@cengage.com**

National Library of New Zealand Cataloguing-in-Publication Data
Viitakangas, Lilian
NCEA accounting, a beginning. Level One / Lilian Viitakangas, Alastair Campbell. NCEA ed.

Includes index.
ISBN 97801702110551.
Accounting. I. Campbell, Alastair (Alastair Scott)
II. Title.

657.044—2 22

Cengage Learning Australia
Level 7, 80 Dorcas Street
South Melbourne, Victoria Australia 3205

Cengage Learning New Zealand
Unit 4B
331 Rosedale Road, Albany, North Shore 0632, NZ

For learning solutions, visit cengage.com.au

Printed in Australia by Ligare.
4 5 6 7 8 19

Table of Contents

ISBN: 9780170211055

Preface

NCEA Accounting – a Beginning – Level 1 is a series of texts that has been specifically written for the 2011 NCEA prescription. As far as possible the material has been organised according to the individual achievement standards. Within the confines of the assessment structure, the thematic approach of previous editions of the text has been maintained. A case study basis continues to be used and a decision-making emphasis is maintained where appropriate.

The textbook covers all of the material for the externally assessed Achievement Standards 1.1 *Demonstrate Understanding of Accounting Concepts for Small Entities*, 1.3 *Prepare Financial Information for Sole Proprietors* and 1.5 *Interpret Accounting Information for Sole Proprietors*, together with the internally assessed Achievement Standard 1.2 *Process Financial Transactions for a Small Entity*.

Terminology and statement formats in this text are taken directly from *New Zealand Equivalents to International Accounting Standards* issued by the *Institute of Chartered Accountants of New Zealand.* Where possible and appropriate, definitions have been simplified to make them more suitable for Level 1 study. However, where such simplification would result in inaccuracies, the formal wording has been used.

The textbook is accompanied by a student workbook which contains all the questions and space in which to answer them. Solutions are provided in the *Teachers' Guide*. This is an overprinted version of the student workbook which provides a quick reference for teachers. An electronic copy of the *Teachers' Guide* is included for use as visual media.

Acknowledgements

The authors and publishers gratefully acknowledge the assistance of the following people in the preparation of this new edition:

Graham McEwan for editing yet another volume and the photographs on page 13;

King's Plant Barn for permission to use photographs of their operation on page 13;

Wiremu and Tuaine Jenkins for meals, lawnmowing and other neighbourly gestures.

The principal author also wishes to acknowledge the generous assistance of co-author Alastair Campbell without whose participation this project would not have been completed.

Dedication

In memory of my most dearly loved mother, June Olive Price, who unfailingly supported and encouraged my writing activities for 17 years.

ISBN: 9780170211055

Introduction to Accounting

- **What is Accounting?**
- **Who uses Financial Information?**
- **The Accounting Entity**
- **Assets, Liabilities and Equity**

Welcome to the world of business decision making! Accounting is the language of business. All of us come into contact with business organisations in many different aspects of daily life. We need to understand business language to live in modern society.

There are many different types of organisations. All of these prepare financial statements to report the results of their activities. Organisations include businesses, clubs and societies and government departments.

In this course you will learn how business organisations prepare and report accounting information. You will also learn to use this information to make decisions about business.

What is Accounting?

In 1966 the American Accounting Association defined accounting as follows:

Accounting is...

the process of identifying, measuring and communicating economic information to permit informed judgements and decisions by the users of the information.

In summary:

- the accountant prepares the economic information in a form that users can understand
- the user makes decisions based on the information.

Economic information is often called **financial** information. Accountants prepare this information. Users make decisions based on both *financial* and *non-financial* information.

Financial information is prepared for both *internal* and *external* users. Internal users include the owner/s and management of the organisation. External users include organisations such as banks, the Inland Revenue Department, potential investors in the business and other interested parties.

The role of the accountant is to present financial information to users so that these people can use the information in making business decisions. The accountant has a responsibility to prepare this information so that it is *understandable*. It must conform with **generally accepted accounting practice**, which means that it is prepared according to the standards prescribed by the New Zealand Institute of Chartered Accountants.

> **Remember!**
>
> The purpose of accounting is to enable *users* to make *business decisions*.

ACCOUNTANT	→	Financial Information	→	USER

Accountants communicate financial information. In order to produce this financial information, an accountant must answer the following questions:

What information do I need?	→	**Identify**
Where does this information belong?	→	**Process**
How can I present this information?	→	**Summarise and Report**
What does this information show?	→	**Analyse**
What do these trends mean?	→	**Interpret**

The information prepared by an accountant is in the form of financial statements which show how the business has performed during the year and its financial position at the end of the year. The accountant will also assist the client by analysing the financial statements and interpreting the results so that he or she can provide the business owner with advice.

Who Uses Financial Information?

You Do! Individuals use financial information to make everyday decisions, such as:

- How much do I need to set aside from my income to meet my expenses?
- How much must I save per week to meet my goals?
- Can I afford to buy a stereo?
- How long will it take me to save the deposit for a car?
- Can I afford to borrow to buy a car?

Managing personal finances requires financial information and a plan of income and expenditure. This plan is a called a **budget**.

Families make important decisions such as:

- Do we buy or rent a house?
- Do we borrow money and buy an expensive car, or pay cash for a cheaper one?

Members of your family who work for employers receive wage slips and tax forms. These are forms of financial information produced by the employers' accounting systems.

Households receive bills for services such as telephone and electricity. These bills are **invoices** or **statements** produced by the supplier's accounting system. Many families use credit cards and need to understand financial information to check transactions on the credit card statements.

When individuals operate a cheque account, the bank's accounting system will produce a **bank statement** which shows all the cheques, deposits and other transactions that have occurred. This statement can be compared against the cheque records, deposit records and EFTPOS receipts and used to prepare a bank reconciliation statement and calculate the actual bank balance.

Families and Households Do!

Employees of businesses are interested in knowing how well a business has performed for several reasons:

- The employee may take pride in belonging to a particular firm and want to find out how successful the efforts of the team of employees have been.
- Employees are concerned about their level of wages or salaries. If a business earns a large profit, employees may bring pressure on management to increase their wages or salaries.
- Employees are concerned about the security of their employment. If a business is successful, they will have more confidence that their jobs are secure than if a business is performing badly.

Employees Do!

Business Managers Do!

People who run a business need to know how well their business is progressing. Decisions they may make include, for example:

- Can the business afford to buy new equipment?
- How should we finance a new building?
- Can we afford to hire more staff?

To make these decisions, business managers need to know how profitable the business is and whether profits are improving or not. They need to know the cash position of the business and how much it owes to lenders. This information is found in the **financial statements**.

Businesses often prepare budgets, which are financial plans for the future. When the financial reports are prepared, the actual results can be compared with the budget to see how well the business has performed. These reports help managers to answer such questions as:

- How well did we do?
- Where did we go wrong?
- How can we improve?

Lenders Do!

Before lending money or selling goods on credit, businesses want to make sure that they will receive any amounts owed to them. For example:

- Banks and other lending institutions want to make sure that their money will be repaid. A business applying for a loan will be required to provide financial statements with its application.
- Suppliers selling goods on credit need to be sure that their accounts will be paid.

Financial information assists lending decisions because the financial statements show the *liquidity* (ability to repay short-term debts), *financial stability* and *cash flow* of a business.

ISBN: 9780170211055

Some people invest in businesses which are run by others. The most common way to invest in a business is to buy shares in companies that are listed on the stock exchange. Investors are interested in answering questions such as:

- How well has the company performed during the year?
- What level of dividend is the company paying?
- Is the company in a sound financial position?
- What is the return on my investment?

These questions can be answered by examining the financial statements of the company.

Investors also need to decide whether to keep their shares or to sell them. New investors want to decide which company would be the most profitable investment for them. They may be looking for a company which will return regular dividend income, or for a company which will produce a capital gain when the shares are sold later.

Investors Do!

Clubs and societies must prepare financial reports which show members the results of the year's activities, including where their money has been spent. Decisions made by clubs include:

- What level of subscriptions will be required next year?
- Should we hold fundraising activities again next year?

Clubs and Societies Do!

The Inland Revenue Department has the task of collecting taxes such as Income Tax, Fringe Benefit Tax and Goods and Services Tax. These taxes are calculated on the basis of financial information.

Inland Revenue Does!

Activities

1 Listed below are some decisions that occur in everyday life.

  a Which programme to watch on television
  b What to buy for lunch
  c How to pay for a new skateboard
  d Whether to lend money to a friend
  e What clothes to wear to the movies
  f What to do on Saturday afternoon.

DO THIS! State whether each of the decisions **a – f** above requires *financial* or *non-financial* information. (Some decisions may require both.)

2 Imagine yourself in each of the following situations.

  a Your friend asks you for a loan of $50 to buy an MP3 player.
  b You want to buy a gaming console on hire purchase. You have $100 deposit and the gaming console costs $599.
  c You are a bank manager. Your neighbour approaches you for a mortgage on her house.
  d You are the manager of a toy factory. You are considering making a new product.
  e Your grandfather has left you $50,000 in his will. You are considering buying a small business.
  f You own a computer store. A new model of computer has been released and you have a lot of the old model left in stock. Another firm has offered to buy all of your old stock at a reduced price.

DO THIS!
  a List the *financial* information you would need before you could make a decision in each of **a – f** above.
  b List one piece of *non-financial* information that would be relevant to each decision.

3 Your business has been saving money for some time and you have decided to buy new equipment. You have approached your bank manager and have an interview next week. The manager has told you to be sure to bring all relevant financial information with you to the interview.

DO THIS!
  a List the information about the equipment purchase that the bank manager would require.
  b State any other *financial* information that you think he will require before he approves the loan.

4 You own a factory which manufactures chips for computerised toys. A company which has been in the toy business for some years has decided to start producing computerised toys and has requested that you supply a large order of chips on credit.

DO THIS!
  a Explain how the *financial* information prepared by this company would help you in making your decision.
  b Identify any *non-financial* information that you would collect before you make your final decision.

Accounting – A Beginning

ISBN: 9780170211055

The Accounting Entity

As we can see from the cartoon above, Brad has started his own business and must now keep accounting records. The first important thing he must learn is to keep his business records separate from his personal records. This idea is known as the accounting entity and can be expressed as:

Accounting entity

The economic affairs of the business are separate and distinct from the affairs of the owner.

The notion of the accounting entity is fundamental to the presentation of accounting information. If we wish to measure the progress and financial position of a business, we must keep the business affairs quite separate from the affairs of the owner. If personal and business affairs are mixed together, incorrect decisions are likely to be made.

If a person owns more than one business the affairs of each business should also be kept separately. This means that each business will have separate financial statements. If we didn't do this, it would be impossible to tell how profitable each individual operation was and to evaluate its financial position.

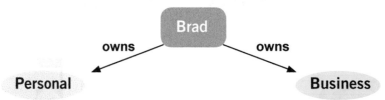

Assets, Liabilities and Equity

Before we can begin learning about the accounting process itself, we must first learn the language of accounting. Accounting has a language all of its own. Some words that we use in everyday life have a special meaning when they are used in an accounting context.

The first terms we will meet are known as **financial elements**. There are five elements:

- Assets
- Liabilities
- Equity
- Income
- Expenses.

In this section we will also meet two more accounting concepts that are used in the preparation of financial statements:

- Monetary measurement
- Historical cost.

Assets

Assets are resources that the business uses in its operations. A full definition of an asset is:

DEFINITION

Asset

An asset is a resource controlled by the entity as a result of past events and from which future economic benefits are expected to flow to the entity.

Examine the photographs opposite of a garden centre:

Some assets which can be seen in the photographs are:

- land
- building
- checkout counters
- computers
- shed
- forklift
- trailer
- pallets
- display racks
- wheelbarrow
- tubs
- shopping cart
- plant trays
- signs
- packaging
- wheelie bin
- inventory (plants, pots, garden mixes for sale).

The business will also have other assets which we cannot see by examining the photographs. Possible additional assets for a garden centre are:

- Cash in the bank
- Accounts receivable (amounts owing by trade customers for goods purchased).

These assets are all resources that will provide future economic benefits to the garden centre. The land and building provide future economic benefits because they house the inventory that is sold to produce cash. Assets such as the forklift and wheelbarrow enable the business to organise and store inventory and display racks enable customers to see what is available. All of the assets are used for the purpose of providing inventory for sale. Accounts receivable provide future economic benefits because they will eventually be turned into cash.

CHECKLIST!

To be classified as a business asset, an item MUST:

- be of *future* economic benefit to the business

  AND

- be under the *present* control of the business

  AND

- arise from a *past* transaction or other event.

To qualify as a business asset, an item must have **all** of these characteristics.

ISBN: 9780170211055

Examples:

1 The **forklift** is an asset because:

- It has *future economic benefit* in that the garden centre uses it to move inventory around so that it can be displayed for sale. Sales will result in economic benefits in the form of cash inflows.
- It is under the *present control* of the garden centre (the owners can stop others from using it).
- It arises from a *past transaction* because the garden centre has bought the forklift.

2 **Accounts receivable** is an asset because:

- It has *future economic benefit* because the garden centre will eventually receive the cash from the customers who owe it.
- It is under the *present control* of the garden centre because no-one else is entitled to receive the cash from these customers.
- It arises from a *past transaction* because the garden centre has already provided the goods and sent out invoices to the customers.

Measuring Assets – Monetary Measurement and Historical Cost

For information about business assets to be meaningful for financial decision-making, it needs to be presented in financial terms. We therefore need:

- a unit of measurement; and
- a time when the asset is measured.

Consider the following example:

Two farmers have the following assets:

Farmer McDonald			Farmer Dagg	
10	hectares land		20	hectares land
50	sheep		40	cows
100	apple trees		1	shed
1	dog		1	house
1	truck		1	horse
1	house		1	tractor
163	???		64	???

Farmer McDonald and Farmer Dagg are having an argument over who has the most assets. Farmer McDonald has 163 assets. She maintains that she is worth far more than Farmer Dagg who, after all, has only 64 assets. How do we decide?

To answer this question we need to measure all the assets using a common unit. This common unit of measure could be chickens. We could calculate how many chickens were equivalent to one cow and how many chickens were equivalent to one hectare of land etc.

The simplest means of comparing the assets of these two farmers involves converting all their assets into dollars. On the face of it, it would seem that Farmer Dagg has, in fact, got the most assets. This is because his assets probably have a higher dollar value than the assets of Farmer McDonald. He has twice as much land which is the most valuable of the assets and he has 40 cows as opposed to 50 sheep. Measured in dollars, one cow is worth several times the amount of one sheep.

Accounting – A Beginning   ISBN: 9780170211055

In accounting, we use the dollar as our unit of measure. We call this principle **monetary measurement**:

DEFINITION

Monetary measurement

All transactions are measured in dollars. The dollar is the common unit of measure.

The next decision we must make is when we measure the assets. Should we use the dollar value when they were purchased or the current market value? In the example above, where we are trying to compare two farmers' assets, it would make sense to use the current value for each of the assets. However, these values can be difficult to determine and are not reliable because they can change from day to day. We would therefore not use these values if we were preparing financial statements for the two farms.

The most reliable measure is to use the **historical cost** of the asset:

DEFINITION

Historical cost

Assets are recorded at the amount of cash paid (or payable) at the time of their acquisition.

In the financial statements, we will also recognise the fact that the future economic benefit of some assets reduces as time goes by. For example, a new truck has a greater future economic benefit than an old one. The idea that assets lose future economic benefit as they are used and become older is called **depreciation**. We will discuss this concept later.

I'm having a problem with this historical cost idea, Aroha. It seems a bit strange to me.

Why? It's easy enough.

Yes, but see that van I bought for the business? I paid $30,000 for it.

I know, that's what the financial statements will show.

Yes, but I got it cheap. I saw one like it for $35,000 the other day. I should show mine at $35,000 as well.

But you paid $30,000, so that's its value to your business.

Don't understand.

By using the amount you paid for the van, we are showing its true historical cost. We can't be sure it's worth $35,000 unless you sell it.

But we could get it valued.

Yes, we could. But, Brad, this is getting very complicated. Historical cost can be verified - we know the value is true because that's what we paid. There are some circumstances when other values can be used, but there are all sorts of rules... I don't really want to go into all that now.

Well what about this thing called depreciation then? How do we work that out?

We base it on the historical cost of the asset. We work out how long you expect it to last, what you think you will get when you sell it, that sort of thing.

Well now I am really confused. How can the depreciation be right if we aren't using the real value of the van?

Depreciation is only an estimate anyway. And I have already told you – the cost of the van to your business is what matters. The historical cost.

OK.OK. Maybe we can look at all this again some other time.

Good idea!

Accounting – A Beginning

ISBN: 9780170211055

Activities

1 A student has made a list of various assets for different types of organisations. The list consists of items **a – j** below.

  a The land of a farmer
  b The inventory of a supermarket
  c The members of a senior citizens club
  d The furniture of a coffee lounge
  e The manager of a factory
  f The books of a public library
  g A truck which has been hired by a garden centre
  h The customers of a dairy
  i The computer of an accountant
  j A machine which has been ordered by a factory and will be delivered next week.

DO THIS!

State whether each of the items **a – j** above is an asset of the organisation concerned. If it is **not** an asset, state why not in terms of the characteristics of assets.

2 You have received an email from a friend whose business owns a large building. He says:

"I've just got my accounts from the accountant. I can't understand why he has shown the building at $100,000. That's what I paid for it. It's worth at least $250,000 now. I am sure these accounts are wrong."

DO THIS!

a Name the accounting concept that has been applied by the accountant.
b Explain why the building is not shown at $250,000 in the financial statements.

3 *Holiday Homes* rents a building for $2,000 per month from *Property Investments Limited*. The building had cost $300,000 and its current market value is $450,000.

DO THIS!

a State which firm will show the building as an asset in its financial statements. Fully explain your choice.
b State the amount that will be shown for the building in the financial statements and justify your answer.

4 *Takapuna Traders* has inventory on hand which cost $30,000 and will sell for $45,000. The manager of *Takapuna Traders* is not sure which figure he should give to the accountant for inclusion in the financial statements.

DO THIS!

Advise the manager which figure is correct and explain why.

ISBN: 9780170211055

Liabilities

Liabilities are amounts owed by a business. This means that, because of some transaction which has taken place in the past, a business has an obligation to either pay money or provide some goods or services in the future. The most common types of liabilities are accounts payable for goods that have been purchased previously, or services such as repairs that have been performed for the business, for which payment has not yet been made. A definition of a liability is:

Liability

A liability is a present obligation of the entity arising from past events, the settlement of which is expected to result in an outflow from the entity of resources embodying economic benefits.

Many businesses will also have bank loans or mortgages which have been taken out to buy land and buildings. Sometimes assets such as trucks may be purchased on hire purchase and the amounts owing for these are also liabilities.

The garden centre we examined in the previous section is likely to have some accounts payable and possibly a mortgage over the land.

CHECKLIST!

To be classified as a business liability, an item MUST:

- require a *future* outflow of economic resources from the business

  AND

- be a *present* obligation of the business

  AND

- arise from a *past* event.

To qualify as a business liability, an item must have **all** of these characteristics.

Sometimes a business will have an obligation to provide goods or services in the future. This usually occurs because a customer has paid in advance – for example, for a magazine subscription, some tuition, or for rent. In these cases, the amount of the liability is the cash received in advance.

Examples:

1 **Accounts payable** is a liability because:
   - The business will have a *future outflow of economic resources* when it uses cash to pay the accounts.
   - The business has a *present obligation* to pay the debt.
   - The obligation arises from a *past transaction* because the business has already received the goods or services.

ISBN: 9780170211055

2 A mortgage is a liability because:

- The business will make a future economic sacrifice when it uses cash to repay the mortgage.
- The business has a present obligation to pay the debt.
- The obligation arises from a past transaction when the business borrowed the money to buy land and buildings.

Measuring Liabilities

Liabilities are measured in the number of dollars that will be required to be paid to satisfy them. For example, if a business receives a power bill for $200, then the amount of the liability is $200.

Equity

The net worth of a business is called **equity**. (This is sometimes called proprietorship because the owner of a business is called the proprietor.) The equity of a business is also known as the business **capital**. The equity of a business equals the assets of the business less its liabilities.

> ### Equity
>
> Equity is the residual interest in the assets of the entity after deducting all its liabilities.

The formula for calculating equity is called the **accounting equation**. It can be written as follows:

$$\text{Equity} = \text{Assets} - \text{Liabilities}$$
$$\text{Eq} = \text{A} - \text{L}$$

We can also write this equation as:

$$\text{Assets} = \text{Liabilities} + \text{Equity}$$
$$\text{A} = \text{L} - \text{Eq}$$

Remember Brad? We met him at the beginning of the chapter when he was talking with Aroha about his new business. Brad runs *Trendy Tourz*, an outdoor adventure business. He has been in business for a short while and has the following business assets and liabilities as at 30 June 2015:

Assets: Cash in the bank $3,500, Accounts receivable $2,000, Outdoor equipment (cost) $18,500, Van (cost) $30,000.

Liabilities: Accounts payable $4,500, Bank loan (due 30 June 2020) $20,000.

Let's calculate the equity of Brad's business. First, we must work out the totals of the assets and liabilities (remember monetary measurement).

Assets		Liabilities	
Cash	$ 3,500	Accounts payable	$ 4,500
Accounts receivable	2,000	Bank loan	20,000
Outdoor equipment (cost)	18,500	(due 30 June 2020)	
Van (cost)	30,000		
Total assets	$54,000	Total liabilities	$24,500

We can now calculate the equity of *Trendy Tourz*:

$$
\begin{aligned}
\text{Eq} &= \text{A} - \text{L} \\
&= \$54,000 - 24,500 \\
&= \$29,500
\end{aligned}
$$

Using the other form of the equation:

$$
\begin{aligned}
\text{A} &= \text{L} + \text{Eq} \\
\$54,000 &= \$24,500 + 29,500
\end{aligned}
$$

This accounting equation forms the basis of the first financial statement we shall meet – the **statement of financial position**. We will look at this statement in the next chapter.

Accounting – A Beginning   ISBN: 9780170211055

Activities

1 A student has made a list of various liabilities for different types of organisations. The list consists of items **a – f** below.

  a A mortgage over the buildings of a factory
  b The wages owing to factory employees for last week
  c The cost of a computer which will be purchased next week
  d The cost of repairs to a truck owned by a courier business, which were done last week but which will be paid for at the end of this month
  e The cost of supplying magazines which have been paid for by subscribers but have not yet been published
  f The rent on a shoe shop for next month which has to be paid at the end of this week.

State whether each of the items **a – f** above is a liability of the organisation concerned. If it is **not** a liability, state why not in terms of the characteristics of liabilities.

2 On 1 October 2017, a business bought a truck that cost $30,000 and paid a deposit of $5,000 cash. The balance of the purchase price was paid on 1 November 2017 from the proceeds of a bank loan.

  a Using the *characteristics of an asset* to help you, explain why the truck is an asset of the business at 1 October.
  b Calculate the liability of the business at 1 October. Explain your answer in terms of the *characteristics of liabilities*.
  c Calculate the liability of the business at 1 November. Explain your answer in terms of the *characteristics of liabilities*.

3 *Takapuna Traders* bought goods (inventory) costing $3,000 on credit from *Shore Supplies* on 1 June 2018. If *Takapuna Traders* pays for the goods before 20 July 2018, a discount of $300 will be allowed. *Takapuna Traders* prepares its financial statements on 30 June each year.

  a Calculate the amount that will be shown for inventory in the financial statements.
  b Name the accounting concept have you applied in your answer to **a** above.
  c Calculate the amount should be shown for accounts payable in the financial statements.
  d Explain your answer to **c** above in terms of *monetary measurement* and the *characteristics of liabilities*.

4 *Bric-a-brac Traders* is a shop that sells second-hand furniture and appliances. You have established the following information at 31 December 2016:

Assets		Liabilities	
Furniture (cost)	$ 5,600	Bank overdraft	$2,500
Appliances (second hand)	10,300	Accounts payable	670
Accounts receivable	565	Hire purchase on shop fittings	
Cash on hand	320	(due 2018)	300
Shop fittings (cost)	900		

DO THIS!

a Calculate the equity of *Bric-a-brac Traders* as at 31 December 2016.
b Explain in terms of an accounting concept why the shop fittings have been shown at $900 when they could now be sold for only $500. You must **name** and **define** the concept in your answer.

5 The following items appear in the business accounts of *Handy Hardware* at 31 March 2018:

Land and buildings (cost)	$150,000	Cash at bank	$12,500
Mortgage on land and		Shop fittings (cost)	6,500
buildings (due 2022)	80,000	Inventory	26,000
Accounts receivable	5,400	Van (cost)	20,000
Accounts payable	3,600		

DO THIS!

a List the assets and liabilities of *Handy Hardware* and calculate the **total assets** and **total liabilities**.
b Define the term *equity*.
c Calculate the equity of *Handy Hardware* as at 31 March 2018.

6 Walter Waiter is a self-employed building consultant trading as *Waiter's Building Consultants*. You have the following information at 31 March 2017:

Assets		Liabilities	
Business car (cost)	$ 22,000	Hire purchase on equipment	
House (cost)	320,000	(due 2019)	$ 15,000
Equipment (cost)	18,500	Mortgage on house (due 2030)	250,000
Boat (cost)	16,500	Wife's VISA card	1,500
Computer (business, cost)	4,500	Bank loan for boat (due 2018)	14,000
Stereo (cost)	1,500	Household telephone bill	120
Freezer (cost)	1,000	Yellow pages advertising invoice	250
Accounts receivable	14,200	Business bank overdraft	1,400

DO THIS!

a Calculate the equity of *Waiter's Building Consultants* as at 31 March 2017.
b Explain, using an example, how you have used *historical cost* in this calculation.
c Explain how you have used the *accounting entity* in this calculation.

Accounting – A Beginning   ISBN: 9780170211055

Applying Accounting Concepts

- **The Statement of Financial Position**
- **Accounting Assumptions**
- **The Income Statement**
- **Capital and Revenue Expenditure**

The Statement of Financial Position

The accounting equation A = L + Eq forms the basis of the first financial statement we shall meet. This is called the **statement of financial position**. It is sometimes called the *balance sheet*. The Statement of Financial Position shows the *financial structure* of the business.

The statement of financial position can be presented in two different formats. We call these the 'T' format and the vertical format. The 'T' format presents the statement in the same form as the accounting equation, A = L + Eq.

In the previous chapter, we learnt that Brad's business, *Trendy Tourz*, had the following assets and liabilities:

Assets		Liabilities	
Cash	$ 3,500	Accounts payable	$ 4,500
Accounts receivable	2,000	Bank loan	20,000
Outdoor equipment (cost)	18,500	(due 30 June 2020)	
Van (cost)	30,000		

We also calculated that the equity of *Trendy Tourz* was $29,500. This information is presented in the 'T' form statement of financial position set out below. The 'T' form statement follows the accounting equation, A = L + Eq.

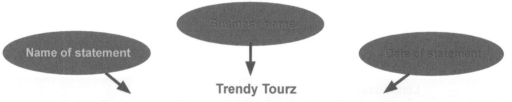

Trendy Tourz
Statement of Financial Position **as at 30 June 2015**

Assets		Liabilities	
Cash	$3,500	Accounts payable	$4,500
Accounts receivable	2,000	Bank loan (due 30 June 2020)	20,000
Outdoor equipment (cost)	18,500		24,500
Van (cost)	30,000	**Equity**	
		Capital	29,500
	$54,000		$54,000

The statement of financial position is shown **as at** a particular date because it is like a photograph of the business at a point in time. As soon as a single transaction takes place, the statement will change. Financial statements are prepared at the close of business on the last day of the **reporting period**.

Important!

- The assets, liabilities and equity are set out in the statement of financial position in exactly the same way as they are in the accounting equation,
A = L + Eq.

- The statement of financial position has a heading. This heading includes:
  - the name of the business, **Trendy Tourz**. This is the name of the accounting entity.
  - the name of the statement, the **Statement of Financial Position**.
  - the date at which the statement was prepared, **30 June 2015**.

The vertical form of the statement of financial position represents the accounting equation in its form Eq = A − L:

Trendy Tourz
Statement of Financial Position as at 30 June 2015

	$	$
ASSETS		
Cash		3,500
Accounts receivable		2,000
Outdoor equipment (cost)		18,500
Van (cost)		30,000
Total assets		$54,000
EQUITY AND LIABILITIES		
Equity		
Capital at end of the month		29,500
Liabilities		
Accounts payable	4,500	
Loan (due 30 June 2020)	20,000	
Total liabilities		24,500
Total equity and liabilities		$54,000

Remember!

The statement of financial position shows the financial *structure* of a business.

Accounting Assumptions

In preparing financial statements, including the statement of financial position above, we have applied two basic accounting assumptions:

- Going concern
- Accrual basis of accounting.

The Going Concern Assumption

When we prepare financial statements, we are assuming that the business will have an indefinite lifetime. This is very important because the way we measure assets and liabilities depends upon the fact that the business will still exist in the future. This means that it will receive economic benefit from its assets and will be required to meet its liabilities. We call this idea the going concern assumption:

Going concern

The entity will continue in existence for the foreseeable future.

If the business assets were going to be sold, then the historical cost of the assets may not be relevant because their market value would be different from this historical cost. In such a case, the going concern assumption would not apply and the financial statements would be prepared differently.

> **Example:**
> The assets of *Trendy Tourz* are shown in the statement of financial position at their historical cost, for example: Van (cost) $30,000. This is the amount that has been paid for the van and represents the future economic benefit that the business will derive from it **if we assume that *Trendy Tourz* will continue to operate**.

Accrual Basis of Accounting

Accounting is concerned with measuring the results of business activities. We must therefore recognise all events relating to the business in each reporting period. Often this means recording transactions that have taken place, but where no cash has changed hands yet. For example, a credit sale is one where the customer buys goods and will pay later when he or she receives an invoice from the business.

When should we record this sale? If we wait until the cash changes hands, then we are not truly representing the activity of the business when the sale was made. Also, it is possible that the cash will be received in the next reporting period.

The idea that transactions are recorded when they occur, which may or may not be at the same time as the cash changes hands, is known as the **accrual basis of accounting**. A more formal definition is:

Accrual basis of accounting

The effects of transactions and other events are recognised when they occur (and not as cash or its equivalent is received or paid) and they are recorded in the accounting records and reported in the financial statements of the periods to which they relate.

ISBN: 9780170211055

This means that transactions must be recorded in the periods that they occur and be shown in the financial statements of those periods. For example, the account receivable generated by a credit sale will be shown as an asset in the statement of financial position even though the business has not yet received the cash.

Period Reporting

Users of financial statements need information on a regular basis. The definition of the accrual basis refers to *reporting periods*. The going concern assumption is not very helpful when it comes to monitoring the results of business activities and making decisions about the financial structure of the business.

Both of the accounting assumptions we have used in preparing the financial statements depend upon the idea that we need to divide the lifetime of a business into periods of time if we want to measure its progress. If we want to compare the performance between periods, then those periods should be of equal length. The headings of financial statements provide users with information as to the dates of those statements and the length of the reporting period.

> **Example:**
> The statement of financial position of *Trendy Tourz* reports two examples of accrual accounting:
>
> - **Accounts receivable** recognises that the business has an asset, because it has made credit sales that have been recorded even though no cash has been received.
>
> - **Accounts payable** recognises that the business has a liability, because it has received goods or services but has not paid for them yet.

More examples:

1 Sometimes a business has a liability at the end of the reporting period for which there have been no entries in the accounting records. For example, it has used a certain amount of electricity but the power bill has not been received, or there may be wages owing to staff since they were last paid. These liabilities are known as **accrued expenses**. Another situation arises when income is received before the goods or services have been provided. A magazine publisher is a good example of this situation. Subscriptions have been received in cash, but the magazines will be published monthly over the course of the subscription period. This is known as **income received in advance.** Both accrued expenses and income received in advance are reported in the statement of financial position.

2 A business may also have assets that are unrecorded at the end of the reporting period. For example, it may have paid rent in advance and not yet have received the economic benefit from it. This is called a **prepayment**. Another example is when interest is due on a term deposit but has not been received. We call this **accrued income**. Both prepayments and accrued income are assets which are reported in the statement of financial position.

Activities

1 The following items have been taken from the statement of financial position of *Blue Tornado Cleaners* prepared at 30 June 2015:

Equipment (cost)	$8,500	Van (cost)	$25,000
Bank loan (due 2020)	5,000	Accounts payable	2,300
Accounts receivable	1,800	Hire purchase on van (due 2017)	10,000
Bank overdraft	1,300	Cleaning supplies	800

DO THIS!

a Prepare this statement of financial position in vertical format.

b Using an example from your statement of financial position, explain how you have applied *monetary measurement*.

c Using an example from your statement of financial position, explain how you have applied *historical cost*.

d Using an example from your statement of financial position, explain how you have applied the *accrual basis of accounting*.

2 Examine the following statement of financial position for *Pete's Panelbeaters*:

Pete's Panelbeaters			
Statement of Financial Position as at 31 March 2017			
Assets		**Liabilities**	
Tools (cost)	$ 5,600	Bank overdraft	$10,000
Van (cost)	11,400	Accounts payable	13,000
Accounts receivable	23,000	Hire purchase on van (due 2022)	2,000
Premises (cost)	160,000	Mortgage on premises (due 2029)	130,000
			155,000
		Equity	
		Capital	45,000
	$200,000		$200,000

DO THIS!

a Prepare this statement of financial position in vertical format.

b Answer the following questions which Pete has asked:

  i How can I improve the cash position of the business?

  ii Why is my house, worth $250,000, not shown in this statement of financial position? After all, I bought it from my profits and it would make things look a lot better.

c Describe **two** ways in which the *going concern assumption* has been applied in this statement of financial position.

d Describe **two** examples of how the *accrual basis of accounting* has been applied in this statement of financial position.

3 The statement of financial position of *Eco Builders* showed the following items:

- Under the heading *Assets* was the entry *'Prepayments, $500'*
- Under the heading *Liabilities* was the entry *'Accrued expenses, $300'*.

You have found that the prepayment was for rent that had paid for three months in advance at the end of the reporting period. The accrued expenses were wages owing to staff that had not been paid at the end of the reporting period.

a Explain how the *prepayment* meets the following characteristics of an asset:
  i past transaction or other event
  ii present control
  iii future economic benefit.
b Explain how the *accrual basis of accounting* has been applied when the prepayment was reported in the statement of financial position.
c Explain how the *accrued expenses* meets the following characteristics of a liability:
  i past transaction or other event
  ii present obligation
  iii future outflow of assets.
d Explain how the *accrual basis of accounting* has been applied when the accrued expenses were reported in the statement of financial position.

4 Jenny Johnson runs a small secretarial business from home, trading as *Jet Jenny*. She has prepared her own business statement of financial position as at 31 March 2018 and has brought it to you for checking.

Jenny's statement of financial position showed total assets of $250,000 and only one liability, which was a bank loan of $5,000. When you examined the statement of financial position you found the following errors:

- Jenny has included her house which cost $220,000 in the statement of financial position of the business.
- At the end of the reporting period, accounts owing by customers were $900 and the business had accounts payable of $400. Jenny had not included these in her statement of financial position.
- When Jenny valued the office equipment, she chose the value that she would receive if she sold it through an advertisement in the paper. This value was $2,000 but the equipment had cost $5,000.
- Jenny's father had lent her $10,000 to start the business and he told Jenny that he would not want the money back for five years. Jenny has recorded this under Capital in the statement of financial position of the business.

a For each of the errors above:
  i identify the accounting concept which has been violated; and
  ii clearly explain the correct accounting treatment and why it is correct.
b Calculate the amount of:
  i total assets
  ii total liabilities
  iii equity

that would appear in the statement of financial position as at 31 March 2018.

ISBN: 9780170211055

Classifying the Statement of Financial Position

The statement of financial position shows the assets, liabilities and equity of the business. Assets and liabilities are further subdivided to enable users of the financial statements to understand them more easily.

Assets

Assets can be classified into two groups: **current assets** and **non-current assets**. Non-current assets are further subdivided into **investment assets**, **property, plant and equipment** and **intangible assets** as in the diagram below.

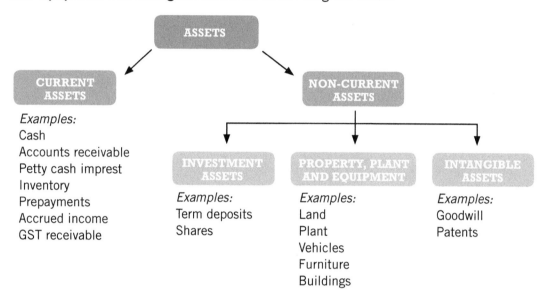

Current assets	Assets that are held for trading or that we expect will turn into cash, or be used up, within the next reporting period. These assets include cash at bank, accounts receivable, stock of goods for resale (inventory), supplies such as cleaning materials and petty cash (small amounts of cash kept on hand to pay expenses).
Non-current assets	Any assets that are not current assets. These assets are expected to be retained in the business beyond the end of the next reporting period. They may be further divided into:
Investment assets	Assets such as term deposits or shares in companies which are expected to be kept in the business for more than one reporting period. These are normally more easily converted into cash than property, plant and equipment (see below).
Property, plant and equipment	Assets which we expect to retain in the business so that it can operate in the future. Property, plant and equipment includes land, buildings, equipment, shop fittings and motor vehicles.
Intangible assets	Assets which are 'untouchable'. One example of an intangible asset is **goodwill**.
	Other examples of intangible assets are copyrights and trademarks. Both of these represent a 'right' but have no physical presence.

Liabilities

Liabilities in the statement of financial position can be classified into two types:
current liabilities and **non-current liabilities**.

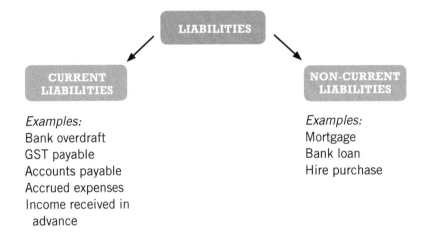

LIABILITIES

CURRENT LIABILITIES

Examples:
Bank overdraft
GST payable
Accounts payable
Accrued expenses
Income received in
    advance

NON-CURRENT LIABILITIES

Examples:
Mortgage
Bank loan
Hire purchase

Current liabilities	Liabilities which we expect will be paid within the next reporting period. It is usually necessary for us to have cash to meet these liabilities. Examples are a bank overdraft, GST payable and accounts payable.
Non-current liabilities	Liabilities that are not current liabilities. These will be paid over a period of time beyond the next reporting period or twelve-month business cycle. They include mortgages, hire purchase payments and long term loans.

A statement of financial position which has assets and liabilities classified under these headings is much more useful for decision-making than one which does not. Separating current assets from other types of assets and current liabilities from other types of liabilities enables us to have some idea of the firm's cash flow or liquidity over the next reporting period. The statement of financial position for *Trendy Tourz* as at 30 June 2015 is reproduced opposite, showing separate classifications for different types of assets and liabilities.

Purpose of the Statement of Financial Position

The statement of financial position is used to show the **financial structure** of the business. It provides users with information about an entity's assets, liabilities and equity that can be used to predict future cash inflows and outflows. In this course, the statement of financial position also provides information about transactions with the owner in the form of contributions and/or drawings. Users can assess:

- the entity's ability to generate cash or provide services in the future
- future borrowing needs of the entity
- the entity's ability to pay drawings to the owner.

There are **two** aspects to financial structure:

- **Liquidity** – the ability of a business to meet its debts in the next reporting period; and

- **Solvency** – the ability of a business to continue operating in the long term.

ISBN: 9780170211055

Trendy Tourz
Statement of Financial Position as at 30 June 2015

	$	$	$
ASSETS			
Non-current assets			
Property, plant and equipment			
Total carrying amount (Note 1)			48,500
Current assets			
Cash		3,500	
Accounts receivable		2,000	
Total current assets			5,500
Total assets			$54,000
EQUITY AND LIABILITIES			
Equity			
Capital at end of the month			29,500
Non-current liabilities			
Loan (due 30 June 2020)		20,000	
Current liabilities			
Accounts payable		4,500	
Total liabilities			24,500
Total equity and liabilities			$54,000

Notes to the statement of financial position

		$
1	*Property, plant and equipment*	
	Outdoor equipment (cost)	18,500
	Van (cost)	30,000
		$48,500

Important!

- Assets are shown at the top, beginning with **non-current** assets.

- A single figure is shown for *property, plant and equipment*. Details of the individual items are shown in a separate note at the bottom of the statement.

- **Current** assets are shown below non-current assets. Since there is more than one current asset, individual balances are shown on an inner column and the total is shown in the outside column. The totals for non-current and current assets are then added to give a figure for **total assets**.

- The equity section is shown next. At this stage it shows only the closing capital.

- Liabilities, separated into **non-current** and **current** liabilities, are shown next. There is only one of each type so no sub-totals are required. The two liabilities are added to give a figure for **total liabilities**.

- Total liabilities are added to equity to give the total for **equity and liabilities**. This is the same as the total assets, following the accounting equation in the form A = Eq + L.

ISBN: 9780170211055

Measuring Liquidity

The statement of financial position for *Trendy Tourz* shows current liabilities deducted from current assets to produce a result called working capital. This calculation illustrates the formula:

$$\text{Working capital} = \text{Current assets} - \text{Current liabilities}$$

The working capital for *Trendy Tourz* is calculated as:

$$\text{Working capital} \quad = \quad \$5,500 - 4,500$$
$$\$1,000$$

The working capital is the measure of the amount of current assets that should be left over after liabilities have been paid in the next reporting period. *Trendy Tourz* should have $1,000 of current assets.

Another measure of the liquidity of a business is given by the current ratio. This ratio measures the relationship between the current assets and the current liabilities in a different way. It is given by the formula:

$$\text{Current ratio} \quad = \quad \frac{\text{Current assets}}{\text{Current liabilities}}$$

We can calculate the current ratio for *Trendy Tourz* as follows:

$$\text{Current ratio} \quad = \quad \frac{\$5,500}{\$4,500}$$
$$= \quad 1.22:1$$

This ratio means that for every $1 of current liabilities, *Trendy Tourz* has $1.22 in assets with which to pay it. Another way of looking at this is to say that the firm has 1.22 times as many current assets as it has current liabilities. Thus the business will not have any problems meeting its debts in the next reporting period, as long *as the accounts receivable pay their debts on time*.

Measuring Solvency

Solvency means that the business will continue to operate in the long term. To be solvent, a business must be able to meet its long term debts.

One way of deciding whether or not a business is solvent is to compare the amount of debt (liabilities) that a business has with the owner's equity. If there is a high proportion of debt, then the business may be at risk of becoming insolvent.

The ratio we use to measure solvency is the equity ratio. It is given by the formula:

$$\text{Equity ratio} \quad = \quad \frac{\text{Equity}}{\text{Total assets}}$$

For *Trendy Tourz*,

$$\text{Equity ratio} \quad = \quad \frac{\$29,500}{\$54,000}$$
$$= \quad 0.55:1$$

ISBN: 9780170211055

A ratio of 0.55:1 means that for every one dollar of business assets Brad has contributed 55 cents. The other 45 cents in the dollar is financed by outsiders or the creditors of the business. This is a reasonably secure position for Brad. Since he has a 55% interest in the business assets, the creditors are unlikely to bring pressure for immediate payment of the amounts owing to them. Thus Brad should not be in the position of having to sell the business assets to pay its debts.

Creditors are often nervous of lending to businesses with an equity ratio of less than 0.5:1 because they are concerned that the business has too much debt and they may not be repaid.

Purpose of the statement of financial position

The statement of financial position shows the *financial structure* of the business. It is used to predict future cash inflows and outflows and assess:

- the entity's ability to generate cash or provide services in the future
- future borrowing needs of the entity
- the entity's ability to pay drawings to the owner.

It can be used to determine:

- the liquidity of the business through calculating the working capital and current ratio; and
- the solvency of the business through calculating the equity ratio.

ISBN: 9780170211055

Activities

Below is a list of items that may be found in a business statement of financial position.

a	Accounts receivable	**f**	Motor vehicles	**k**	Premises
b	Bank overdraft	**g**	Patent	**l**	Equipment
c	Petty cash	**h**	Land	**m**	Inventory
d	Furniture	**i**	Cash	**n**	Goodwill.
e	Mortgage	**j**	Accounts payable		

Classify each of the items **a – n** above under one of the following headings:

Current asset, Property, plant and equipment (PPE), Intangible asset, Current liability or Non-current liability.

The following balances were taken from the accounting records of *Kut Kurtains* on 30 September 2018:

Assets		Liabilities	
Cash	$2,500	Bank loan (due 2023)	$5,000
Office equipment (cost)	3,000	Accounts payable	2,500
Fixtures and fittings (cost)	8,000	Hire purchase on machinery	6,500
Accounts receivable	1,500	(due 2020)	
Machinery (cost)	20,000		

a Prepare a fully classified statement of financial position in vertical form for *Kut Kurtains* as at 30 September 2018.

b Calculate the equity ratio for this business and explain its meaning.

c Calculate the working capital for *Kut Kurtains* and explain the meaning of your calculation.

d Calculate the current ratio for the business and explain the meaning of this ratio.

The following balances are taken from the accounting records of *Betta Biscuits* on 30 June 2016:

Assets		Liabilities	
Accounts receivable	$4,000	Bank overdraft	$2,000
Building (cost)	160,000	Accounts payable	3,000
Motor vehicles (cost)	30,000	Mortgage (due 2036)	85,000
Petty cash	100		
Inventory	5,900		

a Prepare a fully classified statement of financial position in vertical form for *Betta Biscuits* as at 30 June 2016.

b Calculate the equity ratio for this business and explain the meaning of this ratio.

c Calculate the current ratio for the business and explain the meaning of this ratio.

d Explain why it is useful to classify assets and liabilities in the statement of financial position.

Accounting – A Beginning   ISBN: 9780170211055

Income, Expenses and Profit

As we mentioned earlier, the statement of financial position is like a photograph of the business at an instant in time. Every transaction carried out by the business changes the statement of financial position. This means that all the amounts shown for assets, liabilities and equity will change.

It is very important for users of the financial statements to know why the equity has changed. In this section we will examine the reasons for these changes.

Changes in Equity

The statement of financial position of *Trendy Tourz* that was prepared at 30 June 2015 was shown in the previous section. Equity consisted of Capital of $29,500. Below is the statement of financial position that was prepared a month later, on 31 July 2015.

Trendy Tourz
Statement of Financial Position as at 31 July 2015

	$	$	$
ASSETS			
Non-current assets			
Property, plant and equipment			
Total carrying amount (Note 1)			55,000
Current assets			
Cash		5,200	
Accounts receivable		2,800	
Total current assets			8,000
Total assets			$63,000
EQUITY AND LIABILITIES			
Equity			
Capital at end of the month			38,200
Non-current liabilities			
Loan (due 30 June 2020)		19,800	
Current liabilities			
Accounts payable		5,000	
Total liabilities			24,800
Total equity and liabilities			$63,000

Notes to the statement of financial position

1 Property, plant and equipment	$
Computer (cost)	3,000
Outdoor equipment (cost)	22,000
Van (cost)	30,000
	$55,000

If we compare the equity sections of the two statements, we can see that the capital has increased from $29,500 on 30 June to $38,200 on 31 July.

ISBN: 9780170211055

What could be the reasons for this increase? Earlier, we learnt that equity represents the owner's interest in the business assets. Thus, if Brad had contributed or withdrawn assets, we would expect equity to change.

The changes in the capital of *Trendy Tourz* during the month of July are summarised in the following diagram:

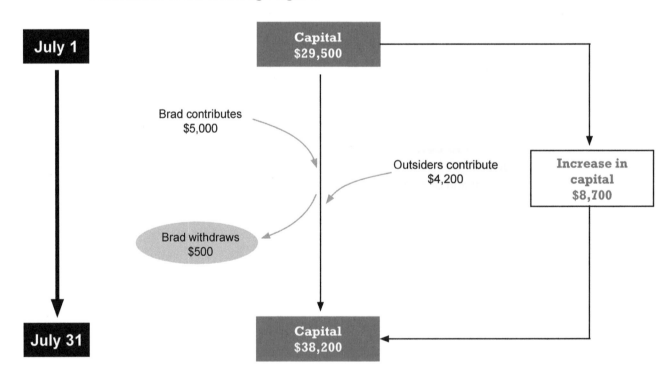

Important!

- The net increase in capital during the month of July was $38,200 – 29,500 = $8,700.
- During the month of July, Brad contributed cash of $5,000 and also withdrew cash of $500. This represents an overall increase in his contribution to the business, from personal sources, of $5,000 – 500 = $4,500. This leaves $4,200 ($8,700 – 4,500) unexplained.

Accounting – A Beginning   ISBN: 9780170211055

Important!

- An increase in capital means an increase in the net assets of the business. Business assets can increase either through transactions with the owners, or through transactions with outside parties.

- The $4,200 represents an increase in the net assets of the business which is due to the transactions which have occurred between *Trendy Tourz* and outside parties. Such an increase is called **profit**.

The statement of financial position, with this information highlighted, is presented below.

Trendy Tourz
Statement of Financial Position as at 31 July 2015

	$	$	$
ASSETS			
Non-current assets			
Property, plant and equipment			
Total carrying amount (Note 1)			55,000
Current assets			
Cash		5,200	
Accounts receivable		2,800	
Total current assets			8,000
Total assets			$63,000
EQUITY AND LIABILITIES			
Equity			
Capital at beginning of the month		29,500	
Contribution by owner		5,000	
Profit for the month		4,200	
Drawings for the month		(500)	
Capital at end of the month			38,200
Non-current liabilities			
Loan (due 30 June 2020)		19,800	
Current liabilities			
Accounts payable		5,000	
Total liabilities			24,800
Total equity and liabilities			$63,000

Notes to the statement of financial position

1 Property, plant and equipment	$
Computer (cost)	3,000
Outdoor equipment (cost)	22,000
Van (cost)	30,000
	$55,000

ISBN: 9780170211055

Activities

1 The following information is available for *Icicles Icecream*
for the year ended 31 March 2018:

Capital at 1 April 2017 $30,000
Profit for the year   45,600
Drawings   25,200

DO THIS!   Prepare the equity section of the statement of financial position as at 31 March 2018.

2 The following balances are taken from the accounting records of *Supa Sweets* on 30 June 2016:

Assets:			**Liabilities:**		
Accounts receivable	$ 3,900		Accounts payable	$ 4,000
Machinery (cost)	60,000		Bank loan (due 2022)	40,000
Petty cash	200		Bank overdraft	1,000
Van (cost)	30,000			
Inventory	5,900			

Equity:		
Capital, 1 July 2015	$43,000
Profit for the year ended 30 June 2016	30,000
Drawings in the year ended 30 June 2016	18,000

DO THIS!   Prepare a fully classified statement of financial position for *Supa Sweets*. You **must** show the changes in equity in your statement.

3 The following balances are taken from the accounting records of *Murray's Mowing Services* on 30 September 2019:

Assets:			**Liabilities:**		
Accounts receivable	$ 2,700		Accounts payable	$ 4,000
Cash	1,500		Bank loan (due 2024)	10,000
Van (cost)	30,000			
Mowers (cost)	6,000			

Equity:		
Capital, 1 October 2018	$12,400
Profit for the year ended 30 September 2019	33,800
Drawings in the year ended 30 September 2019	20,000

DO THIS!   Prepare a fully classified statement of financial position for *Murray's Mowing Services*. You **must** show the changes in equity in your statement.

Accounting – A Beginning   ISBN: 9780170211055

What is profit?

We have already established that the net assets of *Trendy Tourz* increased by $4,200 during July because of transactions that took place between the business and outside parties. We have called this increase **profit**. A formal definition of profit can be given as follows:

Profit

Profit is an increase in the net assets of a business which does not arise from contributions by the owner.

To earn a profit, a business must increase its net assets in some way, but not through transactions with its owner. A profit thus arises through transactions with other, outside parties. A profit arises through the *operations* of the business.

Profit is essentially composed of two elements: income and expenses. It is the difference between income and expenses for a particular period of time and can be represented by the following equation:

$$\textbf{Profit} \quad = \quad \textbf{Income} \quad - \quad \textbf{Expenses}$$

Income and Expenses

Income results from activities such as selling goods or performing services. Types of income include: fees from operating activities, sales of goods, interest earned on investments, a gain on the sale of property, plant and equipment, charging clients fees on overdue accounts, or receiving commission on the sale of goods. Subscriptions paid by the members of clubs are income. When a business earns income, equity increases. A formal definition of income is as follows:

Income

Income is increases in economic benefits during the accounting period in the form of inflows of assets or decreases of liabilities that result in increases in equity, *other than* those relating to contributions from owners.

Note that a contribution by the owner to the business is **not** income. Income is earned only through transactions with *outside parties*.

> **Example:**
> **Tour fees** charged by *Trendy Tourz* are income, because they result in an increase in equity due to an inflow of assets (either cash or accounts receivable) and are **not** contributed by Brad.

Increases in equity thus arise in two ways:

- **contributions** by the owner
- **income** earned through business operations.

Expenses are essentially the costs of producing the income. Examples of expenses include: paying wages, paying rent, writing off bad debts, a loss on the sale of property, plant and equipment, and depreciation. When a business incurs expenses, equity decreases. A formal definition of expenses is as follows:

Expenses

Expenses are decreases in economic benefits during the accounting period in the form of outflows or depletions of assets or incurrences of liabilities that result in decreases in equity, other than those relating to distributions to owners.

Note that a withdrawal (drawing) by the owner from the business is not an expense because it does not help the business to produce income.

> **Example:**
> **Rent** paid by *Trendy Tourz* is an expense because it results in a decrease in equity due to an outflow of cash (an asset) and is **not** a drawing by Brad.

Decreases in equity thus arise in two ways:

- **drawings** by the owner
- **expenses** incurred through business operations.

We now have **four** types of transactions which affect equity. These flows are represented in the following diagram:

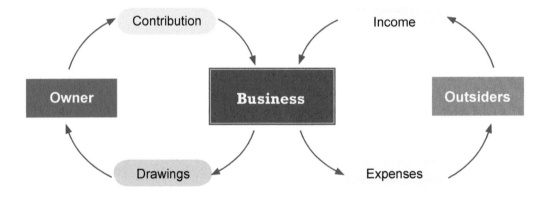

Remember!

Equity is *increased* by:

- Contributions made by the owner
- Income earned by the business.

Equity is *decreased* by:

- Drawings made by the owner
- Expenses incurred by the business.

Summary – Calculating Profit

There are two ways in which the profit for a business can be calculated for any given period of time:

ISBN: 9780170211055

1 Using information about assets and liabilities

We can use information given about the assets and liabilities at two different dates to calculate the profit for the intervening period, as long as we know all the transactions with the owner that have occurred during the period.

To calculate profit, we can reconstruct the *equity section* of the statement of financial position and work backwards to calculate the profit.

Equity

Capital at beginning of the month	29,500	
Contribution by owner	5,000	
Profit for the month	**?**	
Drawings for the month	(500)	
Capital at end of the month		38,200

Profit = $38,200 + 500 – 5,000 – 29,500
   = $4,200

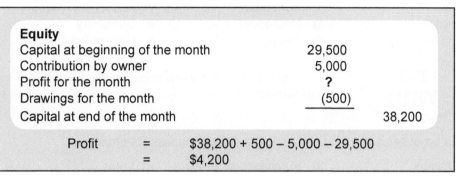

2 Using information about income and expenses

The profit earned by *Trendy Tourz* during July 2015 was $4,200. On investigation, we find that the income for the business in July amounted to $6,900 and total expenses were $2,700. Using the equation:

Profit   =   Income – Expenses
Profit   = $6,900 – 2,700
     = $4,200

Activities

1 Below is a list of items that may be found in a lawyer's financial statements.

a	Fees from clients	**e**	Advertising	**i**	Sales of articles
b	Wages	**f**	Rent paid	**j**	Accountancy fees
c	Electricity	**g**	Insurance	**k**	Stationery
d	Interest from bank	**h**	Telephone rental	**l**	Courier fees.

Classify each of the items above as an *income* or *expense*.

2 Below is a list of items that may be found in a dairy's financial statements.

a	Shop fittings	**g**	Purchases of goods	**m**	Sales
b	Wages	**h**	Mortgage	**n**	Accountancy fees
c	Internet charges	**i**	Accounts receivable	**o**	Insurance
d	Petty cash	**j**	Rates paid	**p**	Accounts payable
e	Advertising	**k**	Drawings	**q**	Van
f	Building	**l**	Inventory	**r**	Capital.

Classify each of the items above under the headings: *asset*, *liability*, *equity*, *income* or *expense*.

3 Mary commenced business with cash of $20,000 on 1 April 2019. At the end of the financial year, 31 March 2020, her equity was $35,000. She had not contributed any more assets to the business during the year, nor had she taken any drawings from it.

Calculate the profit earned by Mary's business during the year.

4 Alesana commenced business as a mobile mechanic on 1 April 2018. He contributed tools costing $5,000, a van costing $10,000 and cash of $3,000 to the business. During the year ended 31 March 2019 he withdrew cash of $22,000. Income for the year was $40,000 and expenses were $15,000.

a Calculate the profit earned by Alesana's business during the year.
b Prepare the equity section of the statement of financial position to show the business profit for the year.

5 Dave's business, *Dave's Diner*, began the year on 1 July 2016 with equity of $73,000. By the end of the year, 30 June 2017, equity had risen to $97,000. During the year Dave contributed a van valued at $15,000 and he also withdrew $12,000 cash for personal use.

Prepare the equity section of the statement of financial position to show the business profit for the year.

ISBN: 9780170211055

The Income Statement

The calculation of the profit for a reporting period is shown in a separate financial statement – the income statement. In this statement, income and expenses are listed separately. We have already established that *Trendy Tourz* reported a profit of $4,200 for the month of July 2015. The income statement showing the individual income and expense items is shown below.

Trendy Tourz
Income Statement for the month ended 31 July 2015

		$	$
Tour fees			6,900
Less: **Expenses**			
	Accounting fees	200	
	Advertising	450	
	Electricity	80	
	Insurance on van	100	
	Interest on loan	135	
	Petrol and oil	500	
	Rent	800	
	Telephone rental	70	
	Tour supplies expense	365	
Total expenses			2,700
Profit for the month			$4,200

The **profitability** of the business can be measured by calculating the profit as a percentage of income from the formula:

$$\text{Profit percentage} = \frac{\text{Profit}}{\text{Income}} \times \frac{100}{1}$$

For *Trendy Tourz*, the profit percentage for July is:

$$\text{Profit \%} = \frac{\$4,200}{\$6,900} \times \frac{100}{1}$$

$$= 60.9\%$$

This means that for each dollar of income, Brad's return is 60.9 cents. The remaining 29.1 cents is used to meet the expenses of running the business.

The Purpose of the Income Statement

The income statement shows the profitability of a business by providing information about income and expenses and disclosing the profit (or loss). It can be used to assess:

- the return to the owner from each dollar of sales (profit percentage)
- the ability of the business to control expenses.

Information from the income statement can be combined with information from the statement of financial position to assist users in predicting the timing and certainty of future cash inflows and outflows.

Activities

1 Waipare's business has a term deposit which earns interest income for the business. One of her business expenses is wages that she pays to staff.

DO THIS!

a Explain why the interest should be recorded as *income* of the business. Do not just give the definition of income.

b Explain why the wages should be recorded as an *expense* of the business. Do not just give the definition of expenses.

2 The following information has been taken from the records of *Chloe's Cleaning Services* for the year ended 30 June 2019.

Cleaning supplies	$ 4,500	Cleaning fees received	$50,000
Van repairs	2,000	Advertising	400
Interest on loan	600	Wages	20,000
Cellphone expenses	350	Petrol	5,000

DO THIS!

a Prepare the income statement for the year.

b Fully explain why the interest on the loan should be recorded as an *expense* of the business.

c Fully explain why the cash that Chloe pays to herself each week is **not** an *expense* of the business.

d Fully explain why the business loan Chloe has taken from the bank is **not** *income* to the business.

3 Your friend Tui Waenga started her own baby-sitting business so that she could save money towards going to university. She is interested in finding out how much profit the business has earned during its first three months and has come to you for assistance. You have discovered the following information for the three months up to 31 March 2017:

- Fees received in cash — $3,500
- Fees still unpaid by clients for March — 400
- Advertising expenses paid — 500
- Amount paid to Tui's mother for hiring her car — 300
- Hire of DVDs to amuse children — 70
- Advertising invoice for February received but not yet paid — 20
- Wages paid for evenings which were double-booked — 700
- Amount spent by Tui on personal expenses — 350
- Amount owing to mother for April car hire — 100
- Amount owing by a client which will not be recovered — 30

DO THIS!

a Prepare the income statement to show the profit Tui has earned for the three-month period.

b Give one example of how you have applied the *accrual basis of accounting* in your statement.

c Give one example of how you have applied the notion of the *accounting entity* in your statement.

d Explain why bad debts is an *expense* of the business.

ISBN: 9780170211055

Gee, Aroha, I'm starting to see why I need an accountant now! All those statements to prepare!

Yes, there are two that you need. Each has a different use. I hope you understand what they mean now.

I think I understand the income statement all right, but I'm still a bit confused about the statement of financial position.

What do you mean?

Well, the income statement shows that the business earned a profit of $4,200 in the month of July.

$4,200?

Yes, that's right.

That doesn't seem right to me. The bank balance increased by much less than that.

If the profit is $4,200 why has the bank account only gone up by $1,700?

What on earth are you talking about?

$4,200? ?$1,700

Oh dear, you're getting confused. The profit is the difference between income and expenses.

I know that.

But the changes in cash came about through various transactions. Some were income, but you also invested $5,000 in the business yourself. You bought equipment too. And there's accrual accounting to consider.

Can you go over it again please?

Well you sold some equipment for $500 and bought more for $4,000. That used up $3,500 of cash. But buying assets is not an expense, so it reduces your cash but not your profit.

And investing your own money in the business doesn't affect the profit either?

No, that's not income. It's a transaction with the owner.

I don't get this equipment business. If I repair it there's an expense. If I buy some, it isn't.

There's a difference between capital and revenue expenditure. You'd better look at this.

ISBN: 9780170211055

Capital and Revenue Expenditure

We have already seen that using the accrual basis of accounting can result in a difference between the profit as shown by the income statement and the change in the bank balance. Another difference arises when we purchase or sell property, plant and equipment. The ideas of **capital expenditure** and **revenue expenditure** help us understand how this difference comes about.

DEFINITION

Capital expenditure

Capital expenditure is any expenditure that creates an asset.

Capital expenditure does **not** affect equity. Any of the following expenditures can be classed as capital expenditure:

- purchase of assets
- improvements to property, plant and equipment which increases its usefulness or extends its useful life
- any expenditure incurred in getting property, plant and equipment to the place and into the condition where it can be used in business operations.

Example:

A business in Auckland bought a biscuit-making machine from a firm in Dunedin. The machine cost $30,000. Freight charges to transport the machine from Dunedin to Auckland were a further $4,000 and the cost of installing the machine in the Auckland factory amounted to $5,000. The staff in the factory had to be trained to use the new machine at a cost of $3,200 and $1,500 was spent on raw materials used in a trial run before saleable biscuits could be produced. Six weeks later the machine developed major faults and repairs cost $5,000.

The capital expenditure (cost of the machine) is calculated as follows:

Remember!

Capital expenditures tend to be of a 'one-off' nature.

Cost of machine	$30,000
Freight	4,000
Installation	5,000
Raw materials (trial runs)	1,500
Total machine cost	$40,500

The amount of capital expenditure involved in the purchase of this machine is $40,500. This includes the original cost of the machine, the costs of freight and installation and also the raw materials which were used before the machine became productive. All of these costs form part of the cost of the asset itself. Freight, installation and the raw material costs are included because they were incurred in order to get the machine into the factory and into the condition where it could be used to make biscuits.

ISBN: 9780170211055

The cost of the repairs six weeks after installation is not included in the cost of the asset. This is because the machine was already producing biscuits before the repairs were found to be necessary. The staff training costs are not included because they are not part of the machine itself. Costs incurred in training staff are related to the staff and not the machine. If new staff were employed, they would have to be trained and this would not affect the cost of the machine.

DEFINITION

Revenue expenditure

Revenue expenditure is the expenditure that is incurred in normal day-to-day operations of the business.

Revenue expenditure involves any costs which are incurred so that the business can produce income from its operations. This type of expenditure does not create an asset. Since operating expenses are incurred in order to produce income, they decrease equity.

Remember!

Revenue expenditures are of a recurring nature.

In the example above, both the repairs to the machine and the staff training costs are revenue expenditure. They are deducted from income to calculate the profit in the income statement.

The major difference between capital and revenue expenditure is the effect on equity:

- Capital expenditure **does not affect** equity because an asset is created.
- Revenue expenditure **decreases** equity because the costs are incurred in producing income. Revenue expenditures are commonly called **expenses** and tend to be of a recurring nature.

Learn!

Capital expenditure *does not affect* equity.

Revenue expenditure *decreases* equity.

Activities

1 The activities below relate to land and a barn.

a Purchase of land
b Fencing land
c Wages for mowing land
d Wages for building fence on land

e Purchase of wood to build extensions to a barn
f Painting the extensions
g Painting the old barn to match the new extensions
h Wages for building the extensions.

DO THIS! State whether each of **a – h** above is capital or revenue expenditure.

2 The activities below relate to a new truck.

a Purchase of a truck
b Painting the firm's name on the truck

c Insurance on the truck for the next year
d Registration of the truck for the next year.

DO THIS! State whether each of **a – d** above is capital or revenue expenditure.

3 The activities below relate to a machine that is used to make spaghetti.

a Purchase of a machine to make spaghetti
b Cartage costs on the machine to the factory
c Customs duty payable on the machine
d Insurance on the machine in transit

e Insurance on the machine for the next year
f Wages paid for installing the machine
g Ingredients used up in practice runs
h Repairs to the machine six months later.

DO THIS! State whether each of **a – h** above is capital or revenue expenditure.

4 Evan Evans decided to set up a minibus business in a small seaside town. Evan purchased a new van to start his business using a loan from the bank for $20,000 and paying the rest himself. He incurred the following costs in the first week:

- Cost of van $30,000
- Signwriting   1,200

- Advertising $ 500
- Seats   5,000

- Insurance for one year $600
- Application fee for the loan   200

DO THIS! Calculate the capital cost of the van.

5 *Paper Products* imported a new drying machine from Italy. The machine cost $45,000 and installation costs amounted to $10,000. This included the cost of an Italian consultant who came to supervise the installation. Freight charges amounted to $3,500 and insurance while the machine was in transit cost $2,600. The staff in the factory spent two weeks learning how to use the machine. The average weekly wages bill for the firm is $15,000 per week. While they were learning, raw materials costing $3,700 were wasted before the machine produced any saleable paper.

DO THIS! Calculate the capital cost of the drying machine.

ISBN: 9780170211055

Accounting Transactions

- **Goods and Services Tax**
- **Source Documents**
- **The Accounting Equation**
- **Recording Assets, Liabilities and Equity**
- **Recording Income and Expenses**

This chapter is concerned with the recording of accounting transactions. We will first examine business documents and discuss Goods and Services Tax (GST). Business documents are usually called **source documents**. The data that are recorded on source documents form the basis of the *input* into the firm's accounting system. Documents must be completed correctly or our accounting information will be inaccurate.

The next section of the chapter is concerned with recording transactions on the accounting equation, A = L + Eq. We met the accounting equation in the first chapter. Finally we will revise the preparation of financial statements.

Goods and Services Tax

GST is a tax imposed by the government and administered by the Inland Revenue Department. GST is an indirect tax. This means that it is not taken from your income (like income tax is) but is charged when you buy goods or pay for services.

Businesses which are registered for GST (this is most businesses except those which are very small) charge GST on all the goods and services they provide. They also pay GST on most of their expenses. Every so often they prepare a GST return and the difference between the GST they have collected and the GST that they have paid is sent to the Inland Revenue Department. (If they have paid more than they have collected, they receive refunds.)

This process is shown in the diagram below.

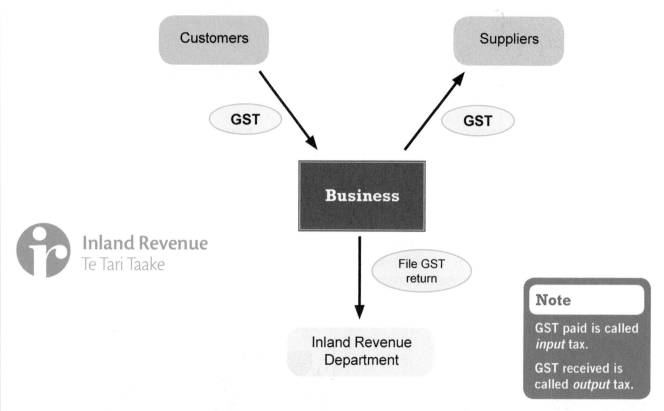

What is GST charged on?

Goods and services tax is charged in New Zealand on almost everything, providing that the supplier is registered for GST. All businesses with expected sales of more than $60,000 (excluding GST) per year must register.

There is no GST charged (or claimable) on the following:

- wages paid
- interest paid or received
- bank charges

- drawings
- loans received
- capital invested in a business.

Calculating GST

GST is added to the selling price of goods or services at the rate of 15%. This represents three twentieths of the pre-GST (or GST exclusive) price. For example:

Remember!

$15\% = {}^3/_{20}$

Normal selling price (GST exclusive)	$100.00
Plus: GST (15% x $100.00)	15.00
GST inclusive selling price	$115.00

The **tax fraction** is the proportion of the total selling price that represents GST. In the above example:

$$\text{Tax fraction} = \frac{\text{GST}}{\text{Total selling price}} = \frac{15}{115} = \frac{3}{23}$$

Accounting – A Beginning

ISBN: 9780170211055

Panel 1:
Do you mean that I have to register for GST as well as keeping all these records? I don't make that much money.

Yes you will. GST registration is based on turnover. You will sell more than $60,000 worth of tours this year.

Panel 2:
What about all those GST returns you have to do?

Its not difficult. Since your business is small we will apply to register you on the PAYMENTS BASIS for GST.

Panel 3:
What does that mean?

You will only have to record GST when you receive or pay cash. Let me explain GST before we go through all that.

Calculating the Tax Fraction

GST is calculated at the rate of 15%. This represents $^3/_{20}$ ths of the price before GST is added. (We call this the GST *exclusive* price.)

$$\frac{15}{100} = \frac{3}{20}$$

We add $^3/_{20}$ths of the GST *exclusive* amount to itself to obtain the GST *inclusive* amount. This can be represented by the diagram below.

GST exclusive price

$^1/_{20}$ $^1/_{20}$

GST inclusive price

The GST *inclusive* amount is thus $^{23}/_{20}$ ths of the GST *exclusive* amount. In other words, the GST component is $^3/_{23}$ rds of the total price. We can also calculate the GST component of a GST inclusive selling price by dividing by 1.15.

Example:
The GST inclusive selling price is $460.

GST component $= \dfrac{3}{23}$ x $460   **OR**   GST component $= \dfrac{\$460}{1.15}$

$\qquad\qquad\quad = \$60$ $\qquad\qquad\qquad\qquad\qquad\qquad\qquad\quad = \$60$

Source Documents

Source documents are the documents where accounting information is first recorded. Before we can input information into an accounting system, we must capture this information in a form which can be used.

Cash Receipts

The most common source documents for cash receipts are cash register tapes, carbon copies of receipts issued and the bank statement.

ISBN: 9780170211055

Cash Register Tape

This is a duplicate of all the dockets given to customers when they buy goods. Two typical cash register tapes are shown below.

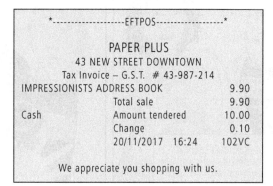

```
*----------------EFTPOS----------------*

            PAPER PLUS
      43 NEW STREET DOWNTOWN
   Tax Invoice – G.S.T.  # 43-987-214
IMPRESSIONISTS ADDRESS BOOK         9.90
         Total sale                 9.90
Cash     Amount tendered           10.00
         Change                     0.10
         20/11/2017  16:24        102VC

   We appreciate you shopping with us.
```

```
*-------------------EFTPOS------------------*
              B P EXPRESS
            GST 20-457-129
         *** TAX INVOICE ***
05 UNLEADED 44.99 L 1.843 $/L      $ 82.92
SALE TOTAL                         $ 82.92
CASH                             NZ$ 85.00
CHANGE                           NZ$  2.10
TAX AMOUNT                         $ 10.82
    21 NOV 2017  08.43 am  0989/02  07
```

Important!

- On the left hand tape, no GST is shown. This is because the price of the goods includes GST.

- On the right hand tape the GST is shown separately at the bottom. Other details include the amount of cash tendered and the change given.

- GST does not have to be shown separately unless the receipt is for more than $1,000 including GST.

Receipt

A receipt is a document issued when a firm receives cash. Most modern receipts are computer-generated. Copies are automatically kept by the computer system. However, there are still some firms that use manually prepared receipts. The details required on a receipt are the same, no matter how it is prepared.

Below is an example of a receipt that has been prepared manually.

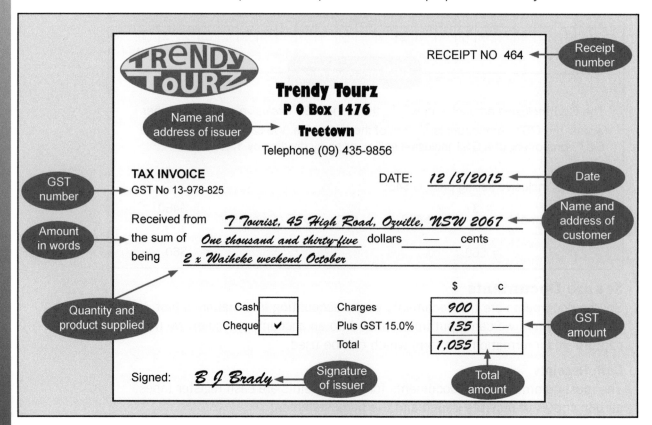

- The name and address of both the supplier and the customer are shown.
- The receipt has a number. This ensures receipts are not issued fraudulently and the money stolen. It also helps to trace a payment if queries arise.
- The date is shown.
- The quantity and nature of goods supplied or services provided is shown.
- The receipt is signed by the person who issues it.
- This receipt is also a tax invoice. For cash sales, a customer can use the receipt to claim back GST.
- The GST is shown separately on this receipt because it is for more than $1,000 including GST.

Bank Statement

There are many transactions where money is deposited directly into a firm's bank account. Internet banking has made this a very common way for businesses to pay their accounts. The bank itself may also deposit interest into the bank account. We will examine bank statements more closely in the next chapter.

Cash Payments

Few business payments are made in actual cash. It is essential to keep accurate business records and for that reason business payments are commonly made in four ways:

- EFTPOS
- Cheque
- Remote banking
- Credit card.

EFTPOS

EFTPOS stands for **Electronic Funds Transfer at Point of Sale**. Specially designed machines are used by retailers to read coded information from a magnetic strip on the back of a plastic card or an electronic chip embedded in the card. When the transaction takes place, the customer's bank account is automatically debited and the retailer's account is credited with the amount of the transaction. As long as there are funds in the customer's bank account, the transaction will be processed.

All EFTPOS transactions produce a receipt like the one opposite.

You should note that this receipt shows details of the vendor, the time, the goods purchased and the GST included in the total amount of the transaction.

It is up to the customer to keep the receipt and update his or her business records. Although details of the transaction will appear on the business bank statement, actual paper receipts can be required for checking by Inland Revenue.

```
            SHELL TREETOWN

          26 JUN 2017 04:43 pm
         TRANSACTION NO 9099/02
            GST# 98 143 769
            *** TAX INVOICE ***

07 ULTRA 35.59 L 1.836 $/L    $            65.34
EFTPOS                             NZ$ 65.34
TAX AMOUNT                          $ 8.52
     *-----------------EFTPOS-----------------*
     MERCHANT:                 11110231010
     TERMINAL:                   31010002
     TIME:                      26JUN17 17:43
     TRAN: 056732           ACCT: CHEQUE
     CARD:              5887650000765412
     PURCHASE:                 NZ$65.34
     TOTAL:                    NZ$65.34
     (00)            ACCEPTED
     *-------------------------------------------*

       THANK YOU FOR SHOPPING WITH US
```

Remote Banking

There are three forms of remote banking:

- telephone banking
- internet banking
- mobile banking

Most banks in New Zealand still operate a system of telephone banking. For a small business, it can be a convenient means of paying business accounts, checking account balances, transferring funds between bank accounts and ordering cheque books or bank statements. The customer's account numbers for commonly paid bills, such as the electricity bill, are coded into the system by the bank and the customer can then access the bank and enter payment instructions via the telephone.

The use of the internet and mobile phones for banking transactions has become extremely common. These methods allow customers remote access to their bank's computer system. The customer can carry out the same sorts of transactions as by telephone banking and access their account information. Mobile phones can also be used as EFTPOS terminals. Most banks have on-line statements and businesses can now elect not to receive paper statements.

Security of access to telephone, internet and mobile banking is very important. Where firm employs staff to pay its accounts, access to PIN numbers and passwords should be restricted and passwords should be changed frequently.

> **Remember!**
>
> Security over access to telephone, internet and mobile banking is extremely important.

Automatic Payments and Direct Debits

An **automatic payment** is an amount paid regularly by the bank on behalf of the account holder for regular expenses such as rent. The amount of the payment is set by the account-holder and cannot be changed without consent.

A **direct debit** is a regular deduction from the bank account but the amount may vary from month to month. In this case the account-holder initially completes a direct debit authority that allows a regular payment to be made and allows the supplier to determine the amount of that payment. For example, the electricity invoice will vary from month to month, so a direct debit authority allows the power company to receive the correct payment each month. Normally, an invoice is sent in plenty of time before the payment is deducted so that the amount can be checked by the business and queried if necessary.

Cheques

Before the invention of internet banking, cheques were the most common method used to pay business expenses. A cheque provides a convenient substitute for sending cash through the mail. It is as good as cash and can be protected so that only the person with rightful ownership to it can use it. However, care must be taken in operating a cheque account to make sure there are sufficient funds available in the bank account to meet the cheques written. If insufficient funds are available, the cheque may 'bounce'. This means that it has been dishonoured by the bank. Not only does this damage the reputation of a customer, but the bank charges involved may be considerable if a lot of cheques are dishonoured.

What is a cheque?

A cheque may be defined as a 'bill of exchange drawn on a banker payable on demand'.

What does this mean? A cheque must:

- be in writing
- be addressed to a bank by a customer
- be signed by the customer

ISBN: 9780170211055

- require the bank to pay on demand a particular sum of money
  - to a bearer (the person who holds the cheque); or
  - to a certain person; or
  - to the order of a certain person.

Providing these conditions are met and there are funds in the account, the bank must pay the cheque.

The most common form of cheque is written on a pre-printed form which is supplied by the bank to the customer. Modern banking practice uses **Magnetic Ink Character Recognition** (MICR) to process cheques quickly. Pre-printed cheques have both the cheque number and the customer's account number recorded in this way on each cheque. However, it is not essential to use these pre-printed forms. While they are more convenient to both customer and bank, any written order which meets the conditions outlined above is a valid cheque.

Parts of a Cheque
The diagram below shows the essential parts of any cheque.

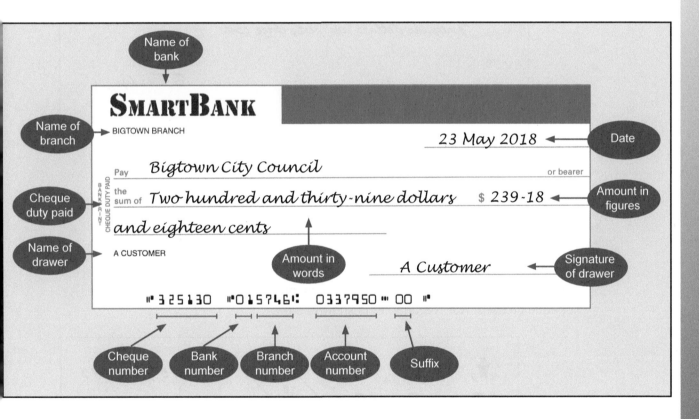

Different types of cheque

1 Open cheques
An open cheque, or bearer cheque, may be cashed by the person holding it. It does not need to be paid into a bank account.

An open cheque commonly contains the words *'Pay Cash'* in which case it is called a **cash cheque**. It may be made payable to a *named party* in which case it is called a **bearer cheque**. However, if the words *'or bearer'* are not crossed out on the cheque, then it can be cashed by any person who presents it for payment to the bank on which it is drawn.

Open cheques are therefore no safer than cash. Two examples of open cheques are shown on the next page.

Cash Cheque

Bank Green TREETOWN BRANCH

Date *10 July 2015*

Pay *Cash*

or bearer $ *50-00*

The sum of *Fifty dollars only*

B BRADY

B Brady

⑈000027 081047402 ⑈ 50

Bearer Cheque

Bank Green TREETOWN BRANCH

Date *12 July 2015*

Pay *Treetown Supermarket*

or bearer $ *49-63*

The sum of *Fortynine dollars and sixty-three cents*

B BRADY

B Brady

⑈000028 081047402 ⑈ 50

2   Crossed cheques

One way of making a cheque safer and preventing it from being cashed by the wrong person is to place two parallel lines across the face of the cheque. A crossed cheque must be paid into a bank account.

Sometimes the words *'Not Negotiable'* are written between the two parallel lines. This means that if a cheque is stolen and passed to a third party, the cheque is invalid since the person who stole it had no right to it in the first place. The words 'Not Negotiable' thus act as a warning to people accepting cheques. A cheque crossed 'Not Negotiable' is shown below.

Not Negotiable Cheque

Since 1996, there has been even greater protection for cheques than was available previously. A crossed cheque containing the words *'Not Transferable'* or *'Account Payee Only'* must be paid into the bank account of the person or firm named on the cheque. Furthermore, the *exact* name of the bank account into

Accounting – A Beginning

ISBN: 9780170211055

which the cheque is to be paid **must** be written on the cheque.

This means that the person receiving the cheque cannot transfer it to a third party. In other words, if you receive a cheque in your name which is crossed in this way you must pay it into **your own** bank account.

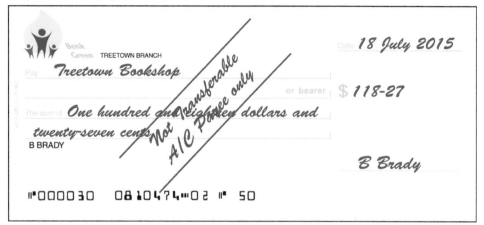

Not Transferable Cheque

Depositing money

When money is deposited by the account holder in a cheque account, a deposit slip is completed. A typical deposit slip is shown below.

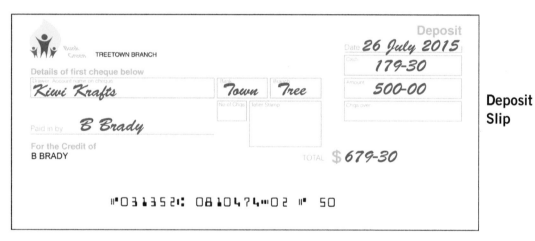

Deposit Slip

Important!

- The person who pays the money into the account must sign the deposit slip. This is not necessarily the account holder as anybody may pay money into a bank account.

- When cash is deposited, most banks require that the amounts of cash and cheques be shown separately. If more than one cheque is deposited, the cheques must be listed separately on the back of the deposit slip.

- Brad has deposited $679.30. This is made up of $179.30 in cash and a cheque for $500.00.

Most business cheque books have cheque butts, which remain in the cheque book when a cheque is removed. A cheque butt provides a space for recording cheque details and for keeping a running balance of the account. Deposit slips in this style of cheque book also have a butt. A typical cheque and a deposit slip which have butts are shown on the next page.

ISBN: 9780170211055

Cheque

13 March 2018

Telecom

BRANCH PRINT
42817 BANK IN CHEQUE DUTY PAID

$ 270·00

571659

SMARTBANK

FREETOWN BRANCH

13 March 2018

Pay   Telecom   or bearer

the sum of   two hundred and seventy $ 270·00

dollars only

FAST FOOD SUPPLIERS LIMITED   KB Sheridan

⑊571659 ⑊030275⑊ 0340514⑊00 ⑊

Deposit Slip

SMARTBANK
Date 6 March 2018

Amount

One thousand dollars

$ 1000·00
(Proceeds of cheques etc. will not be available till cleared.)

Deposited for credit of

Fast Food Suppliers Ltd

Teller

2/95

SMARTBANK

FREETOWN BRANCH

(If more than three cheques record details on reverse.)

Drawer	Bank	Branch
Discount Supermarket	BN2	Thames

Paid in by (Signature)
(Proceeds of cheques etc. will not be available till cleared.)   KB Sheridan

Credit

FAST FOOD SUPPLIERS LIMITED

Date 6 March 2018

Notes	300	00
Coin		
Cheques as per back	700	00
Fees paid	No. of cheques	Teller	Sub total	
			Less charges	
Total $	1000	00

⑊030275⑊ 0340514⑊00 ⑊ 50

Another example of a cheque butt is as follows:

2 June	20 15
To	Private Properties
For	Rent

Bal B/Fwd	695	—
Deposits	230	—
	925	—
This Cheque	690	—
Bal C/Fwd	235	—

231141

The cheque butt shows the following information:

- the number of the cheque (231141)
- the date (2 June 2015)
- the payee (who the cheque was written for – *Private Properties*)
- the amount of the cheque ($690.00).

The cheque butt also provides space to record deposits and thus enables a running balance of the bank account to be kept.

I never knew all that. I've been sending out cash cheques for years.

Well now you do know. You are lucky nothing has gone wrong.

Well......now you mention it.....a cheque got lost once but it was cashed. Must have been stolen...I had to replace it but I didn't get my money back.

To Cash

Accounting – A Beginning

ISBN: 9780170211055

Activities

1 Each of **a** to **l** given below represents the GST *exclusive* selling price of goods.

a $240	**d** $440	**g** $18,000	**j** $600
b $800	**e** $24	**h** $720	**k** $120,000
c $2,000	**f** $88	**i** $1,600	**l** $960

DO THIS!

For each of the above amounts:
i Calculate the GST which would be added to obtain the GST inclusive selling price.
ii Calculate the GST inclusive selling price.

2 Each of **a** to **l** given below represents the GST *inclusive* selling price of goods.

a $92	**d** $46	**g** $736	**j** $1,150
b $1,840	**e** $27,600	**h** $1,104	**k** $3,680
c $1,380	**f** $322	**i** $23,000	**l** $18.40

DO THIS!

For each of the above amounts, calculate the GST which is included in the selling price.

3 During one particular period a business made cash sales of $110,400 (including GST) and paid expenses of $36,800 (including GST). The business is registered for GST on the payments basis.

DO THIS!

a Calculate the GST collected by the business.
b Calculate the GST paid by the business.
c Calculate the amount which will be shown on the GST return prepared for this business. Is this amount payable to the Inland Revenue or will the firm receive a refund?

4 Listed below are some transactions that have occurred for different businesses. The firms are registered for GST on the payments basis.

a Cash sales of $7,820
b Cash purchases of $6,532
c Insurance paid of $1,288
d Capital invested of $4,600
e Interest paid of $193.20
f Rent paid of $2,185
g Cash fees of $3,726
h Cash sale of old equipment of $322

i Interest received of $92
j Wages paid of $4,600
k Advertising paid of $736
l Cash paid for tools, $1,012
m Invoices issued for $552
n Invoices received for $828
o A loan received of $18,400
p Drawings paid to owner of $1,656

DO THIS!

Calculate the GST to be paid to or claimed from Inland Revenue for each of the transactions **a** – **p** above. You should state whether the GST will be **paid** or **claimed back** in each case.

ISBN: 9780170211055

5 Below are two cheques that were written by different people.

Cheque A

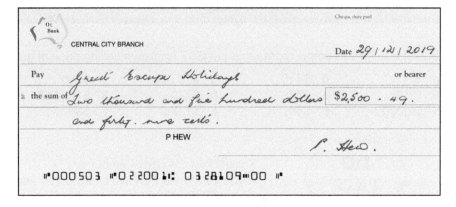

Cheque B

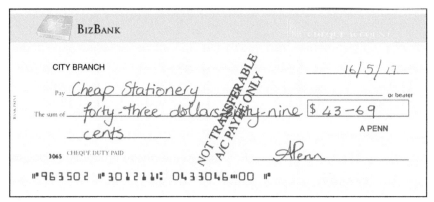

DO THIS!

Answer the following questions about *each* cheque:

a What are the names of the bank and branch which issued this cheque?
b Who is the payee?
c For what amount is this cheque written?
d Name the drawer of this cheque.
e What are the unique numbers of the bank and branch which issued this cheque?
f What is the account number (including suffix) of the drawer of this cheque?
g What is the number of this cheque?
h Is this cheque an open cheque, a bearer cheque or a crossed cheque?

6 You have a cheque account with *Bank Green*. On 16 May 2016, you carried out the following transactions:
- Wrote a cheque for cash, $50.00
- Sent a crossed 'Not Transferable' cheque to the *Townsville City Council* for rates, $320.65
- Wrote a bearer cheque to the *Convenient Petrol Station* for $82.14
- Banked a cheque from your employer, *Crummy Carpenters*, for your wages of $506.87.

DO THIS!

Prepare the cheques and deposit slip in your workbook for the transactions you carried out on 16 May 2016.

ISBN: 9780170211055

7 Each of the cheques shown below contains an error.

Bank Progressive

HIGHTOWN BRANCH

4 - 2 - 2018   19

Pay ___ Cash ___ or Bearer

the sum of ___ Fifty dollars only. ___ $50 - 00

not transferable

I M BROKE   J. M. Broke

⑈ 100930 ⑈ 080273⑈ 0045124⑈00 ⑈

Cheque A

SMARTBANK

MIDTOWN BRANCH

21 DECEMBER 2019

Pay   LETS EAT RESTAURANT   or bearer

the sum of   FORTY NINE DOLLARS 63 CENTS $ 46-93

BANKPRINT CHEQUE DUTY PAID

H UNGER

H Unger

⑈ 275740 ⑈030571⑈ 0314405⑈00 ⑈

Cheque B

Co-opBank

DOWNTOWN BRANCH

6 June 2016

Pay   Grubsup Supermarket   or Bearer

Sixty five dollars and ninety six cents $65-96

Amount in Words   Cheque Duty Paid

not transferable

A SHOPPER

⑈229520 ⑈051865⑈ 7335   ⑈900⑈

Cheque C

DO THIS!

Identify the error in each cheque and explain why it makes the cheque invalid.

ISBN: 9780170211055

8 The following receipts were issued by *Modern Office Supplies* in September 2017:

a On September 10, Harvey Wallbanger paid $46 cash on his account, including $6 GST, Receipt No 465.

b On September 18, Olive Grove settled her account with a cheque for $138 (which includes GST), Receipt No 466.

c On September 21, the office computer was sold to Harry Uphill for $1,200 plus GST. Harry paid by cheque and Receipt No 467 was issued.

d On September 28, April Showers paid her account of $1,267.30 in full by cash and was issued with Receipt No 468.

DO THIS! Prepare the receipts listed above for September 2017. (Your workbook contains forms for these documents.)

9 The following cheques were issued by *Modern Office Supplies* in September 2017:

a On 4 September, Cheque No 001731 for $232.30 was written to *Telecom* for the August telephone bill.

b On 9 September, Cheque No 001732 for $500.00 was written for cash for owner's drawings.

c On 14 September, Cheque No 001733 for $1,016.60 was written for payment on account to *Wholesale Stationery Limited*.

d On 23 September, an open cheque, Cheque No 001734, for $600.00 was written for wages to Owen Charles, one of the staff. Owen wished to bank the cheque into his mother's bank account.

DO THIS! Prepare the cheques listed above for September 2017. You should use the safest format possible when you prepare the cheques. (Your workbook contains forms for these documents.)

10 The following deposits were made at the bank by *Modern Office Supplies* in September 2017:

a On September 11, a deposit of $1,300.20 was made in cash, consisting of notes amounting to $1,250.00 with the balance in coins.

b On September 19, cheques totalling $1,539.47 were banked.

c On September 27, a deposit totalling $2,561.85 was made, consisting of cheques totalling $1,987.45, notes of $380.00 and the balance in coins.

d On September 30, a deposit totalling $4,395.70 was made, consisting of cheques totalling $3,895.50, notes of $475.00 and the balance in coins.

DO THIS! Prepare the deposit slips for the deposits listed above in September 2017. (Your workbook contains forms for these documents.)

Modern Office Supplies

ISBN: 9780170211055

Source Documents for Credit Sales and Purchases

Invoices

When goods are sold on credit the customer is issued with an invoice. A typical invoice for Brad's business (which is now registered for GST) is shown below.

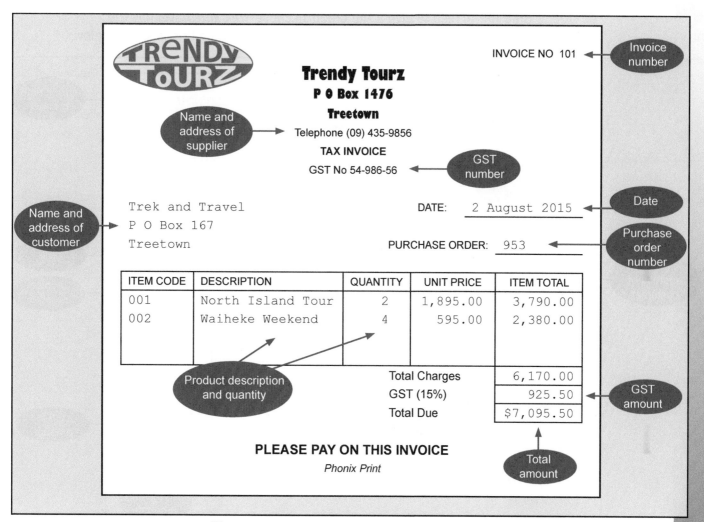

Important!

- The invoice has a number so that it can be traced.

- The name and address of both the firm issuing the invoice and the customer are shown.

- When a travel agent orders holidays from *Trendy Tourz*, a purchase order is completed. This is sent to *Trendy Tourz* and there is a space to enter the number of this **purchase order** on the invoice. This enables the order to be traced back to the purchaser if any problems arise.

- The invoice is a **tax invoice**. This is because *Trendy Tourz* must charge GST on all its sales. At the bottom of the invoice the GST is calculated separately at 15% of the sales value of the tours.

- Carbon copies of manually prepared invoices are kept for the use of the business. The original (top copy) is sent to the customer.

ISBN: 9780170211055

Credit Notes

When customers return goods which they have purchased on credit, a credit note is issued. In the case of *Trendy Tourz*, a credit may be given if a booking is cancelled.

Suppose that *Trek and Travel* had a cancellation for one of the Waiheke Island tours. Brad has agreed to give a full credit because *Trek and Travel* has the potential to become a good client. The credit note recording this is shown below.

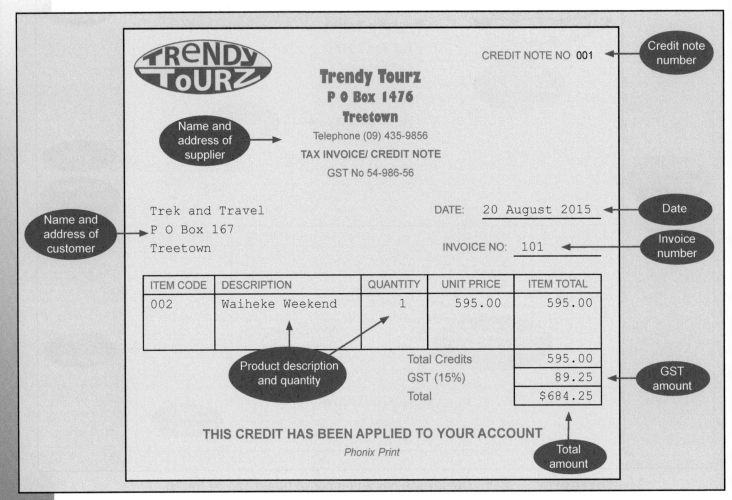

Important!

- The credit note has a number so that it can be traced later if necessary.

- The GST number of the firm is shown on the credit note. This is because the GST records must be adjusted to account for any credits issued.

- The top copy of a credit note is issued to the customer. Carbon copies of manually prepared credit notes are kept so that the business can enter the transactions into its records.

- The number of the original invoice is also shown on the credit note. This is very important when *goods* are returned to a trading business, to ensure that the customer did not purchase the goods from somewhere else. The original invoice should always be checked before a credit note is issued.

ISBN: 9780170211055

Activities

1   The following documents were issued by *Modern Office Supplies* in September 2017:

   a   On 3 September I Spy Detective Agency of 143 Hope Street, Wellstown, purchased 20 reams of A4 paper (Product No 152) at $5.60 per ream (excluding GST), eight packets of A4 envelopes (Product No 231) at $3.20 per packet (excluding GST) and two boxes of staples (Product No 313) at $2.00 per box (excluding GST); Purchase Order No 1022, Invoice No 967.

   b   On 15 September, Reveal Photography of 25 Picture Avenue, Wellstown, purchased ten boxes of photographic paper (Product No 235) at $16.00 per box (excluding GST), two fax rolls (Product No 149) at $4.00 each and one box of ballpoint pens (Product No 168) at $12.00 (excluding GST); Purchase Order No 254, Invoice No 980.

   c   On 5 September I Spy Detective Agency returned three of the reams of A4 paper which had been purchased on 3 September, Credit Note No 127.

   d   On 20 September Reveal Photography returned two of the boxes of photographic paper which had been purchased on 15 September, Credit Note No 128.

     DO THIS!   Prepare the documents for the transactions listed above in September 2017. (Your workbook contains forms for these documents.)

2   *Kiri's Krafts* is a shop specialising in selling New Zealand made craft and souvenir items. The following are regular customers:

Customer Number	Name	Address
10002	Rotorua Souvenirs	P O Box 23-156 Rotorua
10009	Milford Sound Store	23 Te Anau Road Milford
10015	Queenstown Tourist Shoppe	P O Box 1452 Queenstown

The following transactions relate to *Kiri's Krafts* in October 2018:

   a   On 10 October *Rotorua Souvenirs* paid $253.00 on account, Receipt No 1004.

   b   On 15 October *Milford Sound Store* purchased goods on credit for $360.00 excluding GST, Invoice No 008. The goods consisted of six handmade adult T shirts (Product Code 2314) at a price of $40.00 each and four children's T shirts (Product Code 2315) at $30.00 each, Purchase Order No 4367.

   c   On 20 October *Queenstown Tourist Shoppe* purchased goods on credit for $220.00 excluding GST, Invoice No 009. The goods consisted of eight handmade toy sheep (Product Code 1219) at a price of $20.00 each and four stuffed kiwis (Product Code 1306) at $15.00 each, Purchase Order No 56908.

   d   On 25 October *Milford Sound Store* returned one of the adult T shirts that had been purchased on 15 October because the stitching had failed, Credit Note No 127.

   e   On 30 October *Queenstown Tourist Shoppe* returned one of the stuffed kiwis that had been purchased on 20 October because the beak fell off, Credit Note No 128.

   f   On 31 October, *Rotorua Souvenirs* purchased two adult T shirts, four toy sheep and eight stuffed kiwis on credit, Invoice No 010, Purchase Order No 8705.

     DO THIS!   Prepare the documents for the transactions listed above in October 2018. (Your workbook contains forms for these documents.)

Recording Assets, Liabilities and Equity

We can use the accounting equation to record the effect of transactions on business assets, liabilities and equity.

Let's recall the statement of financial position for *Trendy Tourz* as at 31 July 2015. We will use the 'T' form of the equation here since it is easier to record transactions in that form.

Trendy Tourz
Statement of Financial Position as at 31 July 2015

Assets		*Liabilities*	
Cash	$5,200	Accounts payable	$5,000
Accounts receivable	2,800	Bank loan (due 30 June 2020)	19,800
Computer equipment (cost)	3,000		24,800
Outdoor equipment (cost)	22,000		
Van (cost)	30,000	*Equity*	
		Capital	38,200
	$63,000		$63,000

We can set out this statement of financial position in the form of the accounting equation which enables us to record the transactions more easily:

	ASSETS				=	LIABILITIES		+ EQUITY
Cash	**+ Accounts receivable**	**+ Computer equipment**	**+ Outdoor equipment**	**+ Van**	**= Accounts payable**	**+ Bank loan**	**+ Capital**	
5,200	2,800	3,000	22,000	30,000	5,000	19,800	38,200	

TOTAL ASSETS = TOTAL LIABILITIES + EQUITY
= $63,000 = $63,000

ISBN: 9780170211055

We can now begin to record our transactions.

Suppose Brad, the owner of *Trendy Tourz*, contributed a further $5,000 cash to the business on 3 August. We can show this transaction on the accounting equation as follows:

August 3
Brad contributed a further $5,000 cash to the business

August 03

	Cash	+ Accounts receivable	+ Computer equipment	+ Outdoor equipment	+ Van	= Accounts payable	+ Bank loan	+ Capital
	5,200	2,800	3,000	22,000	30,000	5,000	19,800	38,200
Owner contributes $5,000 cash	+ 5,000							+ 5,000
	10,200	2,800	3,000	22,000	30,000	5,000	19,800	43,200

ASSETS = LIABILITIES + EQUITY

You should notice that we have added $5,000 to each side of the accounting equation. When we have carried the balances down, we can check that the equation still balances. Both the left hand side and the right hand side in this case add up to $68,000. We can record further transactions in a similar manner.

August 7
Received $500 from customers on account

August 07

	Cash	+ Accounts receivable	+ Computer equipment	+ Outdoor equipment	+ Van	= Accounts payable	+ Bank loan	+ Capital
	10,200	2,800	3,000	22,000	30,000	5,000	19,800	43,200
Received $500 cash on account	+ 500	− 500						
	10,700	2,300	3,000	22,000	30,000	5,000	19,800	43,200

ASSETS = LIABILITIES + EQUITY

In this case, customers who owed $500 have paid their accounts. Thus the Cash column *increases* by $500. Meanwhile, the amount owed to the business by customers decreases, so $500 is *deducted* from the Accounts receivable column.

August 11
Paid $1,000 owing on accounts payable

August 11

	Cash	+ Accounts receivable	+ Computer equipment	+ Outdoor equipment	+ Van	= Accounts payable	+ Bank loan	+ Capital
	10,700	2,300	3,000	22,000	30,000	5,000	19,800	43,200
Paid $1,000 owing on accounts payable	− 1,000					− 1,000		
	9,700	2,300	3,000	22,000	30,000	4,000	19,800	43,200

ASSETS = LIABILITIES + EQUITY

The Cash column *decreases* by $1,000 (the amount which has been paid) and $1,000 is *deducted* from the Accounts payable column.

ISBN: 9780170211055

August 13
Bought tents for $7,500 and paid a deposit of $2,000 cash

13

Bought tents for $7,500, paid deposit of $2,000 cash

	ASSETS				=	LIABILITIES		+ EQUITY
Cash	+ Accounts receivable	+ Computer equipment	+ Outdoor equipment	+ Van	= Accounts payable	+ Bank loan	+ Capital
9,700	2,300	3,000	22,000	30,000	4,000	19,800	43,200
– 2,000			+ 7,500		+ 5,500		
7,700	2,300	3,000	29,500	30,000	9,500	19,800	43,200

Cash has been paid, so the Cash column *decreases*. The Outdoor equipment column *increases* by the $7,500 cost of the tents. Since only $2,000 of this has been paid so far, the balance of $5,500 is *added* to the Accounts payable column.

August 14
Brad withdrew $600 cash for personal use

14

Brad withdrew $600 cash for personal use

	ASSETS				=	LIABILITIES		+ EQUITY
Cash	+ Accounts receivable	+ Computer equipment	+ Outdoor equipment	+ Van	= Accounts payable	+ Bank loan	+ Capital
7,700	2,300	3,000	29,500	30,000	9,500	19,800	43,200
– 600							– 600
7,100	2,300	3,000	29,500	30,000	9,500	19,800	42,600

Cash has been paid, so the Cash column *decreases* by $600. Cash withdrawn for personal use decreases equity, so the amount is *deducted* from the Capital column.

At 14 August the total of the balances on each side of the equation is $71,900. We can check this by drawing up a trial balance, which is a list of the balances in each column or account. The trial balance helps us to check that the transactions have been entered correctly and that we have carried the balances down correctly.

Trendy Tourz
Trial Balance as at 14 August 2015

Cash	$ 7,100	Accounts payable	$9,500
Accounts receivable	2,300	Bank loan (due 30 June 2020)	19,800
Computer equipment (cost)	3,000	Capital	42,600
Outdoor equipment (cost)	29,500		
Van (cost)	30,000		
	$71,900		$71,900

ISBN: 9780170211055

Activities

1 The following is the statement of financial position of *Pasifika Travel* as at 1 April 2019:

Pasifika Travel Statement of Financial Position as at 1 April 2019			
Assets		**Liabilities**	
Cash	$3,750	Accounts payable	$2,250
Accounts receivable	5,250	Bank loan (due 30 June 2020)	6,000
Furniture and equipment (cost)	3,000		8,250
		Equity	
		Capital	3,750
	$12,000		$12,000

The following transactions occurred during April:

Pasifika Travel
Go WITH US!

Apr 2 Owner contributed more cash, $2,000
    4 Received cash from accounts receivable, $900
    6 Received loan from bank, $5,000
    10 Paid accounts payable, $750
    20 Bought new desk for office on credit, $800
    21 Withdrew cash for personal use, $500
    28 Sold old office desk, cost $250, for $250 cash
    30 Bought new computer costing $5,000 for cash.

DO THIS!

a Record the transactions for the month of April on the accounting equation.
b Prepare the trial balance as at 30 April 2019.

2 At 1 May 2020 *Developmental Surveyors*, a business owned by Darryl Lines, had the following assets and liabilities:

Assets: Cash $2,500, Accounts receivable $13,600, Office equipment $4,500, Surveying equipment $25,000, Van $15,000.
Liabilities: Accounts payable $8,600, Bank loan $15,000.

The following transactions occurred during May:

May 2 Paid $1,500 of accounts payable
    4 Bought surveying equipment costing $2,000, paid cash of $500 as a deposit
    6 Received cash from accounts receivable, $1,900
    10 Borrowed a further bank loan of $10,000
    13 Withdrew cash for personal use, $1,000
    18 Bought wife a car for $10,000 cash from the business bank account
    19 Darryl Lines contributed his own car valued at $5,000 to the business
    25 Received $2,500 on accounts receivable due
    27 Paid accounts payable, $1,800
    31 Withdrew cash for personal use, $1,000.

DO THIS!

a Calculate the equity at 1 May 2020.
b Record the transactions for the month of May on the accounting equation.
c Prepare the trial balance as at 31 May 2020.

ISBN: 9780170211055

Recording Income and Expenses

In Chapter 2 we were introduced to the idea of **profit** as the increase in the net assets of a business which does not arise from a contribution by the owner. We established that the profit was earned through transactions with outside accounting entities.

We also learnt that profit is calculated as the difference between income earned and expenses incurred in a particular period of time:

$$\textbf{Profit} \quad = \quad \textbf{Income} \quad - \quad \textbf{Expenses}$$

- Income is increases in equity during the accounting period arising from inflows of assets or decreases of liabilities, other than from contributions by the owner; and

- Expenses are decreases in equity during the accounting period in the form of outflows of assets or incurrences of liabilities, other than drawings.

These ideas are represented in the following diagram:

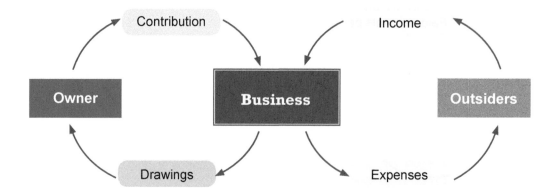

Income results from activities such as selling goods or performing services. Expenses are the costs of producing the income. Examples of expenses include: paying wages, paying rent, writing off bad debts, a loss on the sale of an item of property, plant and equipment, or buying stationery.

When a business earns income, the equity increases. When a business incurs expenses, equity decreases. We now have **four** types of transactions which affect equity.

Remember!

Equity is *increased* by:

- Contributions made by the owner
- Income earned by the business.

Equity is *decreased* by:

- Drawings made by the owner
- Expenses incurred by the business.

ISBN: 9780170211055

Let's return to *Trendy Tourz* and record the remaining transactions for August.

August 16
Received travel fees in cash, $1,950

	ASSETS					=	LIABILITIES		+ EQUITY
Cash	+ Accounts receivable	+ Computer equipment	+ Outdoor equipment	+ Van		= Accounts payable	+ Bank loan	+ Capital
7,100	2,300	3,000	29,500	30,000		9,500	19,800	42,600
+ 1,950								+ 1,950
9,050	2,300	3,000	29,500	30,000		9,500	19,800	44,550

Received travel fees in cash, $1,950

Trendy Tourz charged customers for travel services and they paid in cash. The Cash account *increases* by $1,950. The cash did not come from the owner, so the business has earned **income**. Equity (Capital) thus *increases* by $1,950.

August 18
Paid cash for office stationery, $250

	ASSETS					=	LIABILITIES		+ EQUITY
Cash	+ Accounts receivable	+ Computer equipment	+ Outdoor equipment	+ Van		= Accounts payable	+ Bank loan	+ Capital
9,050	2,300	3,000	29,500	30,000		9,500	19,800	44,550
− 250								− 250
8,800	2,300	3,000	29,500	30,000		9,500	19,800	44,300

Paid cash for office stationery, $250

There has been an outflow of cash to pay for the stationery but it was not a distribution to Brad. The business has therefore paid an **expense**. The *decrease* in assets causes a *decrease* in equity – Capital *decreases* by $250. Since the stationery was paid for in cash, the Cash account also *decreases* by $250.

August 19
Sent invoices to travel agents, $4,500

	ASSETS					=	LIABILITIES		+ EQUITY
Cash	+ Accounts receivable	+ Computer equipment	+ Outdoor equipment	+ Van		= Accounts payable	+ Bank loan	+ Capital
8,800	2,300	3,000	29,500	30,000		9,500	19,800	44,300
	+ 4,500							+ 4,500
8,800	6,800	3,000	29,500	30,000		9,500	19,800	48,800

Sent invoices to agents, $4,500

There has been an inflow of assets (Accounts receivable) to the business. Accounts receivable *increases* by $4,500. The business has earned income, because the inflow of assets did not come from the owner. Equity (Capital) *increases* by $4,500. In this case the income was not received in cash, but charged to customers on account.

ISBN: 9780170211055

August 20
Paid rent, $400

	ASSETS				=	LIABILITIES		+ EQUITY
Cash	+ Accounts receivable	+ Computer equipment	+ Outdoor equipment	+ Van	= Accounts payable	+ Bank loan	+ Capital
8,800	6,800	3,000	29,500	30,000	9,500	19,800	48,800
− 400							− 400
8,400	6,800	3,000	29,500	30,000	9,500	19,800	48,400

Paid rent, $400

There has been an outflow of cash to pay for the rent but it was not a distribution to Brad. The business has therefore paid an **expense**. The *decrease* in assets causes a *decrease* in equity – Capital *decreases* by $400. Since the rent was paid for in cash, the Cash account also *decreases* by $400.

August 22
Wrote off bad debts, $300

	ASSETS				=	LIABILITIES		+ EQUITY
Cash	+ Accounts receivable	+ Computer equipment	+ Outdoor equipment	+ Van	= Accounts payable	+ Bank loan	+ Capital
8,400	6,800	3,000	29,500	30,000	9,500	19,800	48,400
	− 300						− 300
8,400	6,500	3,000	29,500	30,000	9,500	19,800	48,100

Wrote off bad debts, $300

A bad debt is an account receivable that will not be collected. We must therefore *reduce* the amount in the Accounts receivable column by $300. Since an asset has *decreased*, equity (Capital) must also *decrease* by $300. Bad debts are an **expense** even though they are not paid in cash.

August 24
Paid instalment on loan, $350, including interest of $150

	ASSETS				=	LIABILITIES		+ EQUITY
Cash	+ Accounts receivable	+ Computer equipment	+ Outdoor equipment	+ Van	= Accounts payable	+ Bank loan	+ Capital
8,400	6,500	3,000	29,500	30,000	9,500	19,800	48,100
− 350						− 200	− 150
8,050	6,500	3,000	29,500	30,000	9,500	19,600	47,950

Paid loan $350, $150 interest

Cash of $350 has been paid so this is deducted from the Cash account. Of the total $350 payment, $150 is interest so therefore the remaining $200 is a repayment of the loan principal. We must therefore *reduce* the amount in the Bank loan column by $200. The interest on the loan is an **expense**, thus Capital must decrease by $150.

The payment of interest does not reduce the amount of the loan liability that is still owing to the bank. It represents the cost of borrowing money.

Accounting – A Beginning ISBN: 9780170211055

August 27
Received invoice for equipment repairs, $420

	ASSETS					=	LIABILITIES		+ EQUITY
Cash	+ Accounts receivable	+ Computer equipment	+ Outdoor equipment	+ Van	=	Accounts payable	+ Bank loan	+ Capital
8,050	6,500	3,000	29,500	30,000		9,500	19,600	47,950
						+ 420		– 420
8,050	6,500	3,000	29,500	30,000		9,920	19,600	47,530

Received invoice for equipment repairs, $420

The invoice received represents a liability that has been incurred, thus Accounts payable *increases* by $420. The repairs are an **expense** and so equity (Capital) *decreases* by $420.

August 30
Sold old tent that had cost $250 for $50 cash

	ASSETS					=	LIABILITIES		+ EQUITY
Cash	+ Accounts receivable	+ Computer equipment	+ Outdoor equipment	+ Van	=	Accounts payable	+ Bank loan	+ Capital
8,050	6,500	3,000	29,500	30,000		9,920	19,600	47,530
+ 50			– 250					– 200
8,100	6,500	3,000	29,250	30,000		9,920	19,600	47,330

Sold old tent that had cost $250 for $50 cash

In this case an asset was sold at a loss. The tent had cost $250 and so the Outdoor equipment column must be *reduced* by this amount. The Cash column *increases* by only $50 as this was the amount which was received for the tent. The difference, $200, is a **loss on sale** which *reduces* equity (Capital).

The trial balance prepared at 31 August is shown below.

Trendy Tourz
Trial Balance as at 31 August 2015

Cash	$ 8,100	Accounts payable	$9,920
Accounts receivable	6,500	Bank loan (due 30 June 2020)	19,600
Computer equipment (cost)	3,000	Capital	47,330
Outdoor equipment (cost)	29,250		
Van (cost)	30,000		
	$76,850		$76,850

ISBN: 9780170211055

Chapter 3

Activities

1 *Forward Planners* is a city architectural firm owned and operated by Ian Draft. The business has the following assets and liabilities as at 1 July 2018:

Assets: Cash $3,000, Petty cash $100, Accounts receivable $4,500, Office equipment $4,000, Drawing equipment $6,500.

Liabilities: Accounts payable $2,200, Bank loan $8,000.

The following transactions took place during July:

Jul	3	Paid accounts payable, $1,200
	4	Received fees in cash, $1,100
	5	Withdrew $50 petty cash for personal use
	7	Paid cash for stationery supplies, $550
	9	Bought new desk for $500 cash
	10	Paid wages, $400
	12	Sold old desk which had cost $250 for $100 cash
	14	Sent accounts to clients, $600
	15	Received cash fees, $3,200
	16	Paid office cleaning expenses, $300
	19	Paid rent, $1,200
	22	Bought computer costing $3,000, paying $1,000 deposit
	23	Received cash from accounts receivable, $1,500
	24	Ian Draft withdrew $1,000 cash for personal use
	25	Paid telephone rental, $150
	27	Paid for groceries from office bank account, $100
	30	Ian Draft contributed cash to the practice, $3,000.

Forward Planners

DO THIS!

a Calculate the equity at 1 July 2018.
b Record the transactions for the month of July on the accounting equation.
c Prepare the trial balance as at 31 July 2018.

2 Mr I Spark is an electrician who has given you the following information about his business assets and liabilities at 1 September 2017: Cash on hand $150, Bank overdraft $8,500, Tools and ladders $7,000, Van $10,000, Accounts owing to suppliers $4,000, Amount owing from customers $15,000.

The following transactions took place during September:

Sep	2	Contributed a further $8,000 cash to the business from selling his car
	4	Paid accounts payable, $3,000
	5	Received cash from customers on overdue accounts, $3,500
	7	Received fees from customers in cash, $1,200
	8	Sent accounts to customers for work done, $4,200
	10	Paid $20 cash for stamps from cash on hand
	12	Purchased additional tools for cash, $400
	14	Paid personal Visa account from business bank account, $1,200
	17	Paid for the month's petrol, $500
	19	Received invoice from electrical wholesalers, $1,600
	20	Wrote off bad debts, $800
	28	Paid cellphone rental and calls for the month, $300.

Accounting – A Beginning

ISBN: 9780170211055

DO THIS!

a Calculate the equity at 1 September 2017.
b Record the transactions for the month of September on the accounting equation.
c Prepare the trial balance as at 30 September 2017.

3 *Legal Eagles* are solicitors in public practice. They had the following business assets and liabilities as at 1 November 2018:

Assets: Accounts receivable $5,000, Petty cash $100, Office equipment $7,500, Premises $200,000.

Liabilities: Mortgage on premises $150,000, Accounts payable $3,500, Bank overdraft $6,500.

The following transactions took place during November:

Nov 2   Paid wages, $1,600
   3   Received cash from accounts receivable, $1,300
   5   Received account for electricity, $200
   6   Paid deposit for family motor vehicle, $4,000
   7   Paid for general office expenses from petty cash, $50
   9   Received account for business cellphone usage, $300
   10   Received cash from clients on account, $1,650
   13   Received cash for legal services, $3,500
   15   Bought lunch from petty cash, $10
   17   Paid cash for repairs to computer, $400
   19   Bought office computer on credit, $4,500
   20   Paid accounts payable, $500
   21   Built extensions to premises, $20,000 paying a deposit of $5,000 by cheque and raising a mortgage for the balance
   22   Sent accounts to clients for services, $5,700
   23   Paid cash for repairs to electrical wiring, $2,000
   25   Received account for office stationery, $300
   27   Bought computer for $3,000, paying $600 deposit
   28   Sold old printer (cost $600) for $100 cash
   29   Paid accounts payable, $1,200
   30   Wrote off bad debts, $900.

DO THIS!

a Calculate the equity at 1 November 2018.
b Record the transactions for the month of November on the accounting equation.
c Prepare the trial balance as at 30 November 2018.

NEED HELP?

LEGAL EAGLES

YOUR FRIENDLY NEIGHBOURHOOD LAWYERS

The Expanded Accounting Equation

Previously we have used the accounting equation in the form

$$A = L + Eq \qquad \text{or} \qquad Eq = A - L.$$

We have also learnt that there are four types of transactions which affect equity:

> **Remember!**
>
> Equity is *increased* by:
> - Contributions made by the owner
> - Income earned by the business.
>
> Equity is *decreased* by:
> - Drawings made by the owner
> - Expenses incurred by the business.

It is possible to expand the accounting equation so that all four types of transactions that affect equity are recorded separately.

Let's consider the accounting equation again.

$$A = L + Eq$$

But:

$$Eq\ (end) = Eq\ (beginning) + Contributions + Income - Expenses - Drawings$$

Let's suppose we decide that the income and expenses will be recorded separately in the transaction analysis. We will continue to record contributions and drawings by the owner in the equity column, but income and expenses will now be analysed separately.

We can now write the accounting equation as:

$$A = L + Eq + C + I - Ex - D$$

or

$$A = L + (Eq + C - D) + I - Ex$$

By rearranging this equation, we find:

$$A + Ex = L + (Eq + C - D) + I$$

This is called the **expanded accounting equation**. This equation provides the basis for the entire accounting process.

> **Learn!**
>
> $$A + Ex = L + Eq + I$$

Accounting – A Beginning
ISBN: 9780170211055

Let's look at the transactions of *Trendy Tourz* for September:

Sep 2   Invested $5,000 on term deposit from the bank account at
        6% per annum for two years
    5   Paid rent, $800
    8   Sent accounts to travel agents, $4,200
   10   Received $2,000 from customers on account
   11   Bought lifejackets for $3,000, paying $1,000 deposit
   12   Bought food supplies on credit, $350
   13   Paid accounts payable, $2,000
   15   Received fees in cash, $2,500
   17   Paid a loan instalment of $350, including $150 interest
   19   Received $1,700 from customers on account
   20   Paid cash for van repairs, $450
   25   Sold old kayak which had cost $2,500 for $800 cash
   26   Paid cash for stationery, $100
   28   Brad withdrew $1,000 cash for personal use
   29   Received interest of $20 on term deposit
   30   Wrote off a bad debt of $300.

We will record these transactions using the *expanded* accounting equation. The transaction analysis is shown on the next two pages.

This transaction analysis is very similar to the transaction analysis we did using the short form of the accounting equation, A = L + Eq. The only difference is that income and expenses are now recorded in separate sections of the analysis.

We can use the totals obtained in this transaction analysis to prepare an abbreviated trial balance as at 30 September 2015. This trial balance is shown below.

Trendy Tourz
Trial Balance as at 30 September 2015

Cash	$ 4,420	Accounts payable	$10,270
Accounts receivable	6,700	Bank loan (due 30 June 2020)	19,400
Computer equipment (cost)	3,000	Capital	46,330
Outdoor equipment (cost)	29,750	Income	6,720
Van (cost)	30,000		
Term deposit (6%)	5,000		
Expenses	3,850		
	$82,720		$82,720

This is an abbreviated trial balance in which all expenses are combined into a single figure and all income items are combined into a single figure. Later in the course we will prepare a full trial balance which shows all these items separately.

ISBN: 9780170211055

DATE	TRANSACTION		ASSETS		
		Cash	+ Accounts receivable	+ Computer equipment +	
Sep 1	Opening balance	$ 8,100	6,500	3,000	
2	Invested $5,000 on term deposit for two years	− 5,000			
		3,100	6,500	3,000	
5	Paid rent, $800	− 800			
		2,300	6,500	3,000	
8	Sent accounts to travel agents, $4,200		+ 4,200		
		2,300	10,700	3,000	
10	Received $2,000 from customers on account	+ 2,000	− 2,000		
		4,300	8,700	3,000	
11	Bought lifejackets for $3,000, paying deposit of $1,000	− 1,000			
		3,300	8,700	3,000	
12	Bought food supplies on credit, $350				
		3,300	8,700	3,000	
13	Paid accounts payable, $2,000	− 2,000			
		1,300	8,700	3,000	
15	Received fees in cash, $2,500	+ 2,500			
		3,800	8,700	3,000	
17	Paid a loan instalment of $350, including $150 interest	− 350			
		3,450	8,700	3,000	
19	Received $1,700 from customers on account	+ 1,700	− 1,700		
		5,150	7,000	3,000	
20	Paid cash for van repairs, $450	− 450			
		4,700	7,000	3,000	
25	Sold old kayak which had cost $2,500 for $800 cash	+ 800			
		5,500	7,000	3,000	
26	Paid cash for stationery, $100	− 100			
		5,400	7,000	3,000	
28	Brad withdrew $1,000 cash	− 1,000			
		4,400	7,000	3,000	
29	Received interest of $20 on term deposit	+ 20			
		4,420	7,000	3,000	
30	Wrote off a bad debt of $300		− 300		
		4,420	6,700	3,000	

Accounting – A Beginning   ISBN: 9780170211055

ASSETS			+ EXPENSES =	LIABILITIES		+ EQUITY	INCOME
Outdoor equipment +	Van +	Term deposit	+ Expenses	= Accounts + payable	Bank loan	+ Capital +	Income
29,250	30,000			9,920	19,600	47,330	
		+ 5,000					
29,250	30,000	5,000		9,920	19,600	47,330	
			Rent + 800				
29,250	30,000	5,000	800	9,920	19,600	47,330	
							Fees + 4,200
29,250	30,000	5,000	800	9,920	19,600	47,330	4,200
29,250 + 3,000	30,000	5,000	800	9,920 + 2,000	19,600	47,330	4,200
32,250	30,000	5,000	800	11,920	19,600	47,330	4,200
			Supplies + 350	+ 350			
32,250	30,000	5,000	1,150	12,270 − 2,000	19,600	47,330	4,200
32,250	30,000	5,000	1,150	10,270	19,600	47,330	4,200
							Fees + 2,500
32,250	30,000	5,000	1,150	10,270	19,600	47,330	6,700
			Interest +150		− 200		
32,250	30,000	5,000	1,300	10,270	19,400	47,330	6,700
32,250	30,000	5,000	1,300	10,270	19,400	47,330	6,700
			Van expenses + 450				
32,250	30,000	5,000	1,750	10,270	19,400	47,330	6,700
			Loss on sale				
− 2,500			+ 1,700				
29,750	30,000	5,000	3,450	10,270	19,400	47,330	6,700
			Stationery + 100				
29,750	30,000	5,000	3,550	10,270	19,400	47,330	6,700
						Drawings − 1,000	
29,750	30,000	5,000	3,550	10,270	19,400	46,330	6,700
							Interest + 20
29,750	30,000	5,000	3,550	10,270	19,400	46,330	6,720
			Bad debts + 300				
29,750	30,000	5,000	3,850	10,270	19,400	46,330	6,720

ISBN: 9780170211055

Revision – Preparing the Financial Statements

We can use the transaction analysis on the previous page to prepare the financial statements of *Trendy Tourz* for the month of September.

Income Statement

The income statement prepared from the income and expense columns of the transaction analysis. The statement is shown below.

Trendy Tourz
Income Statement for the month ended 30 September 2015

	$	$	$
Revenue			
Tour fees			6,700
Other income			
Interest on term deposit			20
Total income			6,720
Less: **Expenses**			
Tour expenses			
Loss on sale of kayak	1,700		
Tour supplies expense	350		
Van expenses	450		
		2,500	
Administrative expenses			
Bad debts	300		
Rent	800		
Stationery	100		
		1,200	
Finance costs			
Interest on loan		150	
Total expenses			3,850
Profit for the month			$2,870

We can now prepare the statement of financial position. In order to complete the equity section, we need to examine the capital column of the transaction analysis to see what changes have taken place due to transactions with the owner. We see that Brad has made no contributions this month, but has taken drawings of $1,000. The statement of financial position is shown opposite.

Income statement	→ Transfer profit	Statement of financial position

Trendy Tourz

Statement of Financial Position as at 30 September 2015

	$	$	$
ASSETS			
Non-current assets			
Property, plant and equipment			
Total carrying amount (Note 1)		62,750	
Investment			
Term deposit (6%, due 2 September 2017)		5,000	
Total non-current assets			67,750
Current assets			
Cash		4,420	
Accounts receivable		6,700	
Total current assets			11,120
Total assets			$78,870
EQUITY AND LIABILITIES			
Equity			
Capital at beginning of the month		47,330	
Profit for the month		2,870	
Drawings for the month		(1,000)	
Capital at end of the month			49,200
Non-current liabilities			
Bank loan (due 30 June 2020)		19,400	
Current liabilities			
Accounts payable		10,270	
Total liabilities			29,670
Total equity and liabilities			$78,870

Notes to the statement of financial position

1 *Property, plant and equipment*	$
Computer equipment (cost)	3,000
Outdoor equipment (cost)	29,750
Van (cost)	30,000
	$62,750

Well, I'm still waiting to use my computer!

Do you follow the transactions now?

I think so, but I can't see how that has anything to do with the computer.

The computer records the transactions in the same way. It just looks a bit different.

Do you mean we just use a spreadsheet?

We could, but there are accounting packages that are a bit more efficient. We'll get one later.

Activities

1 *Fast 'n Furious* is a firm of painters and decorators owned by Peter Paynter. The firm had the following assets and liabilities as at 1 January 2016:

Assets: Cash $3,000, Accounts receivable $2,250, Ladders and equipment (cost) $3,500, Van (cost) $15,000.

Liabilities: Accounts payable $1,800, Bank loan (due 30 June 2019) $10,000.

The following transactions took place during the month of January:

Jan	2	Received $900 from customers on account
	4	Received fees in cash for decorating done, $800
	5	Paid accounts payable of $500
	7	Received account for van repairs, $450
	8	Paid registration on van, $150
	11	Sent invoices to customers for work done, $1,200
	13	Paid wages for the past fortnight, $800
	14	Paid loan instalment of $300 which included interest of $50
	18	Bought three ladders on credit, $600
	23	Peter Paynter withdrew cash of $900 for personal use
	25	Paid accounts payable of $700
	27	Received $500 from one customer who was invoiced on 11 January
	28	Paid wages for the past fortnight, $800
	29	Sent invoices to customers for work done, $1,900
	31	Wrote off a bad debt of $500.

DO THIS!

Hint

You will need to calculate equity before you begin this question.

a Prepare a transaction analysis using the expanded accounting equation for *Fast 'n Furious* for the month ended 31 January 2016.

b Prepare an abbreviated trial balance for the firm as at 31 January 2016.
   NOTE: You should combine all expenses as a single figure and all income as a single figure in this trial balance.

c Prepare the income statement and a fully classified statement of financial position (in vertical form) for the month of January 2016.

2 *Pampered Pets* is a pet-care service which takes care of animals in their own homes while the owners are away. The firm is owned by I M Helpful who employs a driver to assist her. The business had the following assets and liabilities at 1 December 2017:

Assets: Cash $2,500, Accounts receivable $950, Equipment (cost) $500, Motor vehicles (cost) $30,000.

Liabilities: Accounts payable $700, Bank loan (due 31 July 2020) $15,000.

The following transactions took place during the month of December:

Dec	2	I M Helpful invested her new car, costing $10,000, in the business
	4	Advertised in local paper, paying $50 cash
	7	Received $400 from clients on account
	8	Paid wages of $600 for the previous month
	9	Employed a new driver and paid for uniform expenses, $200
	10	Bought equipment for the new driver, $200, on credit
	12	Sent accounts to clients for feeding services, $800
	15	I M Helpful withdrew $500 cash for personal use
	19	Paid for insurance on one of the vehicles, $500

ISBN: 9780170211055

20	Received account for advertising in the newspaper, $150
21	Banked cash fees, $1,500
23	Paid accounts payable, $550
24	Received $600 cash from clients on account
28	Paid cash for petrol, $300
31	Paid loan instalment of $500, including interest of $150.

Hint

You will need to calculate equity before you begin this question.

DO THIS!

a Prepare a transaction analysis using the expanded accounting equation for *Pampered Pets* for the month ended 31 December 2017.
b Prepare an abbreviated trial balance for the firm as at 31 December 2017.
   NOTE: You should combine all expenses as a single figure and all income as a single figure in this trial balance.
c Prepare a fully classified income statement and a fully classified statement of financial position (in vertical form) for the month of December 2017.

3 *Clear Sight* is an optometry firm owned by Wiremu Happy. The firm had the following assets and liabilities as at 1 May 2016:

Assets: Accounts receivable $3,400, Optical equipment (cost) $47,500, Office equipment (cost) $6,000.
Liabilities: Bank overdraft $2,700, Accounts payable $900, Bank loan (due 31 Jan 2019) $8,000.

The following transactions took place during the month of May:

May 2	Sent accounts to clients, $4,200
4	Bought new computer for $5,600, paying deposit of $1,000. The balance of the payment is due in two months' time.
6	Sold old computer which had cost $3,000 for $800 on credit to a client
7	Wiremu Happy withdrew $1,200 cash for personal use
9	Received $3,300 from clients on account
11	Received cash fees of $1,600
13	Paid accounts payable of $800
14	Bought optical supplies on credit, $1,350
16	Paid monthly vehicle lease of $1,000
18	Bought new cellphone for cash, $500
19	Paid electricity, $150
20	Received invoice for cleaning, $200
22	Sent accounts to clients, $4,500
28	Paid loan instalment of $400 which included interest of $100

Clear Sight

Hint

You will need to calculate equity before you begin this question.

DO THIS!

a Prepare a transaction analysis using the expanded accounting equation for *Clear Sight* for the month ended 31 May 2016.
b Prepare an abbreviated trial balance for the firm as at 31 May 2016.
   NOTE: You should combine all expenses as a single figure and all income as a single figure in this trial balance.
c Prepare the income statement and a fully classified statement of financial position (in vertical form) for the month of May 2016.

4 Fiona Froggitt commenced business as *Valued Vets* on 1 April 2016. The following transactions occurred during the month of April:

Apr 1 Fiona began business with $50,000 cash
2 Purchased equipment for $35,000 cash
3 Borrowed $20,000 as a ten year bank loan
4 Bought a van, paying $30,000 cash
5 Received fees in cash of $800
7 Bought drugs on credit, $600
9 Paid rent for the month, $1,400
11 Fiona withdrew $300 in cash for personal use
13 Sent accounts to clients for fees of $900
14 Paid cash for telephone rental and connection, $200
16 Paid $250 cash to accounts payable
18 Purchased equipment on credit, $2,500
20 Received fees in cash of $1,600
21 Fiona withdrew $400 in cash for personal use
22 Received $300 from customers on account
25 Received invoice for advertising, $100
29 Paid loan instalment of $400, half of which was interest
30 Sent accounts to clients for fees of $1,500.

a Prepare a transaction analysis using the expanded accounting equation for *Valued Vets* for the month ended 30 April 2016.
b Prepare an abbreviated trial balance for the firm as at 30 April 2016.
   NOTE: You should combine all expenses as a single figure and all income as a single figure in this trial balance.
c Prepare the income statement for the month of April 2016.
d Prepare a fully classified statement of financial position (in vertical form) as at 30 April 2016.

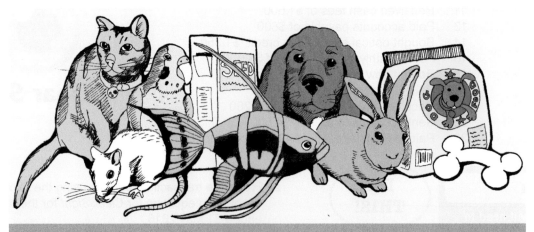

Valued Vets *for Valued Pets*

ISBN: 9780170211055

The General Ledger

This chapter is about the processing of accounting information – the part of the accounting process that is traditionally called **bookkeeping**. Although the emphasis in accounting is on communicating information so that users understand what it means, we must also understand how that information is prepared. In this chapter we will look at accounting for cash transactions using manual accounting systems.

Accounting information is produced by an accounting system. A system may be represented by a diagram as shown below.

The **input** is the daily transaction record of the business. Transactions are recorded on the source documents that we met in Chapter 3, such as cheque butts, invoices, receipts, credit notes etc.

The **process** is the classifying and recording of information in records called journals and ledgers. The information is the summarised in the trial balance which we met in Chapter 3.

The **output** is the financial statements – the income statement and statement of financial position that we met earlier.

The design of accounting systems is a specialised field. The introduction of computers has resulted in the use of accounting 'packages' by many businesses. These packages are software or computer programs which process accounting information. A good system not only processes the information, but also has checking procedures which identify errors and help prevent any dishonest activities.

The best way to learn about the processing part of accounting, or bookkeeping, is to learn about a manual system. In this type of system all the records are hand-written. The work is done by people called bookkeepers. Once you understand a manual system properly, it is relatively easy to transfer your knowledge to a computerised system.

The Chart of Accounts

A ledger is a set of **accounts**. Each column in a transaction analysis represents an account. Each account is given a number for easy reference. The numbers are arranged according to a **chart of accounts**.

The chart of accounts is arranged to suit the particular business. No two businesses will have the same chart of accounts. The chart of accounts for Aroha's business, *Kiwi Krafts*, could look like this:

Kiwi Krafts Chart of Accounts		
100	**Current Assets**	
	110	Cash
	120	Inventory
200	**Non-current Assets**	
	210	Shop Fittings
	220	Van
300	**Current Liabilities**	
	310	GST payable
400	**Long Term Liabilities**	
	410	Loan
500	**Equity**	
	510	Capital
	520	Drawings

The number codes are assigned to leave plenty of room for more accounts to be added later as they are required. The accounts are arranged according to their position in the financial statements. Thus all current asset accounts begin with 1, all non-current assets with 2, and so on.

Note that the **drawings** account appears in the *equity* section. This is because drawings are a negative type of equity account and they appear in the equity section of the statement of financial position.

Note!

Kiwi Krafts is a *trading* business that buys goods and sells them to customers.

It thus has *inventory* listed as one of its current assets.

ISBN: 9780170211055

Recording Balances in the General Ledger

The opening trial balance for *Kiwi Krafts* as at 1 July 2015 is as follows:

Kiwi Krafts
Trial Balance as at 1 July 2015

Cash	$4,500	GST payable	$ 300
Inventory	12,000	Loan (due 31 July 2019)	15,000
Shop fittings (cost)	6,800	Capital	28,000
Van (cost)	20,000		
	$43,300		$43,300

The trial balance is arranged in the same way as the accounting equation:

$$A = L + Eq$$

Assets, which are on the *left* hand side of the accounting equation, appear on the *left* hand side of the trial balance. This is called the **debit** side.

Liabilities and equity, which are on the *right* hand side of the accounting equation, appear on the *right* hand side of the trial balance. This is called the **credit** side.

It is possible to present the trial balance in a different format, known as the three-column form. The trial balance for *Kiwi Krafts* in this format is shown below.

Kiwi Krafts
Trial Balance as at 1 July 2015

	Dr $	Cr $
Cash	$4,500	
Inventory	12,000	
Shop fittings (cost)	6,800	
Van (cost)	20,000	
GST payable		300
Loan (due 31 July 2019)		15,000
Capital		28,000
	$43,300	$43,300

> **Note!**
> • The word debit is abbreviated as Dr.
> • The word *credit* is abbreviated as Cr.

This trial balance contains the same information as the 'T' form trial balance above. However, instead of listing the account *names* on the debit and credit sides of the trial balance, only the *balances* are separated into debit and credit.

Previously we have recorded accounting transactions on a transaction analysis sheet. This was an inefficient way to record a large number of transactions. In practice, all transactions are recorded in a **ledger**, which has a separate page for each account. In this course we are concerned with only one ledger – the **general ledger**. Other ledgers are covered in later courses.

ISBN: 9780170211055

A typical ledger account, in T format, appears as follows:

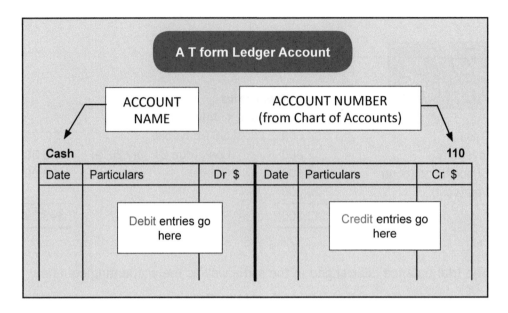

If the balances from the trial balance for *Kiwi Krafts* were entered into the general ledger in T form, it would look like this:

**Kiwi Krafts
General Ledger**

ASSETS

Cash 110

Date	Particulars	$	Date	Particulars	$
Jul 1	Balance	4,500			

Inventory 120

Date	Particulars	$	Date	Particulars	$
Jul 1	Balance	12,000			

Shop fittings 210

Date	Particulars	$	Date	Particulars	$
Jul 1	Balance	6,800			

Van 220

Date	Particulars	$	Date	Particulars	$
Jul 1	Balance	20,000			

=

LIABILITIES

GST payable 310

Date	Particulars	$	Date	Particulars	$
			Jul 1	Balance	300

Loan 410

Date	Particulars	$	Date	Particulars	$
			Jul 1	Balance	15,000

+

EQUITY

Capital 510

Date	Particulars	$	Date	Particulars	$
			Jul 1	Balance	28,000

Important!

- Asset accounts have a **debit** nature.
- Liability and equity accounts have a **credit** nature.
- Total **debit** balances = total **credit** balances.

ISBN: 9780170211055

A typical ledger account, in three-column format, appears as follows:

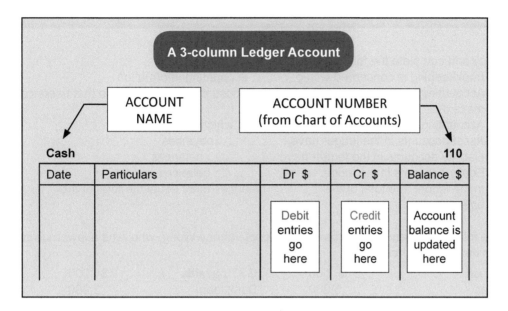

A 3-column Ledger Account

ACCOUNT NAME

ACCOUNT NUMBER (from Chart of Accounts)

Cash   110

Date	Particulars	Dr $	Cr $	Balance $
		Debit entries go here	Credit entries go here	Account balance is updated here

If the balances from the trial balance for *Kiwi Krafts* were entered into the general ledger in 3-column form, it would look like this:

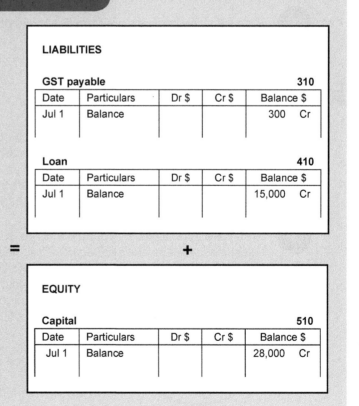

Kiwi Krafts General Ledger

ASSETS

Cash   110

Date	Particulars	Dr $	Cr $	Balance $
Jul 1	Balance			4,500 Dr

Inventory   120

Date	Particulars	Dr $	Cr $	Balance $
Jul 1	Balance			12,000 Dr

Shop fittings   210

Date	Particulars	Dr $	Cr $	Balance $
Jul 1	Balance			6,800 Dr

Van   220

Date	Particulars	Dr $	Cr $	Balance $
Jul 1	Balance			20,000 Dr

=

LIABILITIES

GST payable   310

Date	Particulars	Dr $	Cr $	Balance $
Jul 1	Balance			300 Cr

Loan   410

Date	Particulars	Dr $	Cr $	Balance $
Jul 1	Balance			15,000 Cr

+

EQUITY

Capital   510

Date	Particulars	Dr $	Cr $	Balance $
Jul 1	Balance			28,000 Cr

Important!

- When amounts are entered into the balance column of the 3-column ledger accounts, they **must** be labelled as either **Dr** or **Cr**.

ISBN: 9780170211055

Activities

1. Copy and complete the following sentences:
    a   Bookkeeping is concerned with p .... accounting information.
    b   Accounting emphasises the c .... of accounting information so that users can make d ....
    c   Accounting 'packages' are c .... p .... which ....
    d   Asset accounts in the ledger have .... balances.
    e   Liability accounts in the ledger have .... balances.
    f   Equity accounts in the ledger have .... balances.
    g   In the ledger, the total of the .... balances must equal the total of the .... balances.

2. The following balances are from the books of Johnny Wong, who runs a lawnmowing business, at 1 March 2017:

Cash	$ 500	GST payable	$ 200
Van	5,000	Bank loan	2,000
Mowers	1,600	Capital	4,900

DO THIS!

a   Design a chart of accounts for Johnny's business.
b   Enter the above balances in the general ledger. Make sure you label each account with its correct number from your chart of accounts.
c   Prepare the trial balance as at 1 March 2017.

3. The following balances are from the books of Mere Tupu, financial advisor, at 1 June 2019:

Cash	$6,200	GST payable	$ 2,800
Accounts receivable	3,100	Accounts payable	1,800
Premises	250,000	Mortgage	200,000
Computer	1,600	Capital	56,300

DO THIS!

a   Design a chart of accounts for Mere's business.
b   Enter the above balances in the general ledger. Make sure you label each account with its correct number from your chart of accounts.
c   Prepare the trial balance as at 1 June 2019.

4. You have been asked by your friend Elsie Spark to help her set up the accounts for her electrical business, *Elsie's Electrical*. You have obtained the following information:
    Elsie commenced business on 1 April 2020. At 1 May she has cash of $1,500 in her business bank account and a van which cost $6,000 last month. She owes $4,000 on the van's hire purchase agreement. Elsie has tools which cost $2,500. She owes $200 for household bills and a friend borrowed $1,000 from her last Christmas and has not repaid it.

DO THIS!

a   Calculate the capital of Elsie's business at 1 May 2020.
b   Design a chart of accounts suitable for Elsie's business.
c   Enter the above balances in the general ledger. Make sure you label each account with its correct number from your chart of accounts.
d   Prepare the trial balance as at 1 May 2020.

ISBN: 9780170211055

Transactions – Assets, Liabilities and Equity

The following is a list of the transactions which occurred for Kiwi Krafts in the first week of July 2015:

Jul 2   Aroha contributed $500 cash to the business
4   Aroha paid GST of $300
5   Aroha decided that one of her display racks was not suitable, so she sold it to Brad for cash of $460 which was what she had paid for it last month
6   Aroha bought a new display rack for $1,150 cash.

We will now enter these transactions in the general ledger.

Aroha contributed $500 cash to the business

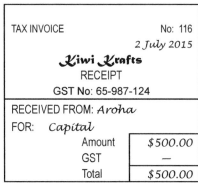

This is a capital contribution which is not subject to GST.

This transaction is recorded on the accounting equation as follows:

	A	+	Ex	=	L	+	Eq	+	I
	Cash						Capital		
Aroha contributed cash, $500	+ 500						+ 500		

When this transaction has been posted to the ledger, the accounts appear as:

General Ledger – T form

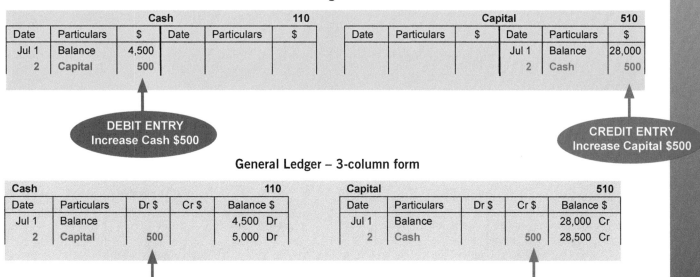

Cash						110
Date	Particulars	$	Date	Particulars	$
Jul 1	Balance	4,500			
2	Capital	500			

Capital						510
Date	Particulars	$	Date	Particulars	$
			Jul 1	Balance	28,000
			2	Cash	500

DEBIT ENTRY Increase Cash $500

CREDIT ENTRY Increase Capital $500

General Ledger – 3-column form

Cash				110
Date	Particulars	Dr $	Cr $	Balance $
Jul 1	Balance			4,500 Dr
2	Capital	500		5,000 Dr

Capital				510
Date	Particulars	Dr $	Cr $	Balance $
Jul 1	Balance			28,000 Cr
2	Cash		500	28,500 Cr

DEBIT ENTRY Increase Cash $500

CREDIT ENTRY Increase Capital $500

Important!

- The Cash account is *increasing*, so we enter the $500 on the *debit* side. This is because Cash is an asset so has a *debit* balance – we want this balance to increase so we make a *debit* entry. In the 3-column format, we then calculate the new balance of the account in the Balance column ($4,500 Dr + 500 Dr = $5,000 Dr). In the T format, balances are calculated at the end of the month.

- The Capital account is also *increasing*, so we enter the $500 on the *credit* side. This is because Capital is an equity account so has a *credit* balance – we want this balance to increase to we make a *credit* entry. In the 3-column format, we can see that the balance is now $28,500 Cr ($28,000 Cr + 500 Cr).

- Each transaction is a *'double entry'*, hence the term **'double-entry bookkeeping'**. This means that

Debit entries	=	Credit entries
$500 Dr	=	$500 Cr

- We call this entry:

Debit	Cash	$500
Credit	Capital	$500

- In the Cash account, we show 'Capital' in the particulars column to show where the other 'half' of the double entry can be found. In the same way, the Capital account has 'Cash' in the particulars column.

Aroha paid GST of $300

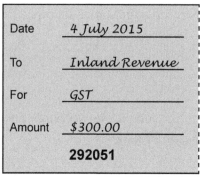

Date	4 July 2015
To	Inland Revenue
For	GST
Amount	$300.00
292051	

NO GST!

This is a GST payment, so no further GST calculation is needed for this transaction.

This transaction is recorded on the accounting equation as follows:

	A	+	Ex	=	L	+	Eq	+	I
	Cash				GST payable				
Aroha paid GST, $300	– 300				– 300				

When this transaction has been posted to the ledger, the accounts appear as:

General Ledger – T form

	Cash				110			GST payable				310
Date	Particulars	$	Date	Particulars	$		Date	Particulars	$	Date	Particulars	$
Jul 1	Balance	4,500	Jul 4	GST payable	300		Jul 4	Cash	300	Jul 1	Balance	300
2	Capital	500										

CREDIT ENTRY
Decrease Cash $300

DEBIT ENTRY
Decrease GST $300

ISBN: 9780170211055

General Ledger – 3-column form

Cash				110
Date	Particulars	Dr $	Cr $	Balance $
Jul 1	Balance			4,500 Dr
2	Capital	500		5,000 Dr
4	GST payable		300	4,700 Dr

GST payable				310
Date	Particulars	Dr $	Cr $	Balance $
Jul 1	Balance			300 Cr
4	Cash	300		—

CREDIT ENTRY
Decrease Cash $300

DEBIT ENTRY
Decrease GST $300

Important!

- The Cash account is *decreasing*. Since this is an asset account which has a *debit* nature, we must use a *credit* entry to decrease its balance. The balance is now $5,000 Dr less 300 Cr = $4,700 Dr.

- The GST payable account is also *decreasing*. This is a liability account which has a *credit* nature, so we use a *debit* entry to decrease its balance. The balance is now $300 Cr less 300 Dr = Nil.

- Once again,

Debit entries	=	Credit entries
$300 Dr	=	$300 Cr

- We call this entry:

Debit	GST payable	$300
Credit	Cash	$300

- In the GST payable account, we show 'Cash' in the particulars column to show where the other 'half' of the double entry can be found. In the same way, the Cash account has 'GST payable' in the particulars column.

July 05

Aroha sold display rack for $460 cash

```
TAX INVOICE                No: 117
                        5 July 2015
          Kiwi Krafts
            RECEIPT
       GST No: 65-987-124
RECEIVED FROM: Trendy Tourz
FOR:   Display rack
          Amount    $400.00
          GST         60.00
          Total     $460.00
```

GST!

GST of $60 has been collected. This must be paid to IRD later, so is a liability.

This transaction is recorded on the accounting equation as follows:

	A	+	Ex	=	L	+	Eq	+	I
	Cash	Shop fittings			GST payable				
Aroha sold display rack for $460 cash	+ 460	– 400			+ 60				

When this transaction has been posted to the ledger, the accounts appear as:

General Ledger – T form

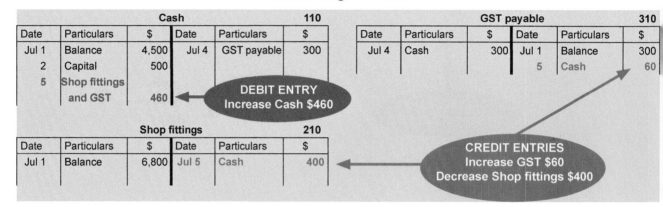

Cash 110

Date	Particulars	$	Date	Particulars	$
Jul 1	Balance	4,500	Jul 4	GST payable	300
2	Capital	500			
5	Shop fittings and GST	460			

DEBIT ENTRY
Increase Cash $460

GST payable 310

Date	Particulars	$	Date	Particulars	$
Jul 4	Cash	300	Jul 1	Balance	300
			5	Cash	60

Shop fittings 210

Date	Particulars	$	Date	Particulars	$
Jul 1	Balance	6,800	Jul 5	Cash	400

CREDIT ENTRIES
Increase GST $60
Decrease Shop fittings $400

General Ledger – 3-column form

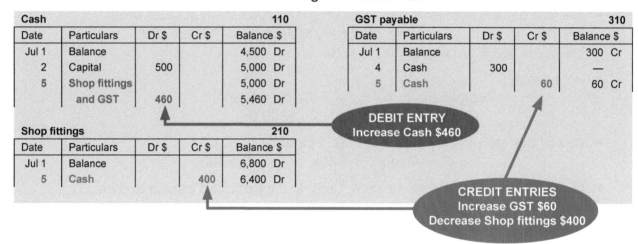

Cash 110

Date	Particulars	Dr $	Cr $	Balance $
Jul 1	Balance			4,500 Dr
2	Capital	500		5,000 Dr
5	Shop fittings			5,000 Dr
	and GST	460		5,460 Dr

DEBIT ENTRY
Increase Cash $460

GST payable 310

Date	Particulars	Dr $	Cr $	Balance $
Jul 1	Balance			300 Cr
4	Cash	300		—
5	Cash		60	60 Cr

Shop fittings 210

Date	Particulars	Dr $	Cr $	Balance $
Jul 1	Balance			6,800 Dr
5	Cash		400	6,400 Dr

CREDIT ENTRIES
Increase GST $60
Decrease Shop fittings $400

Important!

- The Cash account is *increasing*, so requires a *debit* entry.

- The Shop fittings account is an asset account, and therefore has a *debit* nature. It is *decreasing*, and therefore requires a *credit* entry.

- The GST payable account is a liability account which has a *credit* nature. It is *increasing*, so requires a *credit* entry.

- Once again,

Debit entries	=	Credit entries
$460 Dr	=	$400 Cr + $60 Cr

- We call this entry:

Debit	Cash	$460
Credit	Shop fittings	$400
Credit	GST payable	$60

- This entry has **three** parts. The increase in the Cash account comes from two sources: Shop fittings and GST payable. **Both** of these sources must be shown in the particulars column of the Cash account.

- In both the Shop fittings and GST payable accounts, we show 'Cash' in the particulars column.

> **Remember!**
> - T form accounts are balanced at the end of the month.
> - 3-column accounts have a running balance.

Aroha bought display rack for $1,150 cash

Date	*6 July 2015*
To	*Shop Outfitters*
For	*Display rack*
Amount	*$1,150.00*
	292052

GST of $150 has been paid. This will be claimed back from IRD later, so reduces the GST liability.

This transaction is recorded on the accounting equation as follows:

	A		+ Ex	=	L	+ Eq	+ I
	Cash	Shop fittings				GST	
Aroha bought display rack for $1,150 cash	− 1,150	+ 1,000				− 150	

When this transaction has been posted to the ledger, the accounts appear as:

General Ledger – T form

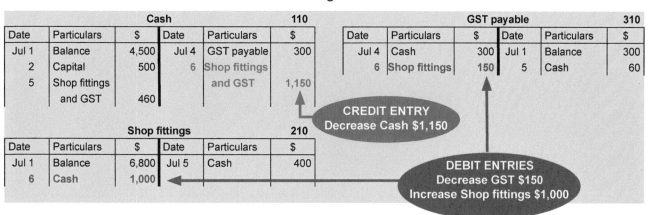

Cash   110

Date	Particulars	$	Date	Particulars	$
Jul 1	Balance	4,500	Jul 4	GST payable	300
2	Capital	500	6	Shop fittings	
5	Shop fittings			and GST	1,150
	and GST	460			

GST payable   310

Date	Particulars	$	Date	Particulars	$
Jul 4	Cash	300	Jul 1	Balance	300
6	Shop fittings	150	5	Cash	60

CREDIT ENTRY Decrease Cash $1,150

Shop fittings   210

Date	Particulars	$	Date	Particulars	$
Jul 1	Balance	6,800	Jul 5	Cash	400
6	Cash	1,000			

DEBIT ENTRIES Decrease GST $150 Increase Shop fittings $1,000

General Ledger – 3-column form

Cash   110

Date	Particulars	Dr $	Cr $	Balance $
Jul 1	Balance			4,500 Dr
2	Capital	500		5,000 Dr
4	GST payable		300	4,700 Dr
5	Shop fittings			
	and GST	460		5,160 Dr
6	Shop fittings			
	and GST		1,150	4,010 Dr

GST Payable   310

Date	Particulars	Dr $	Cr $	Balance $
Jul 1	Balance			300 Cr
4	Cash	300		—
5	Cash		60	60 Cr
6	Cash	150		90 Dr

CREDIT ENTRY Decrease Cash $1,150

Shop fittings   210

Date	Particulars	Dr $	Cr $	Balance $
Jul 1	Balance			6,800 Dr
5	Cash		400	6,400 Dr
6	Cash	1,000		7,400 Dr

DEBIT ENTRIES Decrease GST $150 Increase Shop fittings $1,000

Important!

- The Cash account is *decreasing*, so requires a *credit* entry.

- The Shop fittings account is an asset account, and therefore has a *debit* nature. It is *increasing*, and therefore requires a *debit* entry.

- The GST payable account is a liability account which has a *credit* nature. It is *decreasing*, so requires a *debit* entry.

- Once again,

Debit entries	=	Credit entries
$1,000 Dr + $150 Dr	=	$1,150 Cr

- We call this entry:

Debit	Shop fittings	$1,000
Debit	GST payable	$150
Credit	Cash	$1,150

- This entry has **three** parts. The decrease in the Cash account comes from two sources: Shop fittings and GST payable. **Both** of these sources must be shown in the particulars column of the Cash account.

- In both the Shop fittings and GST payable accounts, we show 'Cash' in the particulars column.

- Note that the GST payable account now has a *debit* balance. The reason for this is that more GST has been paid ($150) than has been received ($60). The difference of $90 is a refund due from the Inland Revenue Department and is therefore an asset at this point.

The trial balance prepared at 7 July is as follows:

Kiwi Krafts
Trial Balance as at 7 July 2015

Cash	$4,010	Loan (due 31 July 2019)	$15,000
GST receivable	90	Capital	28,500
Inventory	12,000		
Shop fittings (cost)	7,400		
Van (cost)	20,000		
	$43,500		$43,500

DEBIT = CREDIT

ISBN: 9780170211055

Summary

The following table shows a summary of the nature of the accounting entries required to enter transactions in ledger accounts.

Type of Account	ASSETS	=	LIABILITIES	+	EQUITY
Nature of Account	Debit		Credit		Credit
To INCREASE balance	Debit		Credit		Credit
To DECREASE balance	Credit		Debit		Debit

The table shows that:

- Asset accounts have a *debit* nature; liabilities and equity accounts have a *credit* nature. This corresponds with the position of the elements in the accounting equation – assets are on the *left hand side* (debit) and both liabilities and equity are on the *right hand side* (credit).

- To **increase** the balance of any account, *follow* the nature of the account:
  - Debit   Assets
  - Credit   Liabilities and Equity

- To **decrease** the balance of any account, *oppose* the nature of the account:
  - Debit   Liabilities and Equity
  - Credit   Assets

Activities

1 Ida Rill is a dentist who is registered for GST on the payments basis. Her business ledger account balances at 1 September 2019 were:

Assets: Cash $6,500, Furniture $2,700, Equipment, $50,000, Computer $5,000.
Liabilities: GST payable $920, Loan $30,000.

The transactions below occurred during September.
(All amounts include GST where appropriate.)

Remember!

To calculate the GST component, multiply by 3 and divide by 23.

Sep 2 Ida contributed $9,200 cash to the business
16 Paid $2,300 cash off the loan
20 Sold an old printer at its cost of $345
27 Paid $920 GST.

DO THIS!

a Calculate Ida's capital at 1 September 2019.
b Enter the balances in the general ledger. Make sure you give each account a number from a suitably designed chart of accounts.
c Enter the transactions listed above in the general ledger.
d Prepare the trial balance as at 30 September 2019.

2 The following transactions relate to separate businesses. (All amounts include GST where appropriate.)

a Owner banked $46,000 cash in a business bank account to start the business
b Bought equipment for $5,750 cash
c Sold old equipment for cash at its cost of $1,380
d Paid GST of $1,150
e Borrowed $11,500 from the bank as a long term loan.

DO THIS!

Enter the transactions above in ledger accounts.
Draw up a separate set of ledger accounts for each transaction.

3 Linda Loo owns and operates a laundromat, *Linda's Laundromat*. Her business is registered for GST on the payments basis. Ledger account balances at 1 October 2018 were:

Assets: Cash $6,500, Computer $3,000, Laundry fittings $5,750, Laundry equipment, $65,000, Premises $190,000.
Liabilities: GST payable $575, Mortgage $70,000.

The transactions listed below occurred during October. (All amounts include GST where appropriate.)

Oct 4 Bought a new dryer for $2,300 cash
7 Sold old dryer for cash at its cost of $690
10 Linda contributed capital of $11,500 to the business
12 A bank loan of $10,000 was received
18 GST payable of $575 was paid
21 A payment of $1,150 was made against the mortgage principal owing
28 A new van was purchased for $34,500 cash

DO THIS!

a Calculate Linda's capital at 1 October 2018.
b Enter the balances in the general ledger. Make sure you give each account a number from a suitably designed chart of accounts.
c Enter the transactions listed above in the general ledger.
d Prepare the trial balance as at 31 October 2018.

4 *Organic Bakers* produces natural breads from certified organic ingredients. The business is registered for GST on the payments basis. Ledger account balances at 1 May 2017 were:

Assets: Cash $13,000, Equipment $8,000, Ovens $35,000
Liabilities: GST payable $1,400, Bank loan $30,000.

The transactions listed below occurred during May.
(All amounts include GST where appropriate.)

May 4   The owner contributed capital of $23,000 to the business
    6   Bought new equipment for $2,300 cash
  10   Sold old equipment for cash at its cost of $2,070
  13   Purchased a van for $27,600 cash
  19   Repaid $2,000 against the bank loan
  23   Purchased oven for $3,450 cash
  28   GST payable of $1,400 was paid.

DO THIS!

a Calculate equity at 1 May 2017.
b Enter the balances in the general ledger. Make sure you give each account a number from a suitably designed chart of accounts.
c Enter the transactions listed above in the general ledger.
d Prepare the trial balance as at 31 May 2017.

5 The following statements relate to recording transactions in the general ledger:

a The opening balances of asset accounts are always debit.
b Decreases in the GST payable account are shown on the credit side.
c In the general ledger, the total of the debit balances should always equal the total of the credit balances.
d When property, plant and equipment is sold for cash, the asset account is credited.
e When a business owner contributes cash to the business, the Capital account is debited.
f When property, plant and equipment is purchased, the asset account is debited.
g A Cash account that is overdrawn will have a debit balance.
h When a business takes a bank loan, the Loan account is credited.
i When GST payable is paid, the Cash account is debited.

DO THIS!

State whether each of the statements **a** to **i** above is **true** or **false**.

Transactions – Income and Expenses

Earlier in the course, we learnt about the transactions which affect equity. We found that:

Equity is increased by:
- Contributions by owners
- Income

Equity is decreased by
- Drawings
- Expenses

Equity is represented by the Capital account in the general ledger. It would be possible to enter income, expenses and drawings into the Capital account like this:

T form ledger

	Capital					510
Date	Particulars	Dr $	Date	Particulars		Cr $
	Expenses			Balance		
	Drawings			Income		

3-column ledger

Capital				510
Date	Particulars	Dr $	Cr $	Balance $
				Balance
			Income	
		Expenses		
		Drawings		

Important!

- Income *increases* capital so is entered in the credit column of the Capital account.
- Expenses and drawings *decrease* capital so they are entered in the debit column of the Capital account.

While this approach will give us the correct closing balance of the Capital account, it will not provide details of income, expenses or drawings. This means that the users of financial statements will not be able to determine how profit was made up, or extract information about the owner's transactions with the business.

Earlier, we expanded the accounting equation so that we could keep income, expenses and drawings in separate accounts.

$$A + Ex = L + Eq + I$$
$$Debit = Credit$$

ISBN: 9780170211055

Important!

- Expenses are on the *left hand side* of the accounting equation. Their balances will thus be **debit** in nature.

- Income is on the *right hand side* of the accounting equation. Income balances will thus be **credit** in nature.

- Drawings represent **negative** equity. Since equity is on the *right hand side* of the accounting equation and has a **credit** nature, drawings will be **debit** in nature.

Let's return to *Kiwi Krafts*. The following are the rest of the transactions for July 2015:

Jul	9	Sales of $4,600 in cash
	11	Aroha paid wages of $230
	15	Aroha withdrew cash for personal use, $460
	17	Paid advertising, $115
	18	Customer returned goods and was given a cash refund of $345
	20	Cash purchases of souvenirs, $690
	21	Paid cash for petrol, $115
	23	Returned goods to supplier for cash refund, $230
	25	Paid rent of $1,150 for the month
	28	Paid loan instalment of $575 including interest of $75
	30	Bought a cash register for $920 cash.

These transactions include income, expense and drawings transactions. Recording these transactions on the accounting equation follows the same pattern as for asset, liability and equity accounts.

Before we can record the transactions for *Kiwi Krafts*, we must expand the chart of accounts to include income, expense and drawings accounts. The expanded chart of accounts is shown below.

**Kiwi Krafts
Chart of Accounts**

KIWI KRAFTS

100 Current Assets		**500 Equity**	
110	Bank	510	Capital
120	Inventory	520	Drawings
200 Non-current Assets		**600 Income**	
210	Shop fittings	610	Sales
220	Van	611	Sales returns
230	Cash register		
		700 Expenses	
300 Current Liabilities		710	Purchases
310	GST payable	711	Purchases returns
		720	Advertising
400 Long Term Liabilities		730	Interest on loan
410	Loan	740	Rent
		750	Van expenses
		760	Wages

We shall now enter the transactions for the rest of July into the general ledger of *Kiwi Krafts*.

Sales of $4,600 in cash

```
CASH REGISTER SUMMARY

    1,795.00  +
      875.00  +
      635.00  +
      320.00  +
       75.00  +
      900.00  +
    4,600.00  T
```

GST of $600 has been collected. This must be paid to IRD later, so is a liability.

Note!

Income for a trading business is called *sales*.

This transaction is recorded on the accounting equation as follows:

A + Cash	Ex	=	L + GST payable	Eq +	I Sales
Sales of $4,600 in cash + 4,600			+ 600		+ 4,000

When this transaction has been posted to the ledger, the accounts appear as:

General Ledger – T form

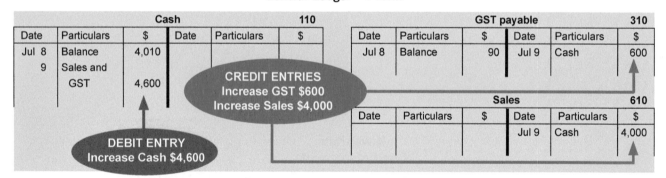

General Ledger – 3-column form

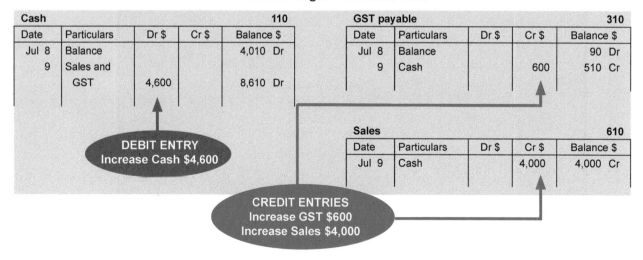

Important!

- The Cash account is *increasing*, so we enter $4,600 on the **debit** side.

- The GST payable account is also *increasing*, so we enter $600 on the **credit** side.

- The Sales account is also *increasing*. Since it is an income account which is on the *right hand side* of the accounting equation, we enter the $4,000 on the **credit** side. This follows the idea that income *increases* equity.

- We call this entry:

Debit	Cash	$4,600
Credit	GST	$600
Credit	Sales	$4,000

Aroha paid wages of $230

Date	11 July 2015
To	A Helper
For	Wages
Amount	$230.00

292053

NO GST!

Wages are exempt from GST so there is no GST recorded on this transaction.

This transaction is recorded on the accounting equation as follows:

A	+	Ex	=	L	+	Eq	+	I
Cash		Wages						

Paid wages, $230   − 230   + 230

When this transaction has been posted to the ledger, the accounts appear as:

General Ledger – T form

Cash   110

Date	Particulars	$	Date	Particulars	$
Jul 8	Balance	4,010	Jul 11	Wages	230
9	Sales and				
	GST	4,600			

CREDIT ENTRY Decrease Cash $230

Wages   760

Date	Particulars	$	Date	Particulars	$
Jul 11	Cash	230			

DEBIT ENTRY Increase Wages $230

General Ledger – 3-column form

Cash   110

Date	Particulars	Dr $	Cr $	Balance $
Jul 8	Balance			4,010 Dr
9	Sales and			
	GST	4,600		8,610 Dr
11	Wages		230	8,380 Dr

CREDIT ENTRY Decrease Cash $230

Wages   760

Date	Particulars	Dr $	Cr $	Balance $
Jul 11	Cash	230		230 Dr

DEBIT ENTRY Increase Wages $230

Important!

- The Cash account is *decreasing*, so we enter $230 on the **credit** side.

- The Wages account is *increasing*. Since it is an expense account which is on the *left hand side* of the accounting equation, we enter the $230 on the **debit** side. This follows the idea that expenses *decrease* equity.

- We call this entry:

Debit	Wages	$230
Credit	Cash	$230

Aroha withdrew $460 cash for personal use

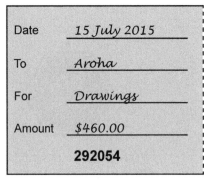

Date	15 July 2015
To	Aroha
For	Drawings
Amount	$460.00
	292054

Drawings are exempt from GST so there is no GST recorded on this transaction.

This transaction is recorded on the accounting equation as follows:

	A +	Ex	=	L	+	Eq	+	I
	Cash					Drawings		
Cash drawings, $460	− 460					− 460		

When this transaction has been posted to the ledger, the accounts appear as:

General Ledger – T form

Cash   110

Date	Particulars	$	Date	Particulars	$
Jul 8	Balance	4,010	Jul 11	Wages	230
9	Sales and		15	Drawings	460
	GST	4,600			

Drawings   520

Date	Particulars	$	Date	Particulars	$
Jul 15	Cash	460			

CREDIT ENTRY
Decrease Cash $460

DEBIT ENTRY
Increase Drawings $460

General Ledger – 3-column form

Cash   110

Date	Particulars	Dr $	Cr $	Balance $
Jul 8	Balance			4,010 Dr
9	Sales and			
	GST	4,600		8,610 Dr
11	Wages		230	8,380 Dr
15	Drawings		460	7,920 Dr

Drawings   520

Date	Particulars	Dr $	Cr $	Balance $
Jul 15	Cash	460		460 Dr

DEBIT ENTRY
Increase Drawings $460

CREDIT ENTRY
Decrease Cash $460

ISBN: 9780170211055

Important!

- The Cash account is *decreasing*, so we enter $460 on the **credit** side.

- Equity is *decreasing* due to drawings, and therefore requires a **debit** entry. However, we need to have a separate account for drawings so that we can record them in the statement of financial position. We therefore enter the $460 in the **debit** column of this Drawings account.

- We call this entry:
Debit	Drawings	$460
Credit	Cash	$460

Paid advertising, $115

Date	17 July 2015
To	Promotions Ltd
For	Advert in paper
Amount	$115.00
	292055

GST of $15 has been paid. This will be claimed back from IRD later, so reduces the GST liability.

This transaction is recorded on the accounting equation as follows:

	A +	Ex =	L +	Eq +	I
	Cash	Advertising	GST payable		
Advertising paid, $115	− 115	+ 100	− 15		

When this transaction has been posted to the ledger, the accounts appear as:

General Ledger – T form

Cash 110

Date	Particulars	$	Date	Particulars	$
Jul 8	Balance	4,010	Jul 11	Wages	230
9	Sales and		15	Drawings	460
	GST	4,600	17	Advertising	
				and GST	115

Advertising 720

Date	Particulars	$	Date	Particulars	$
Jul 17	Cash	100			

GST payable 310

Date	Particulars	$	Date	Particulars	$
Jul 8	Balance	90	Jul 9	Cash	600
17	Cash	15			

CREDIT ENTRY Decrease Cash $115

DEBIT ENTRIES Increase Advertising $100 Decrease GST $15

General Ledger – 3-column form

Cash 110

Date	Particulars	Dr $	Cr $	Balance $
Jul 8	Balance			4,010 Dr
9	Sales and			
	GST	4,600		8,610 Dr
11	Wages		230	8,380 Dr
15	Drawings		460	7,920 Dr
17	Advertising			
	and GST		115	7,805 Dr

Advertising 720

Date	Particulars	Dr $	Cr $	Balance $
Jul 17	Cash	100		100 Dr

GST payable 310

Date	Particulars	Dr $	Cr $	Balance $
Jul 8	Balance			90 Dr
9	Cash		600	510 Cr
17	Cash	15		495 Cr

Important!

- The Cash account is *decreasing*, so we enter $115 on the credit side.

- The GST payable account is also *decreasing*, so we enter $15 on the debit side.

- The Advertising account is *increasing*. Since it is an expense account which is on the *left hand side* of the accounting equation, we enter the $100 on the debit side. This follows the idea that expenses *decrease* equity.

- We call this entry:

Debit	Advertising	$100
Debit	GST payable	$15
Credit	Cash	$115

July
18

Customer returned goods, given a cash refund of $345

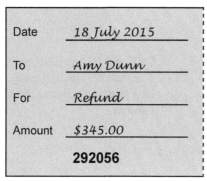

Date	*18 July 2015*
To	*Amy Dunn*
For	*Refund*
Amount	*$345.00*
	292056

GST of $45 has been paid. This will be claimed back from IRD later, so reduces the GST liability.

This transaction is recorded on the accounting equation as follows:

	A +	Ex	=	L +	Eq +	I
	Cash			GST payable		Sales returns
Refund paid, $345	− 345			− 45		− 300

When this transaction has been posted to the ledger, the accounts appear as:

General Ledger – T form

Cash   110

Date	Particulars	$	Date	Particulars	$
Jul 8	Balance	4,010	Jul 11	Wages	230
9	Sales and		15	Drawings	460
	GST	4,600	17	Advertising	
				and GST	115
			18	Sales returns	
				and GST	345

Sales returns   620

Date	Particulars	$	Date	Particulars	$
Jul 18	Cash	300			

GST payable   310

Date	Particulars	$	Date	Particulars	$
Jul 8	Balance	90	Jul 9	Cash	600
17	Cash	15			
18	Cash	45			

CREDIT ENTRY
Decrease Cash $345

DEBIT ENTRIES
Increase Sales returns $300
Decrease GST $45

Accounting – A Beginning   ISBN: 9780170211055

General Ledger – 3-column form

Cash — 110

Date	Particulars	Dr $	Cr $	Balance $
Jul 8	Balance			4,010 Dr
9	Sales and GST	4,600		8,610 Dr
11	Wages		230	8,380 Dr
15	Drawings		460	7,920 Dr
17	Advertising and GST		115	7,805 Dr
18	Sales returns and GST		345	7,460 Dr

Sales returns — 620

Date	Particulars	Dr $	Cr $	Balance $
Jul 18	Cash	300		300 Dr

GST payable — 310

Date	Particulars	Dr $	Cr $	Balance $
Jul 8	Balance			90 Dr
9	Cash		600	510 Cr
17	Cash	15		495 Cr
18	Cash	45		450 Cr

CREDIT ENTRY
Decrease Cash $345

DEBIT ENTRIES
Increase Sales returns $300
Decrease GST $45

Important!

- The Cash account is *decreasing*, so we enter $345 on the credit side.

- The GST payable account is *decreasing*, so we enter $45 on the debit side.

- Income is *decreasing* because we have refunded a customer the money we received when we sold the goods. If income decreases, then equity decreases, and so a debit entry of $300 is required.

- Any sales returns are separated from sales into a **Sales returns** account. This is a **negative** income account (often called *contra income*). A separate account is used so that we can keep track of goods returned.

- We call this entry:

Debit	Sales returns	$300
Debit	GST payable	$45
Credit	Cash	$345

July 20

Cash purchases of souvenirs, $690

Date	*20 July 2015*
To	*Pretty Paua*
For	*Goods*
Amount	*$690.00*
	292057

GST!

GST of $90 has been paid. This will be claimed back from IRD later, so reduces the GST liability.

Important!

This transaction involves the purchase of goods for selling in the shop. We record them in a *Purchases* account in the ledger. Purchases are an *expense*.

We also have an Inventory asset account in the ledger. We only use this account at the *end* of the reporting period when we check our stock levels and record the amount of inventory on hand.

This transaction is recorded on the accounting equation as follows:

	A +	Ex =	L +	Eq +	I
	Cash	Purchases	GST payable		
Cash purchases of souvenirs, $690	– 690	+ 600	– 90		

When this transaction has been posted to the ledger, the accounts appear as:

General Ledger – T form

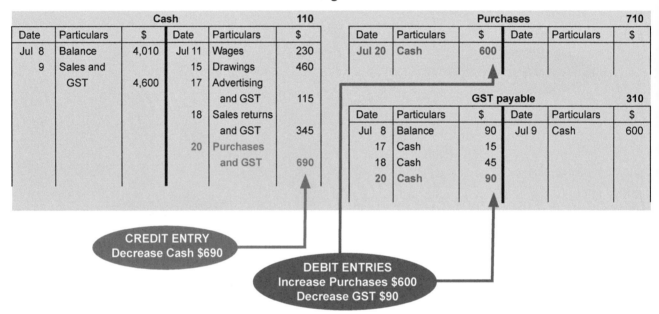

Cash						110
Date	Particulars	$	Date	Particulars	$	
Jul 8	Balance	4,010	Jul 11	Wages	230	
9	Sales and		15	Drawings	460	
	GST	4,600	17	Advertising		
				and GST	115	
			18	Sales returns		
				and GST	345	
			20	Purchases		
				and GST	690	

Purchases					710
Date	Particulars	$	Date	Particulars	$
Jul 20	Cash	600			

GST payable					310
Date	Particulars	$	Date	Particulars	$
Jul 8	Balance	90	Jul 9	Cash	600
17	Cash	15			
18	Cash	45			
20	Cash	90			

CREDIT ENTRY
Decrease Cash $690

DEBIT ENTRIES
Increase Purchases $600
Decrease GST $90

General Ledger – 3-column form

Cash				110
Date	Particulars	Dr $	Cr $	Balance $
Jul 8	Balance			4,010 Dr
9	Sales and			
	GST	4,600		8,610 Dr
11	Wages		230	8,380 Dr
15	Drawings		460	7,920 Dr
17	Advertising			
	and GST		115	7,805 Dr
18	Sales returns			
	and GST		345	7,460 Dr
20	Purchases			
	and GST		690	6,770 Dr

Purchases				710
Date	Particulars	Dr $	Cr $	Balance $
Jul 20	Cash	600		600 Dr

GST payable				310
Date	Particulars	Dr $	Cr $	Balance $
Jul 8	Balance			90 Dr
9	Cash		600	510 Cr
17	Cash	15		495 Cr
18	Cash	45		450 Cr
20	Cash	90		360 Cr

CREDIT ENTRY
Decrease Cash $690

DEBIT ENTRIES
Increase Purchases $600
Decrease GST $90

Important!

- The Cash account is *decreasing*, so we enter $690 on the credit side.

- The GST payable account is also *decreasing*, so we enter $90 on the debit side.

Accounting – A Beginning

ISBN: 9780170211055

- We record the goods in a **Purchases** account in the ledger. Purchases are an *expense* and the account balance is *increasing*, so we enter $600 on the **debit** side. Remember, expenses *decrease* equity.

- You may have noticed that we also have an **Inventory** (asset) account in the ledger. We only use this account at the end of the reporting period when we check our stock levels and record the amount of inventory on hand.

- We call this entry:

Debit	Purchases	$600
Debit	GST payable	$90
Credit	Cash	$690

Paid cash for petrol, $115

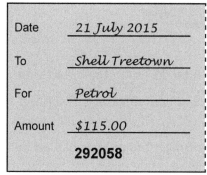

GST of $15 has been paid. This will be claimed back from IRD later, so reduces the GST liability.

This transaction is recorded on the accounting equation as follows:

	A +	Ex =	L +	Eq +	I
	Cash	Van expenses	GST payable		
Cash paid for petrol, $115	− 115	+ 100	− 15		

When this transaction has been posted to the ledger, the accounts appear as:

General Ledger – T form

Cash   110

Date	Particulars	$	Date	Particulars	$
Jul 8	Balance	4,010	Jul 11	Wages	230
9	Sales and		15	Drawings	460
	GST	4,600	17	Advertising and GST	115
			18	Sales returns and GST	345
			20	Purchases and GST	690
			21	Petrol and GST	115

Van expenses   750

Date	Particulars	$	Date	Particulars	$
Jul 21	Cash	100			

GST payable   310

Date	Particulars	$	Date	Particulars	$
Jul 8	Balance	90	Jul 9	Cash	600
17	Cash	15			
18	Cash	45			
20	Cash	90			
21	Cash	15			

CREDIT ENTRY
Decrease Cash $115

DEBIT ENTRIES
Increase Van expenses $100
Decrease GST $15

General Ledger – 3-column form

Cash 110

Date	Particulars	Dr $	Cr $	Balance $
Jul 8	Balance			4,010 Dr
9	Sales and			
	GST	4,600		8,610 Dr
11	Wages		230	8,380 Dr
15	Drawings		460	7,920 Dr
17	Advertising			
	and GST		115	7,805 Dr
18	Sales returns			
	and GST		345	7,460 Dr
20	Purchases			
	and GST		690	6,770 Dr
21	Van expenses			
	and GST		115	6,655 Dr

Van expenses 750

Date	Particulars	Dr $	Cr $	Balance $
Jul 21	Cash	100		100 Dr

GST payable 310

Date	Particulars	Dr $	Cr $	Balance $
Jul 8	Balance			90 Dr
9	Cash		600	510 Cr
17	Cash	15		495 Cr
18	Cash	45		450 Cr
20	Cash	90		360 Cr
21	Cash	15		345 Cr

CREDIT ENTRY
Decrease Cash $115

DEBIT ENTRIES
Increase Van expenses $100
Decrease GST $15

Important!

- The Cash account is *decreasing*, so we enter $115 on the credit side.

- The GST payable account is also *decreasing*, so we enter $15 on the debit side.

- The Van expenses account is *increasing*. Since it is an expense account which is on the *left hand side* of the accounting equation, we enter the $100 on the debit side. This follows the idea that expenses *decrease* equity.

- We call this entry:

Debit	Van expenses	$100
Debit	GST payable	$15
Credit	Cash	$115

Returned goods to supplier for cash refund, $230

TAX INVOICE	No: 118
	23 July 2015

Kiwi Krafts
RECEIPT
GST No: 65-987-124

RECEIVED FROM: *Pretty Paua*	
FOR: *Goods returned*	
Amount	$200.00
GST	30.00
Total	$230.00

GST of $30 has been collected. This must be paid to IRD later, so is a liability.

This transaction is recorded on the accounting equation as follows:

	A	+	Ex	=	L	+	Eq	+	I
	Cash		Purchases returns		GST payable				
Received cash refund of $230 from supplier	+ 230		− 200		+ 30				

ISBN: 9780170211055

When this transaction has been posted to the ledger, the accounts appear as:

General Ledger – T form

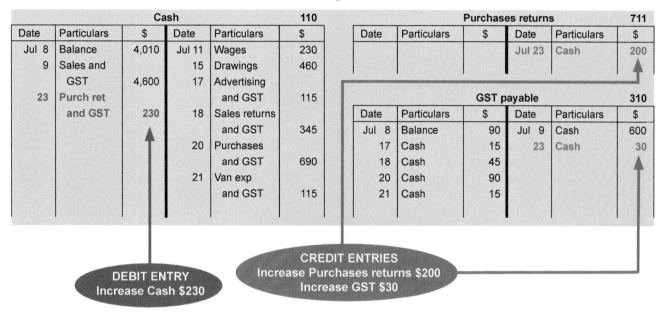

Cash					110
Date	Particulars	$	Date	Particulars	$
Jul 8	Balance	4,010	Jul 11	Wages	230
9	Sales and		15	Drawings	460
	GST	4,600	17	Advertising	
23	Purch ret			and GST	115
	and GST	230	18	Sales returns	
				and GST	345
			20	Purchases	
				and GST	690
			21	Van exp	
				and GST	115

Purchases returns					711
Date	Particulars	$	Date	Particulars	$
			Jul 23	Cash	200

GST payable					310
Date	Particulars	$	Date	Particulars	$
Jul 8	Balance	90	Jul 9	Cash	600
17	Cash	15	23	Cash	30
18	Cash	45			
20	Cash	90			
21	Cash	15			

DEBIT ENTRY
Increase Cash $230

CREDIT ENTRIES
Increase Purchases returns $200
Increase GST $30

General Ledger – 3-column form

Cash				110
Date	Particulars	Dr $	Cr $	Balance $
Jul 8	Balance			4,010 Dr
9	Sales and			
	GST	4,600		8,610 Dr
11	Wages		230	8,380 Dr
15	Drawings		460	7,920 Dr
17	Advertising			
	and GST		115	7,805 Dr
18	Sales returns			
	and GST		345	7,460 Dr
20	Purchases			
	and GST		690	6,770 Dr
21	Van expenses			
	and GST		115	6,655 Dr
23	Purch ret			
	and GST	230		6,885 Dr

Purchases returns				711
Date	Particulars	Dr $	Cr $	Balance $
Jul 23	Cash		200	200 Cr

GST payable				310
Date	Particulars	Dr $	Cr $	Balance $
Jul 8	Balance			90 Dr
9	Cash		600	510 Cr
17	Cash	15		495 Cr
18	Cash	45		450 Cr
20	Cash	90		360 Cr
21	Cash	15		345 Cr
23	Cash		30	375 Cr

DEBIT ENTRY
Increase Cash $230

CREDIT ENTRIES
Increase Purchases returns $200
Increase GST $30

Important!

- The Cash account is *increasing*, so we enter $230 on the **debit** side.

- The GST payable account is *increasing*, so we enter $30 on the **credit** side.

- The purchases expense is decreasing, so we enter the $200 in the **credit** column of Purchases returns. We keep a separate account for purchases returns in the same way as for sales returns.

- We call this entry:

Debit	Cash	$230
Credit	GST payable	$30
Credit	Purchases returns	$200

July 25

Paid rent of $1,150 for the month

Date	25 July 2015
To	Property Holdings
For	Rent
Amount	$1,150.00
	292059

 **GST!**

GST of $150 has been paid. This will be claimed back from IRD later, so reduces the GST liability.

This transaction is recorded on the accounting equation as follows:

A	+	Ex	=	L	+	Eq	+	I
Cash		Rent		GST payable				

Cash paid for rent, $1,150 | − 1,150 | + 1,000 | | − 150

When this transaction has been posted to the ledger, the accounts appear as:

General Ledger – T form

Cash   110

Date	Particulars	$	Date	Particulars	$
Jul 8	Balance	4,010	Jul 11	Wages	230
9	Sales and		15	Drawings	460
	GST	4,600	17	Advertising	
23	Purch ret			and GST	115
	and GST	230	18	Sales returns	
				and GST	345
			20	Purchases	
				and GST	690
			21	Van exp	
				and GST	115
			25	Rent and	
				GST	1,150

Rent   740

Date	Particulars	$	Date	Particulars	$
Jul 25	Cash	1,000			

GST payable   310

Date	Particulars	$	Date	Particulars	$
Jul 8	Balance	90	Jul 9	Cash	600
17	Cash	15	23	Cash	30
18	Cash	45			
20	Cash	90			
21	Cash	15			
25	Cash	150			

CREDIT ENTRY
Decrease Cash $1,150

DEBIT ENTRIES
Increase Rent $1,000
Decrease GST $150

ISBN: 9780170211055

General Ledger – 3-column form

Cash				110
Date	Particulars	Dr $	Cr $	Balance $
Jul 8	Balance			4,010 Dr
9	Sales and GST	4,600		8,610 Dr
11	Wages		230	8,380 Dr
15	Drawings		460	7,920 Dr
17	Advertising and GST		115	7,805 Dr
18	Sales returns and GST		345	7,460 Dr
20	Purchases and GST		690	6,770 Dr
21	Van expenses and GST		115	6,655 Dr
23	Purch ret and GST	230		6,885 Dr
25	Rent and GST		1,150	5,735 Dr

Rent				740
Date	Particulars	Dr $	Cr $	Balance $
Jul 25	Cash	1,000		1,000 Dr

GST payable				310
Date	Particulars	Dr $	Cr $	Balance $
Jul 8	Balance			90 Dr
9	Cash		600	510 Cr
17	Cash	15		495 Cr
18	Cash	45		450 Cr
20	Cash	90		360 Cr
21	Cash	15		345 Cr
23	Cash		30	375 Cr
25	Cash	150		225 Cr

CREDIT ENTRY
Decrease Cash $1,150

DEBIT ENTRIES
Increase Rent $1,000
Decrease GST $150

Important!

- The Cash account is *decreasing*, so we enter $1,150 on the credit side.

- The GST payable account is also *decreasing*, so we enter $150 on the debit side.

- The Rent account is *increasing*. Since it is an expense account which is on the *left hand side* of the accounting equation, we enter the $1,000 on the debit side. This follows the idea that expenses *decrease* equity.

- We call this entry:

Debit	Rent	$1,000
Debit	GST payable	$150
Credit	Cash	$1,150

Paid loan instalment of $575 including interest of $75

BANK PROGRESSIVE

STATEMENT

28 JUL 2015

LOAN REPAYMENT $500.00

INTEREST ON LOAN $75.00

NO GST!

Interest expenses are exempt from GST. The bank loan is a liability and is not subject to GST.

ISBN: 9780170211055

This transaction is recorded on the accounting equation as follows:

	A +	Ex =	L +	Eq +	I
	Cash	Interest	Bank loan		
Instalment paid on loan, $575	− 575	+ 75	− 500		

When this transaction has been posted to the ledger, the accounts appear as:

General Ledger – T form

Cash 110

Date	Particulars	$	Date	Particulars	$
Jul 8	Balance	4,010	Jul 11	Wages	230
9	Sales and GST	4,600	15	Drawings	460
			17	Advertising and GST	115
23	Purch ret and GST	230	18	Sales returns and GST	345
			20	Purchases and GST	690
			21	Van exp and GST	115
			25	Rent and GST	1,150
			28	Loan and Interest	575

CREDIT ENTRY
Decrease Cash $575

Interest on loan 730

Date	Particulars	$	Date	Particulars	$
Jul 28	Cash	75			

Loan 410

Date	Particulars	$	Date	Particulars	$
Jul 28	Cash	500	Jul 8	Balance	15,000

DEBIT ENTRIES
Increase Interest $75
Decrease Loan $500

General Ledger – 3-column form

Cash 110

Date	Particulars	Dr $	Cr $	Balance $
Jul 8	Balance			4,010 Dr
9	Sales and GST	4,600		8,610 Dr
11	Wages		230	8,380 Dr
15	Drawings		460	7,920 Dr
17	Advertising and GST		115	7,805 Dr
18	Sales returns and GST		345	7,460 Dr
20	Purchases and GST		690	6,770 Dr
21	Van expenses and GST		115	6,655 Dr
23	Purch ret and GST	230		6,885 Dr
25	Rent and GST		1,150	5,735 Dr
28	Loan and Interest		575	5,160 Dr

CREDIT ENTRY
Decrease Cash $575

Interest on loan 730

Date	Particulars	Dr $	Cr $	Balance $
Jul 28	Cash	75		75 Dr

Loan 410

Date	Particulars	Dr $	Cr $	Balance $
Jul 8	Balance			15,000 Cr
28	Cash	500		14,500 Cr

DEBIT ENTRIES
Increase Interest $75
Decrease Loan $500

ISBN: 9780170211055

Important!

- The Cash account is *decreasing*, so we enter $575 on the credit side.

- The Loan account is also *decreasing*, so we enter $500 on the debit side.

- The Interest account is *increasing*. Since it is an expense account we enter the $75 on the debit side.

- We call this entry:

Debit	Interest	$75
Debit	Loan	$500
Credit	Cash	$575

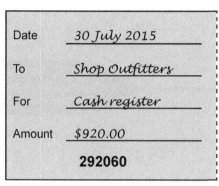

July 30

Bought cash register for $920 cash

Date	*30 July 2015*
To	*Shop Outfitters*
For	*Cash register*
Amount	*$920.00*
	292060

GST!

GST of $120 has been paid. This will be claimed back from IRD later, so reduces the GST liability.

This transaction is recorded on the accounting equation as follows:

	A	+	Ex	=	L	+	Eq	+	I
	Cash		Cash register		GST payable				
Cash paid for cash register, $920	− 920		+ 800		− 120				

When this transaction has been posted to the ledger, the accounts appear as:

General Ledger – T form

Cash — 110

Date	Particulars	$	Date	Particulars	$
Jul 8	Balance	4,010	Jul 11	Wages	230
9	Sales and GST	4,600	15	Drawings	460
23	Purch ret and GST	230	17	Advertising and GST	115
			18	Sales returns and GST	345
			20	Purchases and GST	690
			21	Van exp and GST	115
			25	Rent and GST	1,150
			28	Loan and Interest	575
			30	Cash register and GST	920

Cash register — 230

Date	Particulars	$	Date	Particulars	$
Jul 30	Cash	800			

GST payable — 310

Date	Particulars	$	Date	Particulars	$
Jul 8	Balance	90	Jul 9	Cash	600
17	Cash	15	23	Cash	30
18	Cash	45			
20	Cash	90			
21	Cash	15			
25	Cash	150			
30	Cash	120			

DEBIT ENTRIES
Increase Cash register $800
Decrease GST $120

CREDIT ENTRY
Decrease Cash $920

ISBN: 9780170211055

General Ledger – 3-column form

Cash				110
Date	Particulars	Dr $	Cr $	Balance $
Jul 8	Balance			4,010 Dr
9	Sales and GST	4,600		8,610 Dr
11	Wages		230	8,380 Dr
15	Drawings		460	7,920 Dr
17	Advertising and GST		115	7,805 Dr
18	Sales returns and GST		345	7,460 Dr
20	Purchases and GST		690	6,770 Dr
21	Van expenses and GST		115	6,655 Dr
23	Purch ret and GST	230		6,885 Dr
25	Rent and GST		1,150	5,735 Dr
28	Loan and interest		575	5,160 Dr
30	Cash register and GST		920	4,240 Dr

CREDIT ENTRY
Decrease Cash $920

Cash register				230
Date	Particulars	Dr $	Cr $	Balance $
Jul 30	Cash	800		800 Dr

GST payable				310
Date	Particulars	Dr $	Cr $	Balance $
Jul 8	Balance			90 Dr
9	Cash		600	510 Cr
17	Cash	15		495 Cr
18	Cash	45		450 Cr
20	Cash	90		360 Cr
21	Cash	15		345 Cr
23	Cash		30	375 Cr
25	Cash	150		225 Cr
30	Cash	120		105 Cr

DEBIT ENTRIES
Increase Cash register $800
Decrease GST $120

Important!

- The Cash account is *decreasing*, so we enter $920 on the credit side.

- The GST payable account is also *decreasing*, so we enter $120 on the debit side.

- The Cash register account is a new account and it is *increasing*. Since it is an asset account we enter the $800 on the debit side.

- We call this entry:

Debit	Cash register	$800
Debit	GST payable	$120
Credit	Cash	$920

Preparing the Trial Balance

Now that all the transactions have been recorded in the ledger accounts, we can prepare a trial balance for the month. First, however, we must balance the T form ledger accounts. (The 3-column accounts have running balances so do not require balancing at the end of the month.)

Balancing a T form Ledger Account

When the T form account is used, the debit entries are all on the left hand side of the account and the credit entries are on the right hand side. At the end of the month, we must add both sides and find the difference. This difference will be the closing balance of the account.

The general ledger in T form with all accounts totalled and balanced is shown on pages 118-9 and in 3-column form on pages 120-2.

ISBN: 9780170211055

Balancing a T form Ledger Account

Consider the Bank account of *Kiwi Krafts* at 8 July:

Cash					110
Date	Particulars	$	Date	Particulars	$
Jul 1	Balance	4,500	Jul 4	GST payable	300
2	Capital	500	6	Shop fittings and GST	1,150
5	Shop fittings and GST	460			

The following steps show how to find the closing balance of this account:

STEP 1 Add both sides of the account.

$$\text{Left hand side} = \$4{,}500 + 500 + 460$$
$$= \$5{,}460$$

$$\text{Right hand side} = \$300 + 1{,}150$$
$$= \$1{,}450$$

STEP 2 Find the difference between the two sides.

$$\text{Difference} = \$5{,}460 - 1{,}450$$
$$= \$4{,}010$$

STEP 3 Enter the balance in the account on the side with the smaller total (in this case the right hand or credit side). The date used is usually the last day of the month since this is normally when balancing is carried out. We are balancing weekly here. The account now becomes:

Cash					110
Date	Particulars	$	Date	Particulars	$
Jul 1	Balance	4,500	Jul 4	GST payable	300
2	Capital	500	6	Shop fittings and GST	1,150
5	Shop fittings and GST	460	7	Balance	4,010

STEP 4 Total both sides (they should now have the same total). Transfer the closing balance down to the opposite side so that the account is opened for the next week's transactions. (The next day's date is normally used.)

Cash					110
Date	Particulars	$	Date	Particulars	$
Jul 1	Balance	4,500	Jul 4	GST payable	300
2	Capital	500	6	Shop fittings and GST	1,150
5	Shop fittings and GST	460	7	Balance	4,010
		$5,460			$5,460
Jul 8	Balance	4,010			

Transfer closing balance to become opening balance for the next period.

Kiwi Krafts
General Ledger

Cash   110

Date	Particulars	$	Date	Particulars	$
Jul 8	Balance	4,010	Jul 11	Wages	230
9	Sales and GST payable	4,600	15	Drawings	460
23	Purchases returns and		17	Advertising and	
	GST payable	230		GST payable	115
			18	Sales returns and	
				GST payable	345
			20	Purchases and	
				GST payable	690
			21	Van expenses and	
				GST payable	115
			25	Rent and GST payable	1,150
			28	Loan and interest	575
			30	Cash register and	
				GST payable	920
			31	Balance	4,240
		$8,840			$8,840
Aug 1	Balance	4,240			

Inventory   120

Date	Particulars	$	Date	Particulars	$
Jul 1	Balance	12,000			

Shop fittings   210

Date	Particulars	$	Date	Particulars	$
Jul 8	Balance	7,400			

Van   220

Date	Particulars	$	Date	Particulars	$
Jul 1	Balance	20,000			

Cash register   230

Date	Particulars	$	Date	Particulars	$
Jul 30	Cash	800			

GST payable   310

Date	Particulars	$	Date	Particulars	$
Jul 8	Balance	90	Jul 9	Cash	600
17	Cash	15	23	Cash	30
18	Cash	45			
20	Cash	90			
21	Cash	15			
25	Cash	150			
30	Cash	120			
31	Balance	105			
		$630			$630
			Aug 1	Balance	105

Accounting – A Beginning

ISBN: 9780170211055

Loan   410

Date	Particulars	$	Date	Particulars	$
Jul 28	Cash	500	Jul 1	Balance	15,000
31	Balance	14,500			
		$15,000			$15,000
			Aug 1	Balance	14,500

Capital   510

Date	Particulars	$	Date	Particulars	$
			Jul 8	Balance	28,500

Drawings   520

Date	Particulars	$	Date	Particulars	$
Jul 15	Cash	460			

Sales   610

Date	Particulars	$	Date	Particulars	$
			Jul 9	Cash	4,000

Sales returns   611

Date	Particulars	$	Date	Particulars	$
Jul 18	Cash	300			

Purchases   710

Date	Particulars	$	Date	Particulars	$
Jul 20	Cash	600			

Purchases returns   711

Date	Particulars	$	Date	Particulars	$
			Jul 23	Cash	200

Advertising   720

Date	Particulars	$	Date	Particulars	$
Jul 17	Cash	100			

Interest on loan   730

Date	Particulars	$	Date	Particulars	$
Jul 28	Cash	75			

Rent   740

Date	Particulars	$	Date	Particulars	$
Jul 25	Cash	1,000			

Van expenses   750

Date	Particulars	$	Date	Particulars	$
Jul 21	Cash	100			

Wages   760

Date	Particulars	$	Date	Particulars	$
Jul 11	Cash	230			

The trial balance prepared from the general ledger is shown below.

Kiwi Krafts
Trial Balance as at 31 July 2015

Cash	$ 4,240	GST payable	$ 105
Inventory	12,000	Loan (due 31 July 2019)	14,500
Shop fittings (cost)	7,400	Capital	28,500
Van (cost)	20,000	Sales	4,000
Cash register (cost)	800	Purchases returns	200
Drawings	460		
Sales returns	300		
Purchases	600		
Advertising	100		
Interest on loan	75		
Rent	1,000		
Van expenses	100		
Wages	230		
	$47,305		$47,305

The general ledger in 3-column form is shown below.

Kiwi Krafts
General Ledger

Cash 110

Date	Particulars	Dr $	Cr $	Balance $
Jul 8	Balance			4,010 Dr
9	Sales and GST payable	4,600		8,610 Dr
11	Wages		230	8,380 Dr
15	Drawings		460	7,920 Dr
17	Advertising and GST payable		115	7,805 Dr
18	Sales returns and GST payable		345	7,460 Dr
20	Purchases and GST payable		690	6,770 Dr
21	Van expenses and GST payable		115	6,655 Dr
23	Purch returns and GST payable	230		6,885 Dr
25	Rent and GST payable		1,150	5,735 Dr
28	Loan and interest		575	5,160 Dr
30	Cash register and GST payable		920	4,240 Dr

Inventory 120

Date	Particulars	Dr $	Cr $	Balance $
Jul 1	Balance			12,000 Dr

Shop fittings 210

Date	Particulars	Dr $	Cr $	Balance $
Jul 8	Balance			7,400 Dr

ISBN: 9780170211055

Van   220

Date	Particulars	Dr $	Cr $	Balance $
Jul 1	Balance			20,000 Dr

Cash register   230

Date	Particulars	Dr $	Cr $	Balance $
Jul 30	Cash	800		800 Dr

GST payable   310

Date	Particulars	Dr $	Cr $	Balance $
Jul 8	Balance			90 Dr
9	Cash		600	510 Cr
17	Cash	15		495 Cr
18	Cash	45		450 Cr
20	Cash	90		360 Cr
21	Cash	15		345 Cr
23	Cash		30	375 Cr
25	Cash	150		225 Cr
30	Cash	120		105 Cr

Loan   410

Date	Particulars	Dr $	Cr $	Balance $
Jul 1	Balance			15,000 Cr
28	Cash	500		14,500 Cr

Capital   510

Date	Particulars	Dr $	Cr $	Balance $
Jul 8	Balance			28,500 Cr

Drawings   520

Date	Particulars	Dr $	Cr $	Balance $
Jul 15	Cash	460		460 Dr

Sales   610

Date	Particulars	Dr $	Cr $	Balance $
Jul 9	Cash		4,000	4,000 Cr

Sales returns   611

Date	Particulars	Dr $	Cr $	Balance $
Jul 18	Cash	300		300 Dr

Purchases   710

Date	Particulars	Dr $	Cr $	Balance $
Jul 20	Cash	600		600 Dr

Purchases returns   711

Date	Particulars	Dr $	Cr $	Balance $
Jul 23	Cash		200	200 Cr

Kiwi Krafts
General Ledger

Advertising   720

Date	Particulars	Dr $	Cr $	Balance $
Jul 17	Cash	100		100 Dr

Interest on loan   730

Date	Particulars	Dr $	Cr $	Balance $
Jul 28	Cash	75		75 Dr

Rent   740

Date	Particulars	Dr $	Cr $	Balance $
Jul 25	Cash	1,000		1,000 Dr

Van expenses   750

Date	Particulars	Dr $	Cr $	Balance $
Jul 21	Cash	100		100 Dr

Wages   760

Date	Particulars	Dr $	Cr $	Balance $
Jul 11	Cash	230		230 Dr

The 3-column trial balance prepared from the general ledger is shown below.

Kiwi Krafts
Trial Balance as at 31 July 2015

	$	$
Cash	4,240	
Inventory	12,000	
Shop fittings (cost)	7,400	
Van (cost)	20,000	
Cash register (cost)	800	
GST payable		105
Loan (due 31 July 2019)		14,500
Capital		28,500
Drawings	460	
Sales		4,000
Sales returns	300	
Purchases	600	
Purchases returns		200
Advertising	100	
Interest on loan	75	
Rent	1,000	
Van expenses	100	
Wages	230	
	$47,305	$47,305

ISBN: 9780170211055

Summary

Entering transactions in the ledger is one more step in the accounting process. We have already learnt to prepare financial statements and to calculate some ratios and percentages which help us to interpret these statements. The preparation of the ledger comes before these two steps. In this book, we first learnt to record transactions on the accounting equation using a transaction analysis. This method is not very efficient for a business with a large number of accounts. We have now learnt to use the ledger to replace this transaction analysis. The ledger is used to prepare a trial balance in exactly the same way as we used the transaction analysis.

We can summarise the process so far in a diagram:

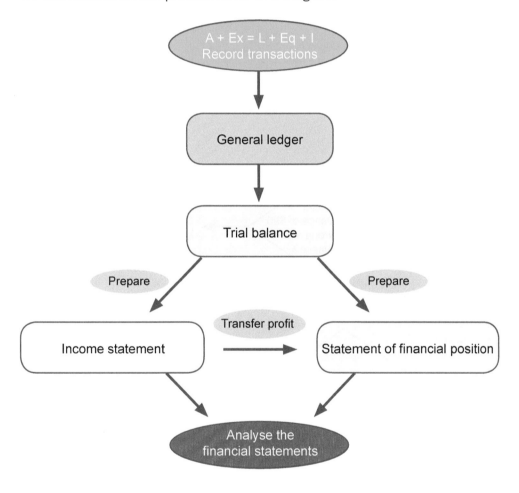

So the trial balance doesn't balance?

There are several reasons that a trial balance may not balance:

- An account may have been left out of the trial balance.

- An account may be on the wrong side of the trial balance.

- An entry may have been posted to the ledger incorrectly:
    - a **debit** entry may have been posted to the **credit** side
    - a **credit** entry may have been posted to the **debit** side
    - one half of an entry may not have been posted at all.

- There may be an arithmetical error in one or more of the accounts.

    The procedure shown on the next page helps to find the error(s).

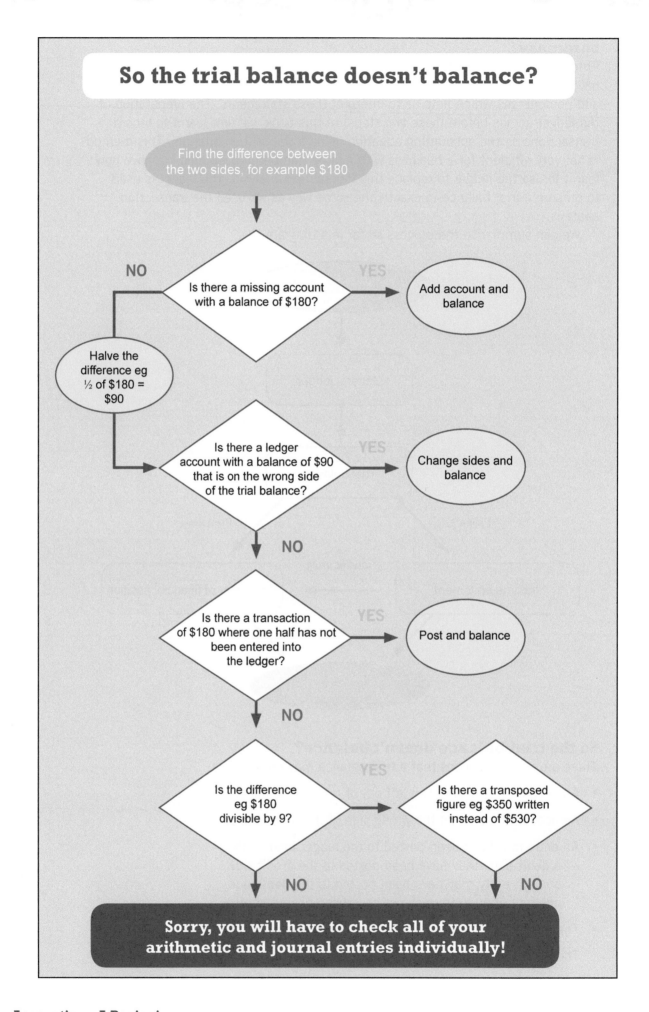

So the trial balance doesn't balance?

Find the difference between the two sides, for example $180

Is there a missing account with a balance of $180? — YES → **Add account and balance**

NO

Halve the difference eg ½ of $180 = $90

Is there a ledger account with a balance of $90 that is on the wrong side of the trial balance? — YES → **Change sides and balance**

NO

Is there a transaction of $180 where one half has not been entered into the ledger? — YES → **Post and balance**

NO

Is the difference eg $180 divisible by 9? — YES → **Is there a transposed figure eg $350 written instead of $530?**

NO   NO

Sorry, you will have to check all of your arithmetic and journal entries individually!

Accounting – A Beginning

ISBN: 9780170211055

Activities

1 Each of the accounts named below has been extracted from a business trial balance.

a Petty cash
b Capital
c Sales
d Telephone expense
e Purchases
f Commission income
g Motor vehicle

h Goodwill
i Shop fittings
j Purchases returns
k GST payable
l Drawings
m Mortgage on premises
n Sales returns.

DO THIS!

State whether each of the accounts would normally have a **debit** or a **credit** balance.

2 The following transactions relate to separate businesses. (All amounts include GST where appropriate.)

a Paid wages in cash, $460
b Cash sales to customers, $1,840
c Cash purchases from suppliers, $920
d Paid GST of $700
e Borrowed $11,500 from the bank as a long term loan.
f Returned goods to suppliers and received a cash refund, $345
g Owner took $690 cash for personal use
h Paid interest of $115 on loan
i Received a loan of $115,000 from the bank
j Paid rent of $1,380
k Refunded customer $460 cash for goods returned.

DO THIS!

Enter the transactions above in ledger accounts. Draw up a separate set of ledger accounts for each transaction.

3 The following Cash account has been taken from the ledger of a local dairy. The account has numerous errors in it, but you may assume that the figures are correct.

Cash				110
Date	Particulars	Dr $	Cr $	Balance $
Apr 1	Balance			2,000 Dr
4	Wages expense		500	1,500 Dr
7	Sales and GST payable	2,000		3,500 Dr
12	Purchases and GST payable		1,600	1,900 Dr
15	Rent expense and GST payable		1,000	900 Dr
20	Telephone expense and GST payable	150		1,050 Dr
22	Loan repaid		2,000	950 Cr
25	Drawings	600		350 Cr
29	Sales and GST payable		5,000	5,350 Cr

DO THIS!

Prepare the Cash account correctly.

4 The following is the chart of accounts of *Outdoor Solutions*, a business which sells and services outdoor equipment. The business is registered for GST on the payments basis.

Outdoor Solutions

Chart of Accounts

100	**Current assets**	**500**	**Equity**
	110 Cash		510 Capital
	120 Inventory		520 Drawings
200	**Non-current assets**	**600**	**Income**
	210 Equipment		610 Servicing fees
	220 Premises		620 Sales
			621 Sales returns
300	**Current liabilities**	**700**	**Expenses**
	310 GST payable		710 Purchases
			711 Purchases returns
400	**Non-current liabilities**		720 Advertising
	410 Mortgage on premises		730 Interest on mortgage
			740 Repairs
			750 Telephone expense
			760 Wages

The owner has just bought a software package to do his accounts but is unsure about coding the transactions. You have been given the following list of transactions and asked to advise him as to the correct accounts to use.

		Debit		Credit	
Example:					
	Bought inventory for cash	710, 310		110	
a	Paid wages				
b	Paid telephone rental				
c	Paid cash for repainting premises				
d	Received servicing fees in cash				
e	Owner took cash for personal use				
f	Sold motor mower for cash				
g	Paid GST				
h	Refunded cash to customer who had been overcharged for servicing				
i	Paid advertising				
j	Owner contributed cash to the business				
k	Paid instalment on mortgage, made up of interest and principal payment				

DO THIS!

For each of the transactions **a – k** above, specify the account numbers for the accounts which are debited and credited respectively. The first one has been done as an example for you to follow.

ISBN: 9780170211055

5 The trial balance of *Safety First*, a swimming school owned by Sandra Fish, is shown below. The firm is registered for GST on the payments basis.

Safety First			
Trial Balance as at 30 June 2019			
Cash	$ 1,750	GST payable	$ 900
Video camera	1,400	Hire purchase on vehicle	15,000
Pool equipment	2,350	Capital – Fish	19,600
Motor vehicle	30,000		
	$35,500		$35,500

The transactions for the month of July are listed below. (All amounts include GST where appropriate.)

Jul	2	Received cash fees from clients, $920
	4	Paid cash for petrol, $115
	6	Paid telephone rental, $230
	9	Paid instalment on hire purchase, $500
	10	Cash drawings, $690
	14	Paid cash for advertising in local paper, $115
	17	Paid $900 GST due
	19	Sandra contributed cash of $2,500 to the business
	22	Received fees of $1,150 in cash
	24	Paid for electricity, $115
	30	Paid personal medical insurance premium from business bank account, $460.

DO THIS!

a Enter the opening balances in the general ledger at 1 July 2019. Make sure you give each account a number from a suitably designed chart of accounts.
b Enter the transactions listed above in the general ledger.
c Prepare the trial balance as at 31 July 2019.

6 *Sweet Tooth* is an ice cream and confectionery business in a shopping mall. The business is registered for GST on the payments basis. The trial balance as at 30 September 2018 was as follows:

Sweet Tooth			
Trial Balance as at 30 September 2018			
Cash	$ 2,800	GST payable	$ 500
Fittings	11,500	Loan	13,000
Equipment	13,300	Capital	14,600
Inventory	500		
	$28,100		$28,100

The transactions for the month of October are listed below. (All amounts include GST where appropriate.)

Oct	7	Cash sales for the week, $1,725
	10	Bought ice cream for cash, $690
	12	Paid electricity, $230
	14	Paid rent, $460
		Cash sales for the week, $1,840
	16	Bought equipment for cash, $1,265
	18	Bought ice cream for cash, $1,035
	20	Withdrew $500 cash to buy Christmas presents

21	Cash sales for the week, $2,760
23	Bought confectionery for cash, $345
28	Paid rent, $460
	Cash sales for the week, $1,150
30	Paid $115 interest on loan.

DO THIS!

a Enter the opening balances in the general ledger at 1 October 2018. Make sure you give each account a number from a suitably designed chart of accounts.
b Enter the transactions listed above in the general ledger.
c Prepare the trial balance as at 31 October 2018.

7 Blodwyn Welsh set up a small gardening shop, *Plantation*, on 1 May 2019. As well as selling plants and gardening supplies, she works as a landscape designer on a contract basis. The business is registered for GST on the payments basis.

The transactions listed below occurred in the month of May. (All amounts include GST where appropriate.)

May 1	Commenced business with $10,000 cash
3	Purchased shop fittings, paying $276 cash
5	Bought plants for cash, $690
6	Returned dead plants to suppliers and received a cash refund, $92
8	Contract fees received, $368
	Cash sales, $2,116
10	Paid shop wages, $345 and advertising, $115
12	Purchased equipment for cash, $575
14	Paid rent, $690
17	Paid shop wages, $345
20	Bought plants for cash, $460
22	Received cash for contracts, $920
24	Paid shop wages, $345
26	Cash sales, $1,725
28	Paid rent, $690
29	Bought plants for cash, $598
30	Cash drawings, $150
31	Paid shop wages, $345.

DO THIS!

a Design a suitable chart of accounts for *Plantation*.
b Enter the transactions listed above in the general ledger.
c Prepare the trial balance as at 31 May 2019.

8 The trial balance of *Elegance*, an upmarket fashion store owned by Betty Barker, is shown below. The firm is registered for GST on the payments basis.

Elegance Trial Balance as at 31 January 2016			
Inventory	$ 26,500	Bank overdraft	$ 650
Shop fittings	3,500	GST payable	150
		Loan	14,000
		Capital – Barker	15,200
	$30,000		$30,000

ISBN: 9780170211055

The transactions for the month of February are listed below. (All amounts include GST where appropriate.)

Feb 7   Cash sales, $2,070
    8   Cash drawings, $230
   13   Paid wages, $345
   14   Paid rent, $920
   19   Cash purchases, $690
   20   Made loan repayment of $600 including $50 interest
   23   Betty contributed cash of $5,000 to the business
   24   Paid cash for extra shop fittings, $460
   25   Cash sales, $3,450
          Paid cash for sewing machine to do alterations, $920
   27   Paid wages, $345
   28   Paid $150 GST due
          Paid rent, $920.

DO THIS!

a Enter the opening balances in the general ledger at 1 February 2016. Make sure you give each account a number from a suitably designed chart of accounts.
b Enter the transactions listed above in the general ledger.
c Prepare the trial balance as at 29 February 2016.

9   The documents below and on the next page relate to the transactions of *Bigger Builders* for the month of January 2017. The firm is registered for GST on the payments basis and had the following ledger balances at 1 January:

Bank $6,700 Dr, Van $20,000 Dr, Tools $8,400 Dr, GST payable $1,200 Cr, Loan $15,000 Cr and Capital $18,900 Cr.

TAX INVOICE	No: 2065
	3 January 2017
Bigger Builders	
RECEIPT	
GST No: 25-987-65	

RECEIVED FROM:	
Big Properties	
FOR: Extensions	
Amount	$8,000.00
GST	1,200.00
Total	$9,200.00

TAX INVOICE	No: 2066
	12 January 2017
Bigger Builders	
RECEIPT	
GST No: 25-987-65	

RECEIVED FROM:	
Bob Bartock	
FOR: Capital	
Amount	$5,000.00
GST	—
Total	$5,000.00

TAX INVOICE	No: 2067
	20 January 2017
Bigger Builders	
RECEIPT	
GST No: 25-987-65	

RECEIVED FROM:	
Dinky Developers	
FOR: Alterations	
Amount	$6,000.00
GST	900.00
Total	$6,900.00

Date	4 January 2017
To	Betta Hardware
For	Skilsaw
Amount	$345.00
	169081

Date	8 January 2017
To	Terrific Timber
For	Materials
Amount	$920.00
	169082

Date	10 January 2017
To	P Paynter
For	Wages
Amount	$1,150.00
	169083

ISBN: 9780170211055

Date	14 January 2017
To	B Bartock
For	Drawings
Amount	$460.00
169084	

Date	16 January 2017
To	Grubby Garage
For	Van repairs
Amount	$690.00
169085	

Date	18 January 2017
To	Housebreakers
For	Materials
Amount	$1,035.00
169086	

Date	19 January 2017
To	B Bartock
For	Drawings
Amount	$460.00
169087	

Date	21 January 2017
To	P Paynter
For	Wages
Amount	$920.00
169088	

Date	23 January 2017
To	Local Garage
For	Petrol
Amount	$115.00
169089	

Date	24 January 2017
To	Local paper
For	Advertising
Amount	$230.00
169090	

Date	28 January 2017
To	Inland Revenue
For	GST
Amount	$1,200.00
169091	

Date	30 January 2017
To	B Bartock
For	Drawings
Amount	$920.00
169092	

STATEMENT

Co-opBank

3 JAN 2017

LOAN ADVANCE $10,000.00

STATEMENT

Co-opBank

31 JAN 2017

LOAN REPAYMENT $270.00
INTEREST ON LOAN $90.00

DO THIS!

a   Enter the opening balances in the general ledger at 1 January 2017. Make sure you give each account a number from a suitably designed chart of accounts.
b   Record the transactions represented by the documents above in the general ledger.
c   Prepare the trial balance as at 31 January 2017.

ISBN: 9780170211055

CHAPTER 5

Cash Journals and Bank Reconciliation

- The Cash Receipts Journal
- Posting Cash Receipts to the Ledger
- The Cash Payments Journal
- Posting Cash Payments to the Ledger
- Bank Reconciliation Statements

Gee Aroha, this is just as bad as those transaction sheets. How do you find anything in there?

Yes it does get a bit complicated. There is an easier way though.

Yes I know, use the computer! I have been telling you that all along. You never listen to me.

I haven't got it set up yet. But we can use a journal to summarise all the cash receipts for the month. Then we just put one figure in the ledger for each account.

That sounds better. I guess you'd better show me if you're not going to get this computer sorted in a hurry.

I will get on to it. I have been so busy since I started this business.

I know the feeling!

When we recorded transactions in the ledger in the previous chapter, we found that the Cash account in the ledger was often very long and complex. It would be difficult to trace the individual cash transactions from looking at the ledger account.

One way of simplifying the ledger account is to summarise all transactions of a similar type before entering them in the Cash account. Cash transactions are of two types: cash receipts and cash payments. Cash receipts are grouped in a summary called the **cash receipts journal** and cash payments in a summary called the **cash payments journal**.

The Cash Receipts Journal

The cash receipts journal is a special type of record that contains only the cash receipts for a period of time. This journal summarises all of the cash receipts and we then make a single entry into each of the relevant ledger accounts. The details of individual receipts can be found in the journal itself so are not required in the ledger.

Let's return to *Kiwi Krafts*. The cash receipts for August 2015 were as follows:

Aug 1   Cash sales, $345

5   Received a loan of $5,000 from AMP bank

10   Received commission in cash $575, Receipt No 1003

15   Cash sales, $460
     Aroha sold an old set of shelves for cash of $230, Receipt No 1004
22   Cash sales, $1,150
     VISA sales, $805
28   Received commission in cash $115, Receipt No 1005
31   Cash sales, $920.

The bank statement showed that interest of $23 had been paid into the bank account on 30 August. The cash receipts journal is shown below.

Kiwi Krafts
Cash Receipts Journal   Page 3

Date	Particulars	Ref	Rec no	Receipts	Cash	GST payable	Sales	Commission	Sundry
Aug 1	Cash sales			345	345	45	300		
5	Loan from AMP bank			5,000	5,000				5,000
10	Commission		1003	575	575	75		500	
15	Cash sales			460		60	400		
	Shop fittings		1004	230	690	30			200
22	Cash sales			1,150	1,150	150	1,000		
	VISA			805	805	105	700		
28	Commission		1005	115	115	15		100	
31	Cash sales			920	920	120	800		
30	Interest		B/S	23	23				23
					$9,623	600	3,200	600	5,223

Receipts column

Cash column

Analysis columns

Important!

- The receipt number is shown beside each transaction. Where the information has come from the bank statement, this is indicated by B/S in the receipt number column.

- There are separate analysis columns for transactions which occur frequently (GST payable, Sales and Commission). If there is only one incidence of a certain kind of transaction, it is shown in the Sundry column.

- When a transaction is recorded, the amount received is entered into the Receipts column. The banking is done daily. The cash amounts entered in the Receipts column are added each day and the total is entered in the Cash column. These totals will be checked against the bank statement later on.

- The amount of each receipt is analysed using the analysis columns. For example, on August 1, cash sales of $345 were received. This $345 includes GST. The amount of the GST ($^3/_{23}$ x $345 = $45) is entered in the GST payable column and the balance ($^{20}/_{23}$ x $345 = $300, or $345 – 45 = $300) is entered in the Sales column.

- The interest is shown at the bottom of the journal because the bank statement is received early in the following month. In the meantime, other transactions have been recorded in correct date order. No GST is deducted from the interest because all financial charges are exempt from GST.

- We have entered the loan when it was received since the business will have been notified by the bank on that day. Similarly, electronic processing allows the VISA sales to be recorded on the day they are made. They are processed separately from physical deposits, so are **NOT** added to the day's bankings in the receipts column, but are entered on a separate line.

Remember!

Electronic transactions are entered on a *separate* line from physical bankings.

Once the monthly totals have been prepared, entries can be made in the ledger. We call this process **posting**. Postings should first be listed at the bottom of the journal as a check to ensure that the journal totals have been calculated correctly. First we must examine each type of transaction in the journal to establish:

- what accounts are to be used; and
- whether debit or credit entries are required.

Account	Type	Increasing/Decreasing	Debit/Credit
Cash	Asset	Increasing	Debit
GST payable	Liability	Increasing	Credit
Sales	Income	Increasing	Credit
Commission	Income	Increasing	Credit
Loan	Liability	Increasing	Credit
Shop fittings	Asset	Decreasing	Credit
Interest	Income	Increasing	Credit

We may now prepare a summary of the ledger postings:

Debit entries	$	Credit entries	$
Cash	9,623	GST payable	600
		Sales	3,200
		Commission	600
		Loan	5,000
		Shop fittings	200
		Interest	23
	$9,623		$9,623

Debit entries = Credit entries

Important!

- This summary is prepared from the totals of the columns in the journal for all except the Sundry column. Since the items in the Sundry column are all of different types, they are recorded separately.

- This summary is prepared before posting is carried out. If the debit entries do not equal the credit entries, the trial balance will not balance. If the posting summary does not balance there is usually either an arithmetical error or an amount which has not been transferred to an analysis column.

Posting Cash Receipts to the Ledger

We have already prepared a summary of the ledger postings. All that remains is to enter the figures in the ledger accounts. The posting process can be summarised as follows:

STEP 1

For all columns in the cash receipts journal **except** the Sundry column:

- Write the account number at the bottom of the column and enter the amount in the ledger account.
- Write CRJ3 in the reference column of the ledger account. This shows that the entry in the ledger was posted from the Cash Receipts Journal, page 3.
- Place a tick in the reference column beside each of the items in a particular analysis column of the journal. This shows that all of the individual items have been posted.
- For good measure, place a tick beside each item in the posting summary as it is posted.

STEP 2

Post each item in the **Sundry** column separately. Write the account number in the reference column beside the particulars of each transaction.

STEP 3

When this process has been completed you should notice that:

- there is an account number at the bottom of each column in the journal (except the Sundry column); and
- there is either an account number or a tick in the reference column beside every single entry in the journal.

When the cash receipts journal has been posted to the ledger, it appears as follows:

Kiwi Krafts
Cash Receipts Journal
Page 3

Date	Particulars	Ref	Rec no	Receipts	Cash	GST payable	Sales	Commission	Sundry
Aug 1	Cash sales	✔		345	345	45	300		
5	Loan from AMP bank	410		5,000	5,000				5,000
10	Commission	✔	1003	575	575	75		500	
15	Cash sales	✔		460		60	400		
	Shop fittings	210	1004	230	690	30			200
22	Cash sales	✔		1,150	1,150	150	1,000		
	VISA	✔		805	805	105	700		
28	Commission	✔	1005	115	115	15		100	
31	Cash sales	✔		920	920	120	800		
30	Interest	630		23	23				23
					$9,623	600	3,200	600	5,223
					110	**310**	**610**	**620**	

Accounting – A Beginning

ISBN: 9780170211055

We have added two new income accounts and one expense account to the chart of accounts for *Kiwi Krafts*: 620 Commission income, 630 Interest income and 770 VISA commission. The updated chart of accounts is:

Kiwi Krafts
Chart of Accounts

100 Current Assets		500 Equity	
110	Bank	510	Capital
120	Inventory	520	Drawings
200 Non-current Assets		600 Income	
210	Shop fittings	610	Sales
220	Van	611	Sales returns
230	Cash register	620	Commission income
		630	Interest income
300 Current Liabilities			
310	GST payable	700 Expenses	
		710	Purchases
400 Long Term Liabilities		711	Purchases returns
410	Loan	720	Advertising
		730	Interest on loan
		740	Rent
		750	Van expenses
		760	Wages
		770	VISA commission

The T form of the general ledger, showing all the relevant ledger accounts after the posting process has been completed, is shown on the next page.

Important!

- There is only **one** posting to each ledger account.

- The reference column shows:
  - the opening balance has been **b**rought **d**own (b/d) from the previous month
  - the journal where each entry has come from: **C**ash **R**eceipts **J**ournal, page **3**
  - the closing balance is **c**arried **f**orward (c/f) to the following month.

- All postings are dated at the end of the month (31 August). Since totals are used, we do not need to list the dates of the individual transactions. If necessary, the cash receipts journal can be used to locate the date of a particular transaction.

- The Particulars column of the Cash account in the ledger shows '*Sundry receipts*'. This is done to save listing all the account names included in the summary figure.

- We will not balance these accounts until after we have processed the cash payments for the month.

Kiwi Krafts
General Ledger

Cash — 110

Date	Particulars	Ref	$	Date	Particulars	Ref	$
Aug 1	Balance	b/d	4,240				
31	Sundry receipts	CRJ3	9,623				

Shop fittings — 210

Date	Particulars	Ref	$	Date	Particulars	Ref	$
Aug 1	Balance	b/d	7,400	Aug 31	Cash	CRJ3	200

GST payable — 310

Date	Particulars	Ref	$	Date	Particulars	Ref	$
				Aug 1	Balance	b/d	105
				31	Cash	CRJ3	600

Loan — 410

Date	Particulars	Ref	$	Date	Particulars	Ref	$
				Aug 1	Balance	b/d	14,500
				31	Cash	CRJ3	5,000

Sales — 610

Date	Particulars	Ref	$	Date	Particulars	Ref	$
				Aug 1	Balance	b/d	4,000
				31	Cash	CRJ3	3,200

Commission income — 620

Date	Particulars	Ref	$	Date	Particulars	Ref	$
				Aug 31	Cash	CRJ3	600

Interest income — 630

Date	Particulars	Ref	$	Date	Particulars	Ref	$
				Aug 31	Cash	CRJ3	23

ISBN: 9780170211055

The relevant accounts from the general ledger in 3-column form are shown below.

Kiwi Krafts
General Ledger

Cash 110

Date	Particulars	Ref	Dr $	Cr $	Balance $
Aug 1	Balance	b/d			4,240 Dr
31	Sundry receipts	CRJ3	9,623		13,863 Dr

Shop fittings 210

Date	Particulars	Ref	Dr $	Cr $	Balance $
Aug 1	Balance	b/d			7,400 Dr
31	Cash	CRJ3		200	7,200 Dr

GST payable 310

Date	Particulars	Ref	Dr $	Cr $	Balance $
Aug 1	Balance	b/d			105 Cr
31	Cash	CRJ3		600	705 Cr

Loan 410

Date	Particulars	Ref	Dr $	Cr $	Balance $
Aug 1	Balance	b/d			14,500 Cr
31	Cash	CRJ3		5,000	19,500 Cr

Sales 610

Date	Particulars	Ref	Dr $	Cr $	Balance $
Aug 1	Balance	b/d			4,000 Cr
31	Cash	CRJ3		3,200	7,200 Cr

Commission income 620

Date	Particulars	Ref	Dr $	Cr $	Balance $
Aug 31	Cash	CRJ3		600	600 Cr

Interest income 630

Date	Particulars	Ref	Dr $	Cr $	Balance $
Aug 31	Cash	CRJ3		23	23 Cr

DEBIT = CREDIT

ISBN: 9780170211055

Activities

1   The transactions listed below are the cash receipts of *Raggs Boutique* for October. (All amounts include GST where applicable.)

Oct 1   Commenced business with $20,000 cash, Receipt No 001
    6   Cash sales, $920
   11   Loan from bank received, $15,000
   14   Cash sales, $1,380
   17   Received commission of $92 for selling handknits, Receipt No 002
   19   Cash sales, $460
   25   Cash sales, $2,530
   27   Received commission of $115 for selling handknits, Receipt No 003
       Cash sales, $2,760
   30   Cash sales, $1,840.

The bank statement showed a direct deposit of $45 for interest on October 31.

Remember!

Post each item in the *Sundry* column individually.

DO THIS!

Record the transactions in the cash receipts journal of *Raggs Boutique* and prepare a ledger posting summary. NOTE: You should use separate analysis columns for *Sales*, *Commission* and *Sundry*.

2   The following list of December's cash receipts is from the business of *Lucy Lawful*, solicitor. (All amounts include GST where applicable.)

Date	Receipt No	Transaction
Dec 1	311	Received cash for fees of $1,380
5	312	Received interest of $460 in cash
8	313	Received cash fees of $1,150
10	314	Sold office computer for $575 cash
12	315	Lucy Lawful contributed $10,000 cash to the business
17	316	Received interest of $690 cash
	317 – 321	Received cash fees totalling $1,035
20		Received $57,500 on loan from *XYZ Bank*
22	322 – 325	Cash fees received totalled $3,450
23	326 – 330	Cash fees received totalled $1,840
28	331	Received interest of $345
30	332 – 334	Cash fees received totalled $3,680.

Hint

Use a separate analysis column when the same type of transaction appears more than once.

DO THIS!

Prepare a cash receipts journal and a posting summary for the month of December.

3   The documents on the next page were issued by *Harry's Hardware* during the week ended 7 June 2019.

DO THIS!

Enter the transactions shown by these documents in a cash receipts journal and prepare a ledger posting summary at the end of the week. NOTE: You should use separate analysis columns for *Paint and paper sales*, *Hardware sales*, *General sales* and *Sundry*.

Accounting – A Beginning   ISBN: 9780170211055

TAX INVOICE	No: 631
	1 June 2019
Harry's Hardware	
RECEIPT	
GST No: 25-987-65	
RECEIVED FROM:	
Andy's Autos	
FOR: Ladders	
Total	$460.00

TAX INVOICE	No: 632
	2 June 2019
Harry's Hardware	
RECEIPT	
GST No: 25-987-65	
RECEIVED FROM:	
Pete's Painters	
FOR: Paint	
Total	$345.00

TAX INVOICE	No: 633
	4 June 2019
Harry's Hardware	
RECEIPT	
GST No: 25-987-65	
RECEIVED FROM:	
Harry	
FOR: Capital	
Total	$5,750.00

TAX INVOICE	No: 634
	5 June 2019
Harry's Hardware	
RECEIPT	
GST No: 25-987-65	
RECEIVED FROM:	
Albany Artists	
FOR: Commission	
Total	$115.00

TAX INVOICE	No: 635
	6 June 2019
Harry's Hardware	
RECEIPT	
GST No: 25-987-65	
RECEIVED FROM:	
Sparky's	
FOR: Electric drill	
Total	$230.00

TAX INVOICE	No: 636
	7 June 2019
Harry's Hardware	
RECEIPT	
GST No: 25-987-65	
RECEIVED FROM:	
Pete's Painters	
FOR: Wallpaper	
Total	$690.00

```
    Harry's
    Hardware

GST No: 25-987-65
  2 June 2019


     13.40 +
     15.90 +
     29.95 +
      9.75 +
     69.00 T


   THANK YOU
   CALL AGAIN
```

```
    Harry's
    Hardware

GST No: 25-987-65
  4 June 2019


      6.70 +
     16.95 +
     29.25 +
     39.10 +
     92.00 T


   THANK YOU
   CALL AGAIN
```

```
    Harry's
    Hardware

GST No: 25-987-65
  7 June 2019


     49.95 +
     19.95 +
     18.95 +
     26.15 +
    115.00 T


   THANK YOU
   CALL AGAIN
```

SuperCity Bank

STATEMENT

3 JUN 2019

LOAN ADVANCE $5,000.00

SuperCity Bank

STATEMENT

4 JUN 2019

TERM DEPOSIT BROKEN $6,000.00

SuperCity Bank

STATEMENT

5 JUN 2019

INTEREST ON DEPOSIT $180.00

SuperCity Bank

STATEMENT

7 JUN 2019

VISA SALES $1,380.00

4 The following is the cash receipts journal of *A Nimmle*, veterinarian. The business is registered for GST on the payments basis.

Date	Particulars	Rec no	Ref	Receipts	Cash	GST payable	Sales	Fees	Sundry
Nov 1	Capital – A Nimmle	101		23,000	23,000	3,000			20,000
3	Cash sales			805		105	700		
	Cash fees			690	1,035	600		90	
6	VISA fees	B/S		805	720	105		700	
10	Cash sales			115		15	100		
	Cash fees			2,300	2,390	300		2,000	
15	Loan – Westpac			18,000	18,000				18,000
18	VISA sales	B/S		920	920	120	800		
21	Cash sales			230		30			
	Cash fees			2,185	2,415	285	1,900		
23	Equipment	102		575	575	75		500	
25	Cash sales			345		45			300
	Cash fees			1,265	720	165	1,100		
28	Interest	B/S		23	27	3			20
				$49,802	4,848	4,600	3,290	38,320	

DO THIS! Correct any errors in the journal and prepare a ledger posting summary. NOTE: You may assume that the figures in the *Receipts* column of the journal are correct.

5 The following list of cash receipts is from the business of *Dine at Home Catering Services*. The business caters for private dinner parties but also receives income from hiring out crockery and cutlery for large events. (All amounts include GST where applicable.)

Date	Receipt No	Transaction
Sep 1	541	Received cash for catering services of $1,380
4	542	Received hire fees in cash of $184
7	543	Received cash for catering services of $1,265
11	544	Sold catering equipment for $230 cash
15	545	Owner contributed $5,000 cash to the business
17	546	Received hire fees of $920 in cash
	547 – 551	Received cash for catering services totalling $1,035
21	B/S	Received $20,000 on loan from *Progressive Bank*
23	552 – 555	Cash for catering services received totalled $3,795
26	556 – 560	Cash for catering services received totalled $2,070
28	561	Received hire fees of $460 in cash
30	562 – 564	Cash for catering services received totalled $2,530.

Relevant ledger balances at 1 September were:

Cash	$ 3,500	Dr
Catering equipment	96,100	Dr
GST payable	500	Cr
Catering services	45,000	Cr
Hire fees	6,200	Cr
Capital	110,000	Cr

In Home Dining

DO THIS!
a Prepare a cash receipts journal and a posting summary for the month of September.
b Post the journal to the ledger.

ISBN: 9780170211055

The Cash Payments Journal

This is the second of the special journals we shall meet in this chapter. The cash payments journal shows all cash payments, and, like the cash receipts journal, analyses them into different categories.

Let's return to *Kiwi Krafts* and examine the cash payments for the month of August. (All the amounts below include GST if applicable.)

Aug 2	Paid cash for towbar for van $276, Cheque No 142
5	Paid rent $460 by automatic payment
9	Cash purchases $690, Cheque No 143
11	Aroha withdrew $500 cash for personal use, Cheque No 144
14	Bought petrol using EFTPOS, $92
16	Paid wages $230, Cheque No 145
18	Paid rent $460 by automatic payment
20	Bought new shelving $920, Cheque No 146
23	Cash purchases $575, Cheque No 147
25	Aroha withdrew $500 cash for personal use, Cheque No 148
26	Paid advertising $161, Cheque No 149
28	Gave a customer a cash refund, $92, Cheque No 150
30	Paid wages $230, Cheque No 151.

The bank statement showed that a payment of $115 was made for interest on the loan on 21 August and VISA commission of $200 had been paid on 31 August. The cash payments journal for *Kiwi Krafts* is shown below.

Kiwi Krafts
Cash Payments Journal — Page 5

Date	Particulars	Ref	Chq no	Cash	GST payable	Purchases	Rent	Wages	Drawings	Sundry
Aug 2	Towbar		142	276	36					240
5	Rent		AP	460	60		400			
9	Cash purchases		143	690	90	600				
11	Drawings		144	500					500	
14	Petrol		EFT	92	12					80
16	Wages		145	230				230		
18	Rent		AP	460	60		400			
20	Shelving		146	920	120					800
23	Cash purchases		147	575	75	500				
25	Drawings		148	500					500	
26	Advertising		149	161	21					140
28	Sales returns		150	92	12					80
30	Wages		151	230				230		
21	Interest on loan		B/S	115						115
31	VISA commission		B/S	200						200
				$5,501	486	1,100	800	460	1,000	1,655

Cash column

Analysis columns

Important!

- There are separate analysis columns for transactions which occur frequently. A *Sundry* column is used for 'one-off' payments each month.

- The cheque number is shown beside each transaction. Automatic payments for rent have AP in this column. EFTPOS transactions are signified by EFT. B/S in this column means that the information has come directly from the bank statement and is not evidenced by any other source document.

- The interest payment is shown at the bottom of the journal because the bank statement was received after the other entries had been made in the journal. This is why it is not in date order.

The effect of these transactions on the accounting equation is shown below.

Account	Type	Increasing/Decreasing	Debit/Credit
Cash	Asset	Decreasing	Credit
GST payable	Liability	Decreasing	Debit
Purchases	Expense	Increasing	Debit
Rent	Expense	Increasing	Debit
Wages	Expense	Increasing	Debit
Drawings	Equity	Decreasing	Debit
Van	Asset	Increasing	Debit
Van expenses	Expense	Increasing	Debit
Shop fittings	Asset	Increasing	Debit
Advertising	Expense	Increasing	Debit
Sales returns	Income	Decreasing	Debit
Interest on loan	Expense	Increasing	Debit

We may now prepare a summary of the ledger postings:

Debit entries	$	Credit entries	$
GST payable	486	Cash	5,501
Purchases	1,100		
Rent	800		
Wages	460		
Drawings	1,000		
Van	240		
Van expenses	80		
Shop fittings	800		
Advertising	140		
Sales returns	80		
Interest on loan	115		
VISA commission	200		
	$5,501		$5,501

Debit entries = Credit entries

ISBN: 9780170211055

Posting Cash Payments to the Ledger

The posting process for the cash payments journal is the same as for cash receipts. The totals are posted from the bottom of each column except for the Sundry column. Items in this column are posted separately. When the cash payments journal has been posted to the ledger, it appears as follows:

Kiwi Krafts
Cash Payments Journal Page 5

Date	Particulars	Ref	Chq no	Cash	GST payable	Purchases	Rent	Wages	Drawings	Sundry
Aug 2	Towbar	220	142	276	36					240
5	Rent	✔	AP	460	60		400			
9	Cash purchases	✔	143	690	90	600				
11	Drawings	✔	144	500					500	
14	Petrol	750	EFT	92	12					80
16	Wages	✔	145	230				230		
18	Rent	✔	AP	460	60		400			
20	Shelving	210	146	920	120					800
23	Cash purchases	✔	147	575	75	500				
25	Drawings	✔	148	500					500	
26	Advertising	720	149	161	21					140
28	Sales returns	611	150	92	12					80
30	Wages	✔	151	230				230		
21	Interest on loan	730	B/S	115						115
31	VISA commission	770	B/S	200						200
				$5,501	486	1,100	800	460	1,000	1,655
				110	310	710	740	760	520	

The complete general ledger in T form is shown below and on the next page.

Kiwi Krafts
General Ledger

Cash 110

Date	Particulars	Ref	$	Date	Particulars	Ref	$
Aug 1	Balance	b/d	4,240	Aug 31	Sundry payments	CPJ5	5,501
31	Sundry receipts	CRJ3	9,623		Balance	c/f	8,362
			$13,863				$13,863
Sep 1	Balance	b/d	8,362				

Inventory 120

Date	Particulars	Ref	$	Date	Particulars	Ref	$
Jul 1	Balance	b/d	12,000				

Shop fittings — 210

Date	Particulars	Ref	$	Date	Particulars	Ref	$
Aug 1	Balance	b/d	7,400	Aug 31	Cash	CRJ3	200
31	Cash	CPJ5	800		Balance	c/f	8,000
			$8,200				$8,200
Sep 1	Balance	b/d	8,000				

Van — 220

Date	Particulars	Ref	$	Date	Particulars	Ref	$
Aug 1	Balance	b/d	20,000	Aug 31	Balance	c/f	20,240
31	Cash	CPJ5	240				
			$20,240				$20,240
Sep 1	Balance	b/d	20,240				

Cash register — 230

Date	Particulars	Ref	$	Date	Particulars	Ref	$
Jul 1	Balance		800				

GST payable — 310

Date	Particulars	Ref	$	Date	Particulars	Ref	$
Aug 31	Cash	CPJ5	486	Aug 1	Balance	b/d	105
	Balance	c/f	219	31	Cash	CRJ3	600
			$705				$705
				Sep 1	Balance	b/d	219

Loan — 410

Date	Particulars	Ref	$	Date	Particulars	Ref	$
Aug 31	Balance	c/f	19,500	Aug 1	Balance	b/d	14,500
				31	Cash	CRJ3	5,000
			$19,500				$19,500
				Sep 1	Balance	b/d	19,500

Capital — 510

Date	Particulars	Ref	$	Date	Particulars	Ref	$
				Aug 1	Balance	b/d	28,500

Drawings — 520

Date	Particulars	Ref	$	Date	Particulars	Ref	$
Aug 1	Balance	b/d	460	Aug 31	Balance	c/f	1,460
31	Cash	CPJ5	1,000				
			$1,460				$1,460
Sep 1	Balance	b/d	1,460				

ISBN: 9780170211055

Sales   610

Date	Particulars	Ref	$	Date	Particulars	Ref	$
Aug 31	Balance	c/f	7,200	Aug 1	Balance	b/d	4,000
				31	Cash	CRJ3	3,200
			$7,200				$7,200
				Sep 1	Balance	b/d	7,200

Sales returns   611

Date	Particulars	Ref	$	Date	Particulars	Ref	$
Aug 1	Balance	b/d	300	Aug 31	Balance	c/f	380
31	Cash	CPJ5	80				
			$380				$380
Sep 1	Balance	b/d	380				

Commission income   620

Date	Particulars	Ref	$	Date	Particulars	Ref	$
				Aug 31	Cash	CRJ3	600

Interest income   630

Date	Particulars	Ref	$	Date	Particulars	Ref	$
				Aug 31	Cash	CRJ3	23

Purchases   710

Date	Particulars	Ref	$	Date	Particulars	Ref	$
Aug 1	Balance	b/d	600	Aug 31	Balance	c/f	1,700
31	Cash	CPJ5	1,100				
			$1,700				$1,700
Sep 1	Balance	b/d	1,700				

Purchases returns   711

Date	Particulars	Ref	$	Date	Particulars	Ref	$
				Aug 1	Balance	b/d	200

Advertising   720

Date	Particulars	Ref	$	Date	Particulars	Ref	$
Aug 1	Balance	b/d	100	Aug 31	Balance	c/f	240
31	Cash	CPJ5	140				
			$240				$240
Sep 1	Balance	b/d	240				

Interest on loan   730

Date	Particulars	Ref	$	Date	Particulars	Ref	$
Aug 1	Balance	b/d	75	Aug 31	Balance	c/f	190
31	Cash	CPJ5	115				
			$190				$190
Sep 1	Balance	b/d	190				

Kiwi Krafts
General Ledger

Rent   740

Date	Particulars	Ref	$	Date	Particulars	Ref	$
Aug 1	Balance	b/d	1,000	Aug 31	Balance	c/f	1,800
31	Cash	CPJ5	800				
			$1,800				$1,800
Sep 1	Balance	b/d	1,800				

Van expenses   750

Date	Particulars	Ref	$	Date	Particulars	Ref	$
Aug 1	Balance	b/d	100	Aug 31	Balance	c/f	180
31	Cash	CPJ5	80				
			$180				$180
Sep 1	Balance	b/d	180				

Wages   760

Date	Particulars	Ref	$	Date	Particulars	Ref	$
Aug 1	Balance	b/d	230	Aug 31	Balance	c/f	690
31	Cash	CPJ5	460				
			$690				$690
Sep 1	Balance	b/d	690				

VISA commission   770

Date	Particulars	Ref	$	Date	Particulars	Ref	$
Aug 31	Cash	CPJ5	200				

Kiwi Krafts
Trial Balance as at 31 August 2015

Cash	$ 8,362	GST payable	$ 219
Inventory	12,000	Loan (due 31 July 2019)	19,500
Shop fittings (cost)	8,000	Capital	28,500
Van (cost)	20,240	Sales	7,200
Cash register (cost)	800	Purchases returns	200
Drawings	1,460	Commission income	600
Sales returns	380	Interest income	23
Purchases	1,700		
Advertising	240		
Interest on loan	190		
Rent	1,800		
Van expenses	180		
Wages	690		
VISA commission	200		
	$56,242		$56,242

ISBN: 9780170211055

The general ledger in 3-column form is shown below.

Kiwi Krafts
General Ledger

Cash 110

Date	Particulars	Ref	Dr $	Cr $	Balance $
Aug 1	Balance	b/d			4,240 Dr
31	Sundry receipts	CRJ3	9,623		13,863 Dr
	Sundry payments	CPJ5		5,501	8,362 Dr

Inventory 120

Date	Particulars	Ref	Dr $	Cr $	Balance $
Jul 1	Balance	b/d			12,000 Dr

Shop fittings 210

Date	Particulars	Ref	Dr $	Cr $	Balance $
Aug 1	Balance	b/d			7,400 Dr
31	Cash	CRJ3		200	7,200 Dr
	Cash	CPJ5	800		8,000 Dr

Van 220

Date	Particulars	Ref	Dr $	Cr $	Balance $
Aug 1	Balance	b/d			20,000 Dr
31	Cash	CPJ5	240		20,240 Dr

Cash register 230

Date	Particulars	Ref	Dr $	Cr $	Balance $
Aug 1	Balance	b/d			800 Dr

GST payable 310

Date	Particulars	Ref	Dr $	Cr $	Balance $
Aug 1	Balance	b/d			105 Cr
31	Cash	CRJ3		600	705 Cr
	Cash	CPJ5	486		219 Cr

Loan 410

Date	Particulars	Ref	Dr $	Cr $	Balance $
Aug 1	Balance	b/d			14,500 Cr
31	Cash	CRJ3		5,000	19,500 Cr

Capital 510

Date	Particulars	Ref	Dr $	Cr $	Balance $
Aug 1	Balance	b/d			28,500 Cr

Drawings 520

Date	Particulars	Ref	Dr $	Cr $	Balance $
Aug 1	Balance	b/d			460 Dr
31	Cash	CPJ5	1,000		1,460 Dr

Kiwi Krafts
General Ledger

Sales   **610**

Date	Particulars	Ref	Dr $	Cr $	Balance $
Aug 1	Balance	b/d			4,000 Cr
31	Cash	CRJ3		3,200	7,200 Cr

Sales returns   **611**

Date	Particulars	Ref	Dr $	Cr $	Balance $
Aug 1	Balance	b/d			300 Dr
31	Cash	CPJ5	80		380 Dr

Commission income   **620**

Date	Particulars	Ref	Dr $	Cr $	Balance $
Aug 31	Cash	CRJ3		600	600 Cr

Interest income   **630**

Date	Particulars	Ref	Dr $	Cr $	Balance $
Aug 31	Cash	CRJ3		23	23 Cr

Purchases   **710**

Date	Particulars	Ref	Dr $	Cr $	Balance $
Aug 1	Balance	b/d			600 Dr
31	Cash	CPJ5	1,100		1,700 Dr

Purchases returns   **711**

Date	Particulars	Ref	Dr $	Cr $	Balance $
Jul 1	Balance	b/d			200 Cr

Advertising   **720**

Date	Particulars	Ref	Dr $	Cr $	Balance $
Aug 1	Balance	b/d			100 Dr
31	Cash	CPJ5	140		240 Dr

Interest on loan   **730**

Date	Particulars	Ref	Dr $	Cr $	Balance $
Aug 1	Balance	b/d			75 Dr
31	Cash	CPJ5	115		190 Dr

Rent   **740**

Date	Particulars	Ref	Dr $	Cr $	Balance $
Aug 1	Balance	b/d			1,000 Dr
31	Cash	CPJ5	800		1,800 Dr

Van expenses   **750**

Date	Particulars	Ref	Dr $	Cr $	Balance $
Aug 1	Balance	b/d			100 Dr
31	Cash	CPJ5	80		180 Dr

Accounting – A Beginning

ISBN: 9780170211055

Wages					760
Date	Particulars	Ref	Dr $	Cr $	Balance $
Aug 1	Balance	b/d			230 Dr
31	Cash	CPJ5	460		690 Dr

VISA commission					770
Date	Particulars	Ref	Dr $	Cr $	Balance $
Aug 31	Cash	CPJ5	200		200 Dr

The 3-column trial balance prepared from the general ledger is shown below.

Kiwi Krafts
Trial Balance as at 31 August 2015

	$	$
Cash	8,362	
Inventory	12,000	
Shop fittings (cost)	8,000	
Van (cost)	20,240	
Cash register (cost)	800	
GST payable		219
Loan (due 31 July 2019)		19,500
Capital		28,500
Drawings	1,460	
Sales		7,200
Sales returns	380	
Commission income		600
Interest income		23
Purchases	1,700	
Purchases returns		200
Advertising	240	
Interest on loan	190	
Rent	1,800	
Van expenses	180	
Wages	690	
VISA commission	200	
	$56,242	$56,242

DEBIT = CREDIT

Remember!

When posting the cash payments journal

- **Credit** the Cash account
- **Debit** all the other accounts.

ISBN: 9780170211055

Activities

1 The cash payments below were made by *I Figure*, an accountant, during March 2016. (All amounts include GST where applicable.)

Date	Cheque no	Transaction
Mar 1	EFT	Cash drawings $1,150
3	702	Paid wages $460
4	703	Paid subscription to the *New Zealand Institute of Chartered Accountants* $920
8	704	Purchased new computer $2,070
10	AP	Paid wages $460
12	705	Paid advertising $230
14	EFT	Cash drawings $1,150
17	AP	Paid wages $460
19	706	Paid insurance $575
21	EFT	Paid personal insurance from business bank account, $690
24	AP	Paid wages $460
27	707	Paid advertising $115
31	AP	Paid wages $460.

> **Remember!**
>
> Wages and interest are *exempt* from GST.

The bank statement showed that bank fees of $23 had been charged on 30 March.

DO THIS!

Record the transactions in the cash payments journal of *I Figure* and prepare a ledger posting summary. NOTE: You should use separate analysis columns for *Drawings*, *Wages*, *Advertising* and *Sundry*.

2 The following cash payments were made by *Whakaturia Waterways* in August 2018. (All amounts include GST where applicable.)

Date	Cheque no	Transaction
Aug 3	AP	Paid rent $460
7	AP	Paid wages $575
8	593	Cash purchases $1,150
10	594	Paid electricity $230
12	595	Cash purchases $1,840
14	AP	Paid wages $575
16	596	Bought equipment $805
17	AP	Paid rent $460
19	EFT	Cash drawings $300
21	AP	Paid wages $575
23	EFT	Paid for petrol $115
25	597	Cash purchases $345
28	AP	Paid wages $575
30	598	Paid cellphone account $46
31	AP	Paid rent $460.

> **Remember!**
>
> Post each item in the *Sundry* column individually.

The bank statement showed that interest of $345 on a bank loan had been charged on 20 August.

DO THIS!

Record the transactions in the cash payments journal of *Whakaturia Waterways* and prepare a ledger posting summary. NOTE: You should use separate analysis columns for *Purchases*, *Drawings*, *Wages* and *Sundry*.

3 The documents below relate to *Andy's Appliances* for October 2019.
(All amounts include GST where applicable.)

Date	4 October 2019
To	Always Ready
For	Purchases
Amount	$805.00

211451

Date	8 October 2019
To	Power Provision
For	Electricity
Amount	$460.00

211452

Date	10 October 2019
To	Electrix
For	Purchases
Amount	$2,300.00

211453

Date	13 October 2019
To	Advantage
For	EFTPOS system
Amount	$1,610.00

211454

Date	15 October 2019
To	Promo Design
For	Advertising
Amount	$920.00

211455

Date	18 October 2019
To	Insuresafe
For	House insurance
Amount	$575.00

211456

Date	24 October 2019
To	APG Warehouse
For	Purchases
Amount	$1,035.00

211457

Date	28 October 2019
To	Go Garage
For	Van repairs
Amount	$690.00

211458

Date	30 October 2019
To	Greenfuel
For	Petrol for van
Amount	$115.00

211459

OurBank

STATEMENT

13 OCT 2019

| CASH WITHDRAWAL | $1,500.00 |
| S JONES WAGES | $2,300.00 |

OurBank

STATEMENT

27 OCT 2019

RENT	$3,450.00
CASH WITHDRAWAL	$1,000.00
S JONES WAGES	$2,300.00

DO THIS!

Enter the transactions shown by these documents in a cash payments journal and prepare a ledger posting summary.

ISBN: 9780170211055

4 *Free Ride Legal Consultants* commenced business on 1 July 2018. The following are the partially completed cash receipts and payments journals for the month of July:

Free Ride Legal Consultants
Cash Receipts Journal
Page1

Date	Particulars	Rec No	Ref	Receipts	Cash	GST payable	Fees	Interest	Sundry
Jul 1	Capital	101		10,000	10,000				
3	Cash fees	102		345	345				
5	Interest	103		230	230				
8	Cash fees	104		460	460				
	Loan	B/S		5,750	5,750				
11	Interest	B/S		150	150				
17	VISA	B/S		920	920				
	Interest	B/S		350	350				
20	Cash fees	105		1,035	1,035				
25	Cash fees	106		690	690				
28	Interest	107		200	200				
					$20,130				

Free Ride Legal Consultants
Cash Payments Journal
Page1

Date	Particulars	Chq No	Ref	Cash	GST payable	Station-ery	Wages	Draw-ings	Postage & Courier	Sundry
Jul 1	Copy paper	521		92						
3	Electricity	522		230						
5	Wages	AP		690						
7	Drawings	523		2,300						
9	Telephone	524		230						
12	Desk	525		1,035						
	Wages	AP		690						
14	Computer	526		4,600						
16	Rent	527		2,300						
19	Wages	AP		690						
21	Drawings	528		2,300						
23	Pens and paper	529		69						
25	Stamps	530		115						
26	Courier	531		161						
	Wages	AP		690						
30	Drawings	532		2,300						
				$18,492						

The firm's chart of accounts is shown below.

FREE RIDE LEGAL CONSULTANTS
Chart of Accounts

100 **Current assets**
    110   Cash

200 **Non-current assets**
    210   Office furniture
    220   Office equipment

300 **Current liabilities**
    310   GST payable

400 **Non-current liabilities**
    410   Loan

500 **Equity**
    510   Capital
    520   Drawings

600 **Income**
    610   Fees
    620   Interest

700 **Expenses**
    705   Electricity
    710   Postage and courier
    715   Rent
    720   Stationery
    725   Telephone expense
    730   Wages

ISBN: 9780170211055

DO THIS!

a Complete the cash receipts and payments journals given above. (These have been reproduced in your workbook.)
b Prepare posting summaries for each journal and post the journals to the ledger.
c Prepare the trial balance as at 31 July 2018.

 5

The following summaries are from the cash receipts and payments journals of *Premium Pet Supplies* for the month of January 2017:

Premium Pet Supplies
Cash Receipts Journal

Cash	GST payable	Sales	Commission	Sundry
16,040	1,440	9,000	600	5,000

Premium Pet Supplies
Cash Payments Journal

Cash	GST payable	Purchases	Wages	Drawings	Advertising	Sundry
12,495	1,395	8,000	800	1,000	300	1,000

The *Sundry* column in the cash receipts journal contains a single receipt which was a long term loan from the bank of $5,000. The *Sundry* column of the cash payments journal contains payments for electricity $120, telephone expense $80 and rent $800.

The trial balance of the firm as at 31 December 2016 is shown below.

Premium Pet Supplies
Trial Balance as at 31 December 2016

Cash	$ 1,200	GST payable	$ 200
Inventory	18,000	Sales	120,000
Shop fittings	2,500	Capital	30,000
Advertising	3,200		
Electricity	900		
Purchases	96,000		
Rent	8,000		
Telephone expense	800		
Wages	9,600		
Drawings	10,000		
	$150,200		$150,200

DO THIS!

a Post the cash receipts journal and the cash payments journal to the ledger. NOTE: You should use a suitable chart of accounts for your ledger.
b Prepare the trial balance as at 31 January 2017.

6 The trial balance of *Electronix* as at 28 February 2018 is shown below.

Electronix			
Trial Balance as at 28 February 2018			
Inventory	$ 7,200	Bank overdraft	$ 2,600
Shop fittings	5,000	GST payable	400
Van	20,000	Capital	60,000
Advertising	3,000	Sales	75,500
Electricity	1,400	Commission income	1,500
Purchases	40,000		
Rent	22,000		
Telephone expense	1,700		
Van expenses	4,200		
Wages	19,000		
Drawings	16,500		
	$140,000		$140,000

The firm uses the following chart of accounts:

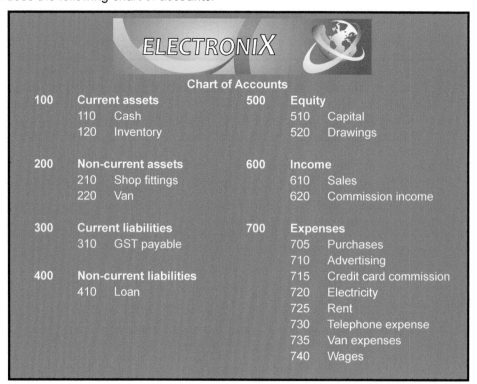

		ELECTRONIX		
		Chart of Accounts		
100	**Current assets**		500	**Equity**
110	Cash		510	Capital
120	Inventory		520	Drawings
200	**Non-current assets**		600	**Income**
210	Shop fittings		610	Sales
220	Van		620	Commission income
300	**Current liabilities**		700	**Expenses**
310	GST payable		705	Purchases
			710	Advertising
400	**Non-current liabilities**		715	Credit card commission
410	Loan		720	Electricity
			725	Rent
			730	Telephone expense
			735	Van expenses
			740	Wages

The following transactions occurred during March 2018:

Mar 1 Cash sales, $690
3 Paid $138 for advertising, Cheque No 134
4 Received commission of $92, Receipt No 346
   Cash sales, $552
5 Owner paid personal medical insurance, $920, Cheque No 135
   Paid wages of $460 by automatic payment
6 Cash sales, $736
7 Purchased goods for cash $920, Cheque No 136
   Paid electricity of $138, Cheque No 137
9 Cash sales, $345
11 Received loan of $10,000 from Co-op Bank
12 Paid wages of $460 by automatic payment
14 Cash sales, $552
   Received $184 commission, Receipt No 347
   MasterCard sales, $621

17 Purchased goods for cash $1,380, Cheque No 138
18 Paid rent for the month of $2,300 by automatic payment
19 Paid wages of $460 by automatic payment
     Paid $115 for petrol using EFTPOS
20 Cash sales, $345
     VISA sales, $690
22 Owner withdrew $460 cash for personal use by EFTPOS
24 Paid telephone $230, Cheque No 139
25 Cash sales, $1,380
26 Bought shop fittings $575, Cheque No 140
     Paid wages of $575 by automatic payment
27 Purchased goods for cash $1,955, Cheque No 141
28 Paid $230 for repairs to van, Cheque No 142
29 Cash sales $920
30 Paid advertising $207, Cheque No 143.

Hint

Total cash receipts = $17,107

Total cash payments = $11,549

The bank statement at 31 March showed MasterCard commission of $12 and VISA commission of $14 had both been paid on 31 March.

DO THIS!

a Prepare the cash journals for March and a ledger posting summary for each journal.
b Post the journals to the ledger.
c Prepare the trial balance as at 31 March 2018.

7 *Xtreme* is a business owned by Riki Payne that imports and sells sporting equipment. The business has a retail store and also sells on credit to wholesale customers.
The trial balance as at 30 September 2017 is shown below.

Xtreme Trial Balance as at 30 September 2017			
Inventory	$23,000	Accounts payable	$ 5,400
Cash	22,100	GST payable	1,200
Office equipment (cost)	15,000	Capital	58,000
Vehicle (cost)	35,000	Sales	103,780
Advertising	2,500	Commission income	12,500
Electricity	3,000	Loan (6%, due May 2021)	49,600
Interest	1,780		
Office expenses	8,220		
Purchases	45,000		
Sales commission	3,700		
Shop rent	24,000		
Telephone expense	1,580		
Vehicle expenses	3,160		
VISA commission	440		
Wages	18,000		
Drawings	24,000		
	$230,480		$230,480

The firm's chart of accounts is shown on the next page.

The following transactions occurred during October 2017:

Oct 1 Cash sales, $1,035
         Purchased new computer system for $2,760 cash, Cheque No 722
         Riki paid for son's school trip from the business bank account $230, Cheque No 723
      3 Paid wages by automatic payment, $470
         Cash sales, $1,794
      4 Received commission $690, Receipt No 219
         Paid telephone account of $184, Cheque No 724
      5 Cash sales, $575

7 Paid accounts payable $5,400, Cheque 725
   Cash purchases, $2,875, Cheque No 726
8 Cash sales, $1,058
   VISA sales, $1,380
10 Paid wages by automatic payment, $470
   Purchased goods for cash $1,610, Cheque No 727
17 Paid wages by automatic payment, $470
   Cash sales, $437
18 Cash purchases, $2,875, Cheque No 728
   Cash sales, $2,415
   Received commission $851, Receipt No 220
20 Owner withdrew $1,500 using EFTPOS
21 VISA sales, $322
   Paid rent of $3,450 by automatic payment
24 Paid wages by automatic payment, $470
   Paid advertising, $851, Cheque 729
   Cash sales, $1,610
   Paid for petrol, $69, using EFTPOS
25 Cash sales, $2,139
   Paid electricity, $391, Cheque No 730
26 Paid $368 for repairs to vehicle, Cheque No 731
   Paid sales commission, $460, Cheque No 732
31 Paid wages by automatic payment, $470.

<table>
<tr><td>Hint</td></tr>
<tr><td>Total cash receipts = $14,306</td></tr>
<tr><td>Total cash payments = $26,004</td></tr>
</table>

The bank statement at 31 October showed a loan repayment was made on 10 October of $340 and $245 interest on the loan was paid on the same day. VISA commission of $46 had been paid on 31 October.

XTREME
Chart of Accounts

100	**Current assets**		500	**Equity**	
	110	Cash		510	Capital
	120	Inventory		520	Drawings
200	**Non-current assets**		600	**Income**	
	210	Office equipment		610	Sales
	220	Vehicle		620	Commission income
300	**Current liabilities**		700	**Expenses**	
	310	GST payable		705	Advertising
	320	Accounts payable		710	Electricity
				715	Interest
400	**Non-current liabilities**		720	Office expenses
	410	Loan		725	Purchases
				730	Sales commission
				735	Shop rent
				740	Telephone expense
				745	Vehicle expenses
				750	VISA commission
				755	Wages

DO THIS!

a Prepare the cash journals for October and a ledger posting summary for each journal.

b Post the journals to the ledger. Prepare the trial balance as at 31 October 2017.

ISBN: 9780170211055

Bank Reconciliation Statements

Banks regularly issue statements of account to all account-holders. A bank statement is a record of all the transactions which have occurred in the account, prepared from the bank's point of view. Most banks now have statements available on-line through internet banking. Customers can also receive paper statements through the mail, but this is becoming less common.

There are often differences between the cash journals and the bank statement prepared by the bank. For example, there may be automatic payments from the bank account which have not been recorded in the cash journals, or deposits into the bank account made directly by debtors or by the bank itself. Sometimes people forget to record transactions in the journals.

As well as transactions which appear on the bank statement but do not appear in the cash journals, there might be transactions which appear in the cash journals but have not yet been processed by the bank. Examples of these are deposits which have been made after the close of business for the day, or cheques which have not been banked by the people who have received them.

The cash journals of *Kiwi Krafts* for September 2015 are shown below, before they have been totalled for the month.

Kiwi Krafts
Cash Receipts Journal   Page 4

Date	Particulars	Ref	Rec no	Receipts	Cash	GST	Sales	Commission	Sundry
Sep 1	Cash sales			414	414	54	360		
6	Commission		1006	276	276	36		240	
12	Cash sales			575	575	75	500		
	VISA			920	920	120	800		
18	Capital		1007	5,000	5,000				5,000
22	VISA			1,150	1,150	150	1,000		
	Commission		1008	115	115	15		100	
28	Cash sales			345	345	45	300		

Kiwi Krafts
Cash Payments Journal

Date	Particulars	Ref	Chq no	Cash	GST	Purchases	Rent	Wages	Drawings	Sundry
Sep 4	Rent		AP	460	60		400			
5	EFTPOS machine		152	1,035	135					900
8	Cash purchases		153	299	39	260				
12	Drawings		EFT	500					500	
14	Wages		AP	230				230		
18	Rent		AP	460	60		400			
19	Cash purchases		154	690	90	600				
20	Drawings		EFT	500					500	
26	Petrol		EFT	276	36					240
28	Wages		AP	230				230		
29	Advertising		155	115	15					100

It is important to make sure that there is agreement between the bank statement and the business records. Preparing a bank reconciliation statement enables us to do this. The bank statement for September is shown below.

Branch	Treetown	
Address	25 Tower Road Treetown	
Contact	Customer Services Centre Ph. (07) 361-2000	

Kiwi Krafts
PO Box 23-156
Treetown

Customer Number	08-6515-7335976-00
Opening date	1 September 2015
Statement number	**3** Page No **1**
Overdraft Limit	$0

Date	Transaction	Debit/Withdrawal	Deposit	Balance
01 Sep	**Opening Balance**			**8362.00**
02 Sep			414.00	8776.00
04 Sep	TOWN RENTALS	460.00		8316.00
07 Sep	215152	1035.00		7281.00
07 Sep			276.00	7557.00
12 Sep	EFTPOS TERMINAL	500.00		7057.00
12 Sep	VISA		920.00	7977.00
13 Sep			575.00	8552.00
14 Sep	A HELPER WAGES	230.00		8322.00
18 Sep	TOWN RENTALS	460.00		7862.00
18 Sep	TUI'S TRINKETS		230.00	8092.00
19 Sep			5000.00	13092.00
19 Sep	215153	299.00		12793.00
20 Sep	EFTPOS TERMINAL	500.00		12293.00
21 Sep	LOAN INTEREST	180.00		12113.00
21 Sep	LOAN PRINCIPAL	200.00		11913.00
22 Sep	VISA		1150.00	13063.00
26 Sep	TREETOWN MOTORS	276.00		12787.00
26 Sep			115.00	12902.00
28 Sep	A HELPER WAGES	230.00		12672.00
30 Sep	FEE	46.00		12626.00
30 Sep 15	**Closing Balance**			**12626.00**

The reconciliation process is shown on the next page.

ISBN: 9780170211055

STEP 1

Compare the bank statement with the cash journals

After comparing the bank statement against the cash journals for *Kiwi Krafts*, we find the following differences:

Items in the bank statement but not in the cash journals:
- *Tui's Trinkets* made a deposit of $230 on 18 September.
- On 21 September payments were made for interest on the loan of $180 and loan principal of $200.
- On 30 September a bank fee of $46 was charged.

Items in the cash journals but not in the bank statement:
- Cheque numbers 154 ($690) and 155 ($115) had not been presented at the bank.
- The deposit of $345 made on 28 September did not appear on the bank statement.

STEP 2

Update the cash journals and prepare the Bank account

When the deposit from *Tui's Trinkets* and the payments for loan principal, interest and bank fees have been entered in the cash journals and the journals have been totalled for the month, they appears as follows:

Kiwi Krafts
Cash Receipts Journal   Page 4

Date	Particulars	Ref	Rec no	Receipts	Cash	GST	Sales	Commission	Sundry
Sep 1	Cash sales			414	414	54	360		
6	Commission		1006	276	276	36		240	
12	Cash sales			575	575	75	500		
	VISA			920	920	120	800		
18	Capital		1007	5,000	5,000				5,000
22	VISA			1,150	1,150	150	1,000		
	Commission		1008	115	115	15		100	
28	Cash sales			345	345	45	300		
18	Tui's Trinkets		B/S	230	230	30	200		
					9,025	525	3,160	340	5,000

Kiwi Krafts
Cash Payments Journal   Page 6

Date	Particulars	Ref	Chq no	Cash	GST	Purchases	Rent	Wages	Drawings	Sundry
Sep 4	Rent		AP	460	60		400			
5	EFTPOS machine		152	1,035	135					900
8	Cash purchases		153	299	39	260				
12	Drawings		EFT	500					500	
14	Wages		AP	230				230		
18	Rent		AP	460	60		400			
19	Cash purchases		154	690	90	600				
20	Drawings		EFT	500					500	
26	Petrol		EFT	276	36					240
28	Wages		AP	230				230		
29	Advertising		155	115	15					100
21	Loan interest		B/S	180						180
	Loan principal		B/S	200						200
30	Bank fee		B/S	46						46
				5,221	435	860	800	460	1,000	1,666

Note!

- The deposit made by *Tui's Trinkets* which did not appear in the bank statement is highlighted in the cash receipts journal above.

- The payments for interest on loan, loan principal and bank fee which do not appear in the bank statement have been highlighted in the cash payments journal above.

 STEP 3

Complete and balance the Cash account in the ledger

The ledger accounts in T form and 3-column form are as follows:

			Cash					110
Date	Particulars	Ref	$	Date	Particulars	Ref	$	
Sep 1	Balance	b/d	8,362	Sep 30	Sundry payments	CPJ6	5,221	
30	Sundry receipts	CRJ4	9,025		Balance	c/f	12,166	
			$17,387				$17,387	
Oct 1	Balance	b/d	12,166					

Cash   110

Date	Particulars	Ref	Dr $	Cr $	Balance $
Sep 1	Balance	b/d			8,362 Dr
30	Sundry receipts	CRJ4	9,025		17,387 Dr
	Sundry payments	CPJ6		5,221	12,166 Dr

 STEP 4

Prepare the bank reconciliation statement

A reconciliation form is often provided on the back of the statement sent by the bank. However, with the popularity of electronic banking, many firms elect not to receive paper statements. We can prepare a similar statement ourselves. The bank reconciliation statement for *Kiwi Krafts* as at 30 September 2015 is shown below.

Kiwi Krafts
Bank Reconciliation Statement as at 30 September 2015

		$	$
Balance as per bank statement			12,626
Plus: *Deposit not credited*			345
			12,971
Less: *Unpresented cheques*			
	#154	690	
	#155	115	
			805
Balance as per Cash account			$12,166

ISBN: 9780170211055

Activities

 1 Daisy Driver operates a companionship and driving service for elderly and disabled people. The following is a list of transactions taken from the cash journals for December 2016:

Receipts			Payments			
Date	Transaction	Amount	Date	Chq no	Transaction	Amount
Dec 14	Cash fees	$580.00	Dec 4	718	Car registration	$129.58
21	Cash fees	100.00	6	EFT	Petrol	43.46
			10	EFT	Cash drawings	40.00
			13	AP	Insurance	29.12
			14	719	Tyre	144.45
			16	EFT	Cash drawings	60.00
			19	720	Advertising	146.20
			20	721	Uniform	140.00
Total receipts		**$680.00**	**Total payments**			**$732.81**

The balance of the Cash account in the ledger at 1 December was $714.20 Dr. Daisy received the following bank statement early in the new year:

SMARTBANK

Address	23 Downtown Road
	Uptown
Contact	Customer Services Centre
	Ph. (07) 361-2000

Ms Daisy Driver
234 Smart Street
Uptown

Customer Number	02-3125-985647-00
Opening date	1 December 2016
Statement number	**10** Page No **1**
Overdraft Limit	$100.00

Date	Transaction	Debit/Withdrawal	Deposit	Balance
01 Dec	**Opening Balance**			**714.20**
05 Dec	684718	129.58		584.62
06 Dec	Local Motors	43.46		541.16
10 Dec	Driver, Daisy	40.00		501.16
13 Dec	Insuresafe	29.12		472.04
14 Dec			580.00	1052.04
16 Dec	684719	144.45		907.59
16 Dec	Driver, Daisy	60.00		847.59
19 Dec	684720	146.20		701.39
31 Dec 16	**Closing Balance**			**701.39**

DO THIS!

a Prepare the Cash ledger account of Daisy's business for the month of December 2016.

b Prepare the bank reconciliation statement as at 31 December 2016.

ISBN: 9780170211055

2 *Window Washers* is a small business owned by Winny Willams who washes shop windows part-time under contract while her children are at school. The following transactions occurred during September 2018:

Receipts			Payments			
Date	Transaction	Amount	Date	Chq no	Transaction	Amount
Sep 2	Cash fees	$300.00	Sep 10	EFT	Petrol	$89.00
16	Cash fees	300.00	12	291	Cleaning supplies	16.40
30	Cash fees	300.00	20	EFT	Cash drawings	400.00
			26	292	Van registration	177.00
Total receipts		**$900.00**	**Total payments**			**$682.40**

The balance of the Cash account in the ledger at 1 September was $492.49 Cr. Winny received the following bank statement early in October:

Co-opBank

Branch	Invertown	
Address	46 Lake Road	
	Invertown	
Contact	Customer Services Centre	
	Ph. (07) 361-2000	

Ms W Williams
20 Soames Street
Invertown

Customer Number	07-3210-465879-00
Opening date	03 September 2018
Statement number	8 Page No 1
Overdraft Limit	$500.00

Date	Transaction	Debit/Withdrawal	Deposit	Balance	
03 Sep	Opening Balance			492.49	OD
04 Sep			300.00	192.49	OD
10 Sep	Caltex Invertown	89.00		281.49	OD
14 Sep	354291	16.40		297.89	OD
18 Sep			300.00	2.11	
20 Sep	Williams W	400.00		397.89	OD
30 Sep	Fee	1.50		399.39	OD
01 Oct 18	Closing Balance			399.39	OD

Hint

Winny's bank statement shows that her bank account is overdrawn. You should treat this as a *negative* opening balance in the bank reconciliation statement.

DO THIS!

a Prepare the Cash ledger account of *Window Washers* for the month of September 2018. NOTE: You will need to calculate an updated balance for total payments before you begin.
b Prepare the bank reconciliation statement as at 30 September 2018.

3 *Perfect Print* is a small photographic printing business owned by Peter Porter. The following transactions occurred during May 2018:

Receipts			Payments			
Date	Transaction	Amount	Date	Chq no	Transaction	Amount
May 8	Cash fees	$1,000.00	May 15	EFT	Cash drawings	$300.00
22	Cash fees	1,000.00	19	723	Computer	1,450.00
			20	724	Printer	800.00
			26	725	Advertising	720.00
Total receipts		**$2,000.00**	**Total payments**			**$3,270.00**

ISBN: 9780170211055

The balance of the Cash account in the ledger at 1 May was $101.65 Dr. Peter received the following bank statement early in June:

		Branch	Kamo
		Address	123 Kamo Road
			Whangarei
		Contact	Customer Services Centre
			Ph. (07) 361-2000
		Customer Number	09-3026-096814-00

 **Bank Green**

Mr Peter Porter
83 Marae Drive
Whakapara

Opening date	01 May 2018
Statement number	**15** Page No **1**
Overdraft Limit	$750.00

Date	Transaction	Debit/Withdrawal	Deposit	Balance	
01 May	**Opening Balance**			**101.65**	
01 May	Fee	5.00		96.65	
01 May	Service Commitment Fee	5.00		91.65	
01 May	Interest	2.68		88.97	
08 May			1000.00	1088.97	
15 May	Porter, Peter	300.00		788.97	
21 May	546723	1450.00		661.03	OD
22 May			1000.00	338.97	
25 May	546724	800.00		461.03	OD
31 May 18	**Closing Balance**			**461.03**	**OD**

DO THIS!

a Prepare the Cash ledger account of *Perfect Print* for the month of May 2018. NOTE: You will need to calculate updated balances for total receipts and total payments before you begin.

b Prepare the bank reconciliation statement as at 31 May 2018.

4 *Help4U* is a gardening and handyman service owned and operated by Ruth Rewi. Ruth usually works on her own, but hires occasional labour for heavy lifting work. The following transactions occurred during August 2019:

Receipts			Payments			
Date	Transaction	Amount	Date	Chq no	Transaction	Amount
Aug 14	Cash fees	$701.14	Aug 4	142	Tools	$85.32
21	Cash fees	832.65	16	143	Storage	200.00
31	Dividend	79.60		EFT	Cash drawings	100.00
			22	EFT	Petrol	36.08
				EFT	Garden supplies	83.41
				144	Personal shopping	29.50
			23	145	Advertising	100.00
				DD	Cellphone account	45.60
			30	EFT	Cash drawings	100.00
				146	Wages – Joe	200.00
				EFT	Garden supplies	54.87
Total receipts		**$1,613.39**	**Total payments**			**$1,034.78**

The balance of the Cash account in the ledger at 1 August was $201.19 Dr. The bank statement for August is shown on the next page.

ISBN: 9780170211055

	Ourßank		Branch Address	Homesville 89 Ordinary Drive Homesville

OurßAnk

Branch Address — Homesville, 89 Ordinary Drive, Homesville

Contact — Customer Services Centre Ph. (07) 361-2000

Ms R Rewi
67 Porterhouse Lane
Homesville

Customer Number — 06-3651-958421-00

Opening date — 02 August 2019
Statement number — **16** Page No **1**
Overdraft Limit — $500.00

Date	Transaction	Debit/Withdrawal	Deposit	Balance
02 Aug	**Opening Balance**			**201.19**
03 Aug	Activity Fee	7.10		194.09
04 Aug	Interest		11.20	205.29
05 Aug	Withholding Tax	3.70		201.59
14 Aug			701.14	902.73
15 Aug	482142	85.32		817.41
15 Aug	Rewi R	100.00		717.41
18 Aug	482143	200.00		517.41
22 Aug	Highway Service Station	36.08		481.33
22 Aug	Gardenmart	83.41		397.92
22 Aug	Safer Insurance 456912Z004	45.91		352.01
23 Aug	Telecom	45.60		306.41
24 Aug	482145	100.00		206.41
26 Aug	482144	29.50		176.91
29 Aug			832.65	1009.56
30 Aug	Rewi R	100.00		909.56
30 Aug	Gardenmart	54.87		854.69
30 Aug 19	**Closing Balance**			**854.69**

DO THIS!

a Prepare the Cash ledger account of *Help4U* for the month of August 2019. NOTE: You will need to calculate updated balances for total receipts and total payments before you begin.

b Prepare the bank reconciliation statement as at 31 August 2019.

5 *Tere's Tax Services* specialises in preparing GST and tax returns for small businesses. The firm is owned and operated by Teresa Thomas on her own, but during the busy tax season she employs senior high school students to prepare some of the GST returns.

The balance of the Cash account in the ledger at 1 September was $631.29 Dr. The transactions from the cash receipts and cash payments journals and the bank statement for September are shown on the next page.

DO THIS!

a Prepare the Cash ledger account of *Tere's Tax Services* for the month of September 2017. NOTE: You will need to calculate updated balances for total receipts and total payments before you begin.

b Prepare the bank reconciliation statement as at 30 September 2017.

ISBN: 9780170211055

Receipts

Date		Transaction	Amount
Sep	11	Cash fees	$310.20
	17	Cash fees	422.32
	22	Term deposit	500.00
	24	Cash fees	306.56
	30	Cash fees	100.00
Total receipts			**$1,639.08**

Payments

Date		Chq no	Transaction	Amount
Sep	1	EFT	Petrol	$133.00
	6	218	Copy paper	12.80
	7	EFT	Cash drawings	50.00
	9	219	Advertising	70.00
	12	AP	Insurance	15.70
	12	EFT	Stationery	56.00
	19	220	Stamps and courier	59.17
	20	EFT	Petrol	133.00
	20	DD	Power	107.82
	21	221	Cellphone account	110.50
	22	222	WOF	42.75
	23	223	Stationery	18.50
	26	224	Car repairs	95.41
	27	EFT	Transfer	1000.00
	28	EFT	Petrol	113.96
Total payments				**$2,018.61**

SuperCity Bank

Branch	Totaraville
Address	93 Main Street Totaraville
Contact	Customer Services Centre Ph. (07) 361-2000
Customer Number	07-3096-588796-00

Ms T Thomas
43 Parity Place
Totaraville

Opening date	1 September 2017
Statement number	**6** Page No **1**
Overdraft Limit	$100.00

Date	Transaction	Debit/Withdrawal	Deposit	Balance
01 Sep	**Opening Balance**			**631.29**
01 Sep	Shell Wellstown	133.00		498.29
02 Sep	Interest 12-3096-588796-72		315.30	813.59
07 Sep	124218	12.80		800.79
07 Sep	Thomas, T	50.00		750.79
10 Sep	124219	70.00		680.79
11 Sep			310.20	990.99
11 Sep	Fee	5.80		985.19
12 Sep	Total Insurance 4309862Z001	15.70		969.49
12 Sep	Super Stationery	56.00		913.49
12 Sep	Total Insurance 4309862Z002	29.93		883.56
17 Sep			422.32	1305.88
17 Sep	124220	59.17		1246.71
20 Sep	Shell Wellstown	133.00		1113.71
20 Sep	Northpower	107.82		1005.89
22 Sep	Interest 12-3096-588796-71		89.88	1095.77
22 Sep	Principal 12-3096-588796-71		500.00	1595.77
24 Sep			306.56	1902.33
24 Sep	124221	110.50		1791.83
24 Sep	124222	42.75		1749.08
26 Sep	124223	18.50		1730.58
27 Sep	Transfer to 12-3096-588796-73	1000.00		730.58
28 Sep	Shell Wellstown	113.96		616.62
28 Sep	Thomas, T	20.00		596.62
30 Sep 17	**Closing Balance**			**596.62**

ISBN: 9780170211055

6 Extracts from the cash receipts and payments journals of *Tick Tock Jewellers* for May 2017 and the bank statement for the month are shown below.

Date	Cash Receipts	Rec No	Amount $
May 2	Cash sales		920.23
4	Repairs	112	46.69
8	Cash sales		738.30
12	Commission	113	92.00
16	Cash sales		1,104.00
18	Repairs	114	115.46
22	T Tock – Capital	115	5,000.00
24	Cash sales		2,369.23
31	Cash sales		1,726.38
	Total to date		$12,112.29

Date	Cash Payments	Chq No	Amount $
May 1	Advertising	451	116.15
3	Purchases	452	644.00
5	Electricity	DD	230.46
8	Telephone	453	92.00
12	Drawings	EFT	1,000.00
15	Purchases	454	738.30
19	Wages	AP	1,350.00
21	Rent	AP	2,530.00
26	Drawings	EFT	1,000.00
28	Purchases	455	506.00
31	Advertising	466	128.69
	Total to date		$8,335.60

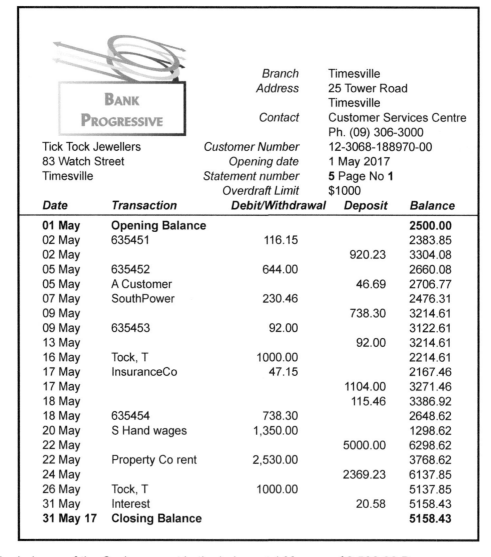

BANK PROGRESSIVE

Tick Tock Jewellers
83 Watch Street
Timesville

Branch	Timesville
Address	25 Tower Road Timesville
Contact	Customer Services Centre Ph. (09) 306-3000
Customer Number	12-3068-188970-00
Opening date	1 May 2017
Statement number	**5** Page No **1**
Overdraft Limit	$1000

Date	Transaction	Debit/Withdrawal	Deposit	Balance
01 May	**Opening Balance**			**2500.00**
02 May	635451	116.15		2383.85
02 May			920.23	3304.08
05 May	635452	644.00		2660.08
05 May	A Customer		46.69	2706.77
07 May	SouthPower	230.46		2476.31
09 May			738.30	3214.61
09 May	635453	92.00		3122.61
13 May			92.00	3214.61
16 May	Tock, T	1000.00		2214.61
17 May	InsuranceCo	47.15		2167.46
17 May			1104.00	3271.46
18 May			115.46	3386.92
18 May	635454	738.30		2648.62
20 May	S Hand wages	1,350.00		1298.62
22 May			5000.00	6298.62
22 May	Property Co rent	2,530.00		3768.62
24 May			2369.23	6137.85
26 May	Tock, T	1000.00		5137.85
31 May	Interest		20.58	5158.43
31 May 17	**Closing Balance**			**5158.43**

The balance of the Cash account in the ledger at 1 May was $2,500.00 Dr.

DO THIS!

a Prepare the Cash ledger account of *Tick Tock Jewellers* for the month of May 2017. NOTE: You will need to calculate updated balances for total receipts and total payments before you begin.

b Prepare the bank reconciliation statement as at 31 May 2017.

ISBN: 9780170211055

7 The following is a list of cheques and other payments for *Musik Master*, a retailer of musical instruments owned by Mike Masters, for the month of August 2018:

Cheque No	For	$	Cheque No	For	$
621590	Advertising	46.69	621595	Purchases	690.46
621591	Purchases	364.32	621596	Stationery	90.85
EFT	Drawings	500.00	621597	Advertising	46.00
621592	Purchases	920.00	621598	Shop counter	1,265.00
621593	Cleaning	69.00	AP	Rent	3,795.00
DD	Electricity	231.15	621599	Signwriting	573.85
AP	Wages	1265.00	EFT	Drawings	1,500.00
621594	Telephone	232.30	621600	Stationery	82.80

The bank statement that was received in early September is shown below.

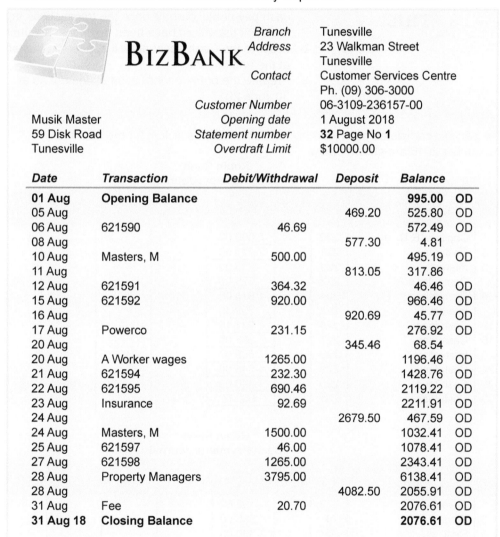

BizBank

Branch	Tunesville
Address	23 Walkman Street
	Tunesville
Contact	Customer Services Centre
	Ph. (09) 306-3000
Customer Number	06-3109-236157-00
Opening date	1 August 2018
Statement number	**32** Page No **1**
Overdraft Limit	$10000.00

Musik Master
59 Disk Road
Tunesville

Date	Transaction	Debit/Withdrawal	Deposit	Balance	
01 Aug	**Opening Balance**			**995.00**	**OD**
05 Aug			469.20	525.80	OD
06 Aug	621590	46.69		572.49	OD
08 Aug			577.30	4.81	
10 Aug	Masters, M	500.00		495.19	OD
11 Aug			813.05	317.86	
12 Aug	621591	364.32		46.46	OD
15 Aug	621592	920.00		966.46	OD
16 Aug			920.69	45.77	OD
17 Aug	Powerco	231.15		276.92	OD
20 Aug			345.46	68.54	
20 Aug	A Worker wages	1265.00		1196.46	OD
21 Aug	621594	232.30		1428.76	OD
22 Aug	621595	690.46		2119.22	OD
23 Aug	Insurance	92.69		2211.91	OD
24 Aug			2679.50	467.59	OD
24 Aug	Masters, M	1500.00		1032.41	OD
25 Aug	621597	46.00		1078.41	OD
27 Aug	621598	1265.00		2343.41	OD
28 Aug	Property Managers	3795.00		6138.41	OD
28 Aug			4082.50	2055.91	OD
31 Aug	Fee	20.70		2076.61	OD
31 Aug 18	**Closing Balance**			**2076.61**	**OD**

All cash received during the month was for cash sales except for the transaction on 16 August which was from the sale of old shop fittings. There was a deposit of $1,150.00 made on 31 August that did not appear on the bank statement. The ledger bank balance at 1 August was $995.00 Cr.

DO THIS!

a Prepare the cash receipts and payments journals of *Musik Master* for the month of August 2018.
b Prepare the Cash account in the ledger for the month of August 2018.
c Prepare the bank reconciliation statement as at 31 August 2018.

8 The cash receipts journal of *S Ossage Butchery* for June 2017 totalled $3,250 and the cash payments journal totalled $2,925. When the journals were compared with the bank statement, the following differences were found:

- A payment of $90 for insurance was in the bank statement but not in the cash payments journal.
- A deposit of $180 which was made on 30 June did not appear in the bank statement.
- Cheques #312 ($75), #314 ($120) and #315 ($230) had not been presented at the bank.

The balance of the Cash account in the ledger at 1 June was $1,900 Dr. The bank statement had a closing balance of $2,380.

DO THIS!

a Calculate the updated totals of the cash receipts and cash payments journals once the transactions from the bank statement have been taken into account.

b Prepare the Cash account as it appears in the ledger at the end of June.

c Prepare the bank reconciliation statement as at 30 June 2017.

9 The partially completed cash journals for *Robin Runn*, solicitor, for the month of September 2016 are shown below.

Robin Runn
Cash Receipts Journal   Page 1

Date	Particulars	Rec No	Ref	Receipts	Cash	GST payable	Fees	Interest	Sundry
Sep 1	Capital – R Runn	220		5,000.00					
3	Cash fees	221		2,771.50					
5	Interest	222		630.00					
	Computer sold	223		575.00					
9	Cash fees	224		1,518.00					
	Interest	225		759.46					
12	Cash fees	226		921.15					
16	Cash fees	227		966.00					
20	Interest	228		569.00					
24	Cash fees	229		4,048.00					
28	Cash fees	230		1,840.00					
30	Cash fees	231		632.50					

Robin Runn
Cash Payments Journal   Page 1

Date	Particulars	Chq No	Ref	Cash	GST payable	Wages	Drawings	Stationery	Sundry
Sep 1	Advertising	582		92.69					
3	Wages	AP		500.00					
5	Rent	AP		2,300.00					
7	Stationery	583		303.60					
12	Printer	584		230.69					
14	Telephone	DD		404.80					
	Drawings	EFT		1,800.00					
15	Wages	AP		500.00					
17	Stationery	585		46.69					
19	Car insurance	586		809.60					
28	Stamps	587		116.15					
29	Stationery	588		151.80					
30	Drawings	EFT		1,800.00					

The balance of the Cash account in the ledger at 1 September was $1,200.00 Dr. Robin received the following bank statement early in October:

ISBN: 9780170211055

Oz Bank

Branch	Tinseltown
Address	165 Hollywood Drive
	Tinseltown
Contact	Customer Services Centre
	Ph. (09) 306-3000
Customer Number	07-3081-643879-00
Opening date	1 September 2016
Statement number	**23** Page No **1**
Overdraft Limit	$5000

Robin Runn Solicitors
43 Thugg Lane
Tinseltown

Date	Transaction	Debit/Withdrawal	Deposit	Balance
01 Sep	**Opening Balance**			**1200.00**
02 Sep	Insurance	46.23		1153.77
02 Sep			5000.00	6153.77
03 Sep			2771.50	8925.27
03 Sep	121582	92.69		8832.58
03 Sep	Susan Handy Wages	500.00		8332.58
04 Sep	A Robber		276.00	8608.58
05 Sep			1205.00	9813.58
07 Sep	Commercial Rentals	2300.00		7513.58
09 Sep			2277.46	9791.04
09 Sep	121583	303.60		9487.44
13 Sep			921.15	10408.59
13 Sep	121584	230.69		10177.90
14 Sep	Runn R	1800.00		8377.90
14 Sep	Telstra	404.80		7973.10
17 Sep			966.00	8939.10
17 Sep	Susan Handy Wages	500.00		8439.10
20 Sep			569.00	9008.10
20 Sep	A Robber		276.00	9284.10
22 Sep	121586	809.60		8474.50
25 Sep			4048.00	12522.50
25 Sep	121587	116.15		12406.35
29 Sep			1840.00	14246.35
30 Sep	Runn R	1800.00		12446.35
30 Sep	Fee	18.40		12427.95
30 Sep 16	**Closing Balance**			**12427.95**

DO THIS!

a Complete the cash receipts and payments journals of *Robin Runn* for the month of September 2016.

b Prepare the Cash account in the ledger as it would appear at the end of September.

c Prepare the bank reconciliation statement as at 30 September 2016.

10 On 1 August 2016 Tama HeiHei commenced business in a small souvenir shop, *Tama's Trinkets*. Tama sells souvenirs to the public and also sells carvings he has made to other shops in the area. The business is registered for GST on the payments basis.

Below is a record of the shop's transactions for the month of August.

Aug 1 Commenced business with $15,000.00 cash, Receipt No 101
2 Bought shop fittings for $1,840.00 cash, Cheque No 151
3 Purchased souvenir inventory paying cash of $2,760.00, Cheque No 152

ISBN: 9780170211055

5   Sold goods for cash, $575.00
6   Purchased goods for $920.00 cash, Cheque No 153
7   Paid $138.00 cash for advertising, Cheque No 154
10   Paid rent of $460.00 by automatic payment
     VISA payment for cash sales, $460.00
12   Customer returned goods for a cash refund of $92.69, Cheque No 155
15   Tama took $800.00 cash for personal use by EFTPOS
18   Sold goods for cash $922.30 and by VISA $413.54
19   Purchased shop fittings costing $1,288.00 for cash, Cheque No 156
22   Purchased souvenirs for $805.00 cash, Cheque No 157
24   Paid telephone rental of $206.54, Cheque No 158
     Paid rent of $460.00 by automatic payment
27   Paid $310.50 cash for advertising, Cheque No 159
29   Tama took $500.00 cash for personal use by EFTPOS
31   Sold goods for cash, $1,518.46.

The August bank statement is shown below.

OurßBank

		Branch	Totaraville
		Address	23 Rimu Street
			Totaraville
		Contact	Customer Services Centre
			Ph. (09) 306-3000
		Customer Number	12-3019-324157-00
Tama's Trinkets		Opening date	1 August 2016
167 Wood Road		Statement number	1 Page No 1
Totaraville		Overdraft Limit	$0

Date	Transaction	Debit/Withdrawal	Deposit	Balance
01 Aug	**Opening Balance**			0.00
01 Aug			15000.00	15000.00
01 Aug	Transfer to 12-3019-324157-70	5000.00		10000.00
04 Aug	431152	2760.00		7240.00
04 Aug	Cheque books	18.40		7221.60
05 Aug	431151	1840.00		5381.60
05 Aug			575.00	5956.60
09 Aug	431153	920.00		5036.60
10 Aug	Town Properties Rent	460.00		4576.60
10 Aug	431154	138.00		4438.60
10 Aug	VISA		460.00	4898.60
15 Aug	EFTPOS	800.00		4098.60
18 Aug	VISA		413.54	4512.14
19 Aug			922.30	5434.44
23 Aug	Safer Insurance	92.46		5341.98
24 Aug	Town Properties Rent	460.00		4881.98
25 Aug	431157	805.00		4076.98
28 Aug	431159	310.50		3766.48
28 Aug	431158	206.54		3559.94
30 Aug	EFTPOS	500.00		3059.94
31 Aug	Interest		23.69	3083.63
31 Aug 16	**Closing Balance**			**3083.63**

Hint

The transfer on 01 August is to a term deposit.

DO THIS!

a Prepare a chart of accounts for *Tama's Trinkets*.
b Enter the above transactions in the cash receipts and cash payments journals of *Tama's Trinkets*, post to the ledger and prepare the trial balance as at 31 August 2016.
c Prepare the bank reconciliation statement as at 31 August 2016.

CHAPTER 6

Preparing Financial Statements

- **The Income Statement**
- **Financial Statements from a Trial Balance**
- **Accrual Basis of Accounting**
- **Adjusting the Trial Balance**

This chapter is about the preparation of financial statements for sole trading businesses. In Chapter 2 we introduced the following financial statements:

- The **statement of financial position**, which shows the assets, liabilities and equity of the business at the end of the reporting period according to the accounting equation in the form: Eq = A − L.

- The **income statement**, which shows the income and expenses for a reporting period and calculates the profit for the period.

The Income Statement

In Chapter 2, Aroha prepared the income statement for Brad's business, *Trendy Tourz*. This statement is shown on page 43. It shows a profit for the month of $4,200.

The income statement can be made more useful if expenses are classified into different types. This gives users a means of assessing how well the business is controlling expenses in different areas of its operation.

Classifying Expenses

The expenses of a business may be classified into various groups. Each group contains types of expenses which have a similar nature.

Trendy Tourz is a **service** business. It provides tourism services to its customers. Other services include plumbers, mechanics, accountants, lawyers and so on.

The other main type of business is a **trading** business. These businesses buy goods and sell them to customers at a profit.

The classification of expenses depends on the type of business for which the financial statements are being prepared. A common classification for a service business is shown in the diagram below.

Remember!

Trading businesses buy goods and sell them at a profit.

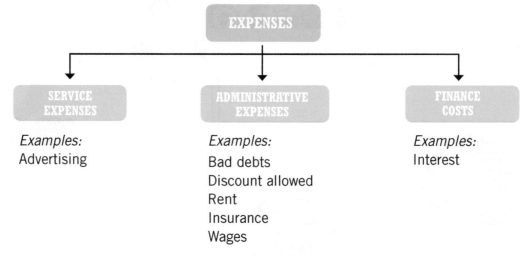

EXPENSES

SERVICE EXPENSES	ADMINISTRATIVE EXPENSES	FINANCE COSTS
Examples: Advertising	*Examples:* Bad debts Discount allowed Rent Insurance Wages	*Examples:* Interest

Service expenses are those incurred in order to increase the sales of a business (such as advertising) and to provide the service itself. For example, an electrician would include the cost of supplies such as wiring and switches, travel costs to go to the jobs (including all vehicle expenses and depreciation on vehicles) and wages for the staff who actually work on the jobs.

For trading businesses, this category is called *Distribution costs* and includes expenses incurred in obtaining sales, such as advertising, sales commissions and salespeople's wages and also expenses incurred in delivering goods such as freight and delivery van expenses.

Administrative expenses are those expenses which are incurred in order to organise the business. These include all expenses relating to managing and accommodating the business. Examples of administrative expenses are:

- Rent
- General expenses
- Office wages
- Postage
- Bad debts

- Office salaries
- Insurance
- Electricity
- Stationery
- Discounts allowed for prompt payment.

- Telephone and internet
- Repairs
- Rates
- Accountancy fees

Finance costs are those incurred in financing, or obtaining cash, for the business. The only items under this heading are interest expenses such as interest on a mortgage, loan or bank overdraft.

Other expenses are those which do not fit into any of the above groups. We will not be concerned with those expenses in this course. *Trendy Tourz* is a **service organisation** because it provides services to customers but does not sell goods.

The income statement shows the income earned for the period and the expenses incurred during the period. It then calculates the profit:

$$\textbf{Profit} \quad = \quad \textbf{Income} \quad - \quad \textbf{Expenses}$$

Remember!

If expenses are *greater* than income, the business reports a *loss*.

The fully classified income statement for *Trendy Tourz* is shown below for the month ended 31 July 2015.

Trendy Tourz
Income Statement for the month ended 31 July 2015

	$	$	$
Revenue			
Tour fees			6,900
Less: **Expenses**			
Tour expenses			
Advertising	450		
Insurance on van	100		
Petrol and oil	500		
Tour supplies expense	365		
		1,415	
Administrative expenses			
Accounting fees	200		
Electricity	80		
Rent	800		
Telephone rental	70		
		1,150	
Finance costs			
Interest on loan		135	
Total expenses			2,700
Profit for the month			$4,200

Important!

- *Income* includes **revenue** and **other income**.
- In this example the income is all from tour fees. Since tours are the main activity of the business, we use the heading **Revenue** here.

Activities

1 The table below shows a number of different expenses.

		Distribution cost	Administrative expense	Finance cost
a	Rent		✓	
b	Discount allowed			
c	Postage and stationery			
d	Sales commissions			
e	Interest			
f	Legal fees			
g	Advertising			

DO THIS!

Classify each expense by placing a tick in the correct box. (The first one has been done for you.)

2 The information below relates to *Paul's IT Services* for the year to 30 June 2016:

Expenses		**Income**	
Advertising	$ 4,000	Contract fees	$100,000
Car expenses	3,200		
Computer repairs	2,500		
Depreciation on computers	3,000		
Interest on loan	900		
Rent	20,000		
Stationery expenses	1,000		
Telephone expenses	1,400		
Wages	30,000		

DO THIS!

Prepare a fully classified income statement for *Paul's IT Services*. You should classify expenses as *Computing expenses*, *Administrative expenses* or *Finance costs*.

3 The information below relates to *Great Gardeners* for the year to 31 March 2015:

Fees received in cash	$90,000
Fees still unpaid by clients for March	10,000
Advertising expenses paid	2,500
Van expenses paid	5,400
Cellphone expenses paid	700
Advertising invoice for March received but not yet paid	400
Wages paid	50,000
Accountancy fees paid	1,600
Tools purchased	650
Interest on loan	100

DO THIS!

Prepare a fully classified income statement for *Great Gardeners*. You should classify expenses as *Gardening expenses*, *Administrative expenses* or *Finance costs*.

Accounting – A Beginning

ISBN: 9780170211055

The statement of financial position shows the assets, liabilities and equity of the business. In this course, it incorporates the statement of changes in equity.

Assets

In Chapter 2, we classified assets into two groups: **current assets** and **non-current assets**. Non-current assets were further subdivided into **investment assets**, **property, plant and equipment** and **intangible assets**.

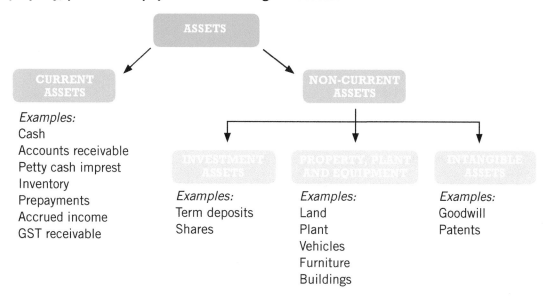

Current assets	Assets that are held for trading or that we expect will turn into cash, or be used up, within the next reporting period. These assets include cash at bank, accounts receivable, stock of goods for resale (inventory), supplies such as cleaning materials and petty cash (small amounts of cash kept on hand to pay expenses).
Non-current assets	Any assets that are not current assets. These assets are expected to be retained in the business beyond the end of the next reporting period. They may be further divided into:
Investment assets	Assets such as term deposits or shares in companies which are expected to be kept in the business for more than one reporting period. These are normally more easily converted into cash than property, plant and equipment (see below).
Property, plant and equipment	Assets which we expect to retain in the business so that it can operate in the future. Property, plant and equipment includes land, buildings, equipment, shop fittings and motor vehicles.
Intangible assets	Assets which are 'untouchable'. One example of an intangible asset is **goodwill**.
	Other examples of intangible assets are copyrights and trademarks. Both of these represent a 'right' but have no physical presence.

Liabilities

In Chapter 2, liabilities in the statement of financial position were classified into two types: **current liabilities** and **non-current liabilities**.

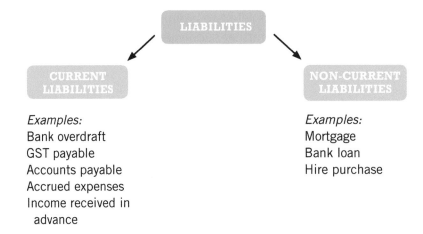

	LIABILITIES	
CURRENT LIABILITIES		**NON-CURRENT LIABILITIES**
Examples:		*Examples:*
Bank overdraft		Mortgage
GST payable		Bank loan
Accounts payable		Hire purchase
Accrued expenses		
Income received in advance		

Current liabilities   Liabilities which we expect will be paid within the next reporting period. It is usually necessary for us to have cash to meet these liabilities. Examples are a bank overdraft, GST payable and accounts payable.

Non-current liabilities   Liabilities that are not current liabilities. These will be paid over a period of time beyond the next reporting period or twelve-month business cycle. They include mortgages, hire purchase payments and long term loans.

Ahhhh....I remember now. You calculate the profit in the income statement and then add it to the opening capital.

Yes, the profit increases your equity.

But why are my drawings shown in the statement of financial position? Aren't they an expense?

No, remember what I told you about the accounting entity. Drawings are a personal expense, not a business expense. You have to keep personal and business affairs separate.

Oops! I think I have put them in the wrong place in the computer chart of accounts. Can we fix that?

Yes, I will do a journal entry for you. Anything else?

I was wondering about GST. Is it an asset or a liability?

Well that's a bit tricky. If the IRD owes you money, it's a current asset. If you owe them, it's a current liability. The computer will sort that out for you.

Equity

The equity section of the statement of financial position shows the changes in equity between the beginning and end of the reporting period. The statement of financial position of *Trendy Tourz*, which we prepared in Chapter 2, is shown below. We see that Brad contributed $5,000 and withdrew $500 during the year. The profit is also shown in this section of the statement because it represents an increase in Brad's equity. Profit *increases* equity – drawings *decrease* equity.

Trendy Tourz
Statement of Financial Position as at 31 July 2015

	$	$	$
ASSETS			
Non-current assets			
Property, plant and equipment			
Total carrying amount (Note 1)			55,000
Current assets			
Cash		5,200	
Accounts receivable		2,800	
Total current assets			8,000
Total assets			$63,000
EQUITY AND LIABILITIES			
Equity			
Capital at beginning of the month		29,500	
Contribution by owner		5,000	
Profit for the month		4,200	
Drawings for the month		(500)	
Capital at end of the month			38,200
Non-current liabilities			
Loan (due 30 June 2020)		19,800	
Current liabilities			
Accounts payable		5,000	
Total liabilities			24,800
Total equity and liabilities			$63,000

Notes to the statement of financial position

1 *Property, plant and equipment*	$
Computer (cost)	3,000
Outdoor equipment (cost)	22,000
Van (cost)	30,000
	$55,000

Activities

1 The following list of assets and liabilities has been taken from the chart of accounts of *Recycle*:

a	Machinery	**h**	Accounts receivable
b	GST payable	**i**	Bank overdraft
c	Computer	**j**	Accounts payable
d	Bank loan (5 years)	**k**	Land
e	Goodwill	**l**	Mortgage
f	Cellphone	**m**	GST receivable
g	Cash	**n**	Inventory.

Classify each of the items **a – n** above under one of the following headings:

Current asset, Property, plant and equipment (PPE), Intangible asset, Current liability or *Non-current liability*.

2 The following balances are taken from the accounting records of *Value Video:*

Assets:			Liabilities:		
	Accounts receivable	$ 400		Accounts payable	$ 6,000
	DVD and video library (cost)	80,000		Bank loan (due 2020)	60,000
	Petty cash	100		GST payable	2,700
	Computer equipment (cost)	30,000			
	Cash	7,000			
	Inventory of snacks	2,900			

Equity:		
	Capital, 1 April 2015	$31,300
	Profit for the year ended 31 March 2016	45,000
	Drawings in the year ended 31 March 2016	24,600

Prepare a fully classified statement of financial position for *Value Video*. You **must** show the changes in equity in your statement.

3 The following balances are taken from the accounting records of *Pete's Painters:*

Assets:			Liabilities:		
	Accounts receivable	$18,900		Accounts payable	$ 3,000
	Cash	4,500		Bank loan (due 2022)	15,000
	Van (cost)	34,000			
	Tools and ladders (cost)	5,000			
	Paint supplies on hand	800			
	GST receivable	1,200			

Equity:		
	Capital, 1 July 2016	$19,500
	Profit for the year ended 30 June 2017	62,700
	Drawings in the year ended 30 June 2017	35,800

Prepare a fully classified statement of financial position for *Pete's Painters*. You **must** show the changes in equity in your statement.

ISBN: 9780170211055

Financial Statements from a Trial Balance

We have already been introduced to the **trial balance**, which is a list of the account balances in the ledger after all the transactions for the period have been posted. The trial balance can be used to prepare the income statement and the statement of financial position. We can represent this process as follows:

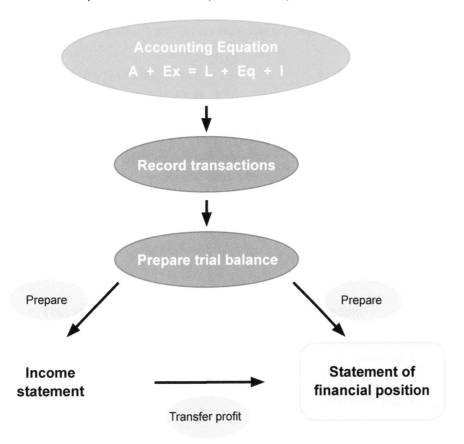

Consider the following example:

The trial balance below was prepared for *Super Snooper Detective Agency*:

	Super Snooper Detective Agency Trial Balance as at 31 March 2017				
IEx	Advertising	$ 2,100		Capital, 1 April 2016	$45,950
	Cash	3,400	R	Fees	56,700
	Camera (cost)	1,700	OI	Gain on sale of camera	200
IEx	Car expenses	3,400		GST payable	1,000
	Cellphone (cost)	1,200		Loan (due 31 October 2024)	20,000
	Drawings	30,000			
AEx	Electricity	1,400			
FC	Interest	2,600			
	Motor vehicle (cost)	35,000			
	Office equipment (cost)	7,500			
IEx	Photographic expenses	3,100			
AEx	Postage and stationery	1,150			
AEx	Rent	6,500			
AEx	Telephone expense	1,800			
IEx	Wages	23,000			
		$123,850			$123,850

STEP 1

Identify and classify income and expense accounts

The trial balance shown on the previous page has all income and expense accounts highlighted. *Super Snooper Detective Agency* is a service organisation. We therefore need a name to use for service expenses. We will call these *Investigative expenses*. The following abbreviations have been used beside the account names on the trial balance:

Income		*Expenses*	
R	Revenue	**IEx**	Investigative expenses
OI	Other income	**AEx**	Administrative expenses
		FC	Finance costs

Income items have *credit* balances and therefore appear on the right hand side of the trial balance. Expenses have *debit* balances and appear on the left hand side of the trial balance.

STEP 2

Prepare the income statement

Super Snooper Detective Agency
Income Statement for the year ended 31 March 2017

	$	$	$
Revenue			
Fees			56,700
Other income			
Gain on sale of camera			200
Total income			56,900
Less: **Expenses**			
Investigative expenses			
Advertising	2,100		
Car expenses	3,400		
Photographic expenses	3,100		
Wages	23,000		
		31,600	
Administrative expenses			
Electricity	1,400		
Postage and stationery	1,150		
Rent	6,500		
Telephone expense	1,800		
		10,850	
Finance costs			
Interest		2,600	
Total expenses			45,050
Profit for the year			$11,850

Accounting – A Beginning

ISBN: 9780170211055

Important!

- *Income* includes **revenue** and **other income**.

- In this example, there are two types of income: fees and the gain on sale of the camera.

- Fees come from investigative services, which are the main activity of the business. Thus the fees are shown under the **Revenue** heading.

- The gain on sale of the camera is incidental to the operation of the business, so we show this as **Other income**.

STEP 3

Identify the assets, liabilities and equity

The trial balance below has all asset, liability and equity accounts highlighted. The following abbreviations have been used beside the account names on the trial balance:

Assets	*Liabilities*
CA Current assets	**CL** Current liabilities
NCA Non-current assets	**NCL** Non-current liabilities

Equity
C Capital
D Drawings

- Assets have *debit* balances and therefore appear on the *left hand side* of the trial balance.
- Liabilities have *credit* balances and appear on the *right hand side* of the trial balance.
- Equity items appear on both sides of the trial balance. Capital is positive equity and appears on the right hand side because it has a *credit* balance.
- The drawings account represents negative equity, thus has a *debit* balance and appears on the left hand side.

Super Snooper Detective Agency
Trial Balance as at 31 March 2017

	Advertising	$ 2,100	**C**	Capital, 1 April 2016	$45,950
CA	Cash	3,400		Fees	56,700
NCA	Camera (cost)	1,700		Gain on sale of camera	200
	Car expenses	3,400	**CL**	GST payable	1,000
NCA	Cellphone (cost)	1,200	**NCL**	Loan (due 31 October 2024)	20,000
D	Drawings	30,000			
	Electricity	1,400			
	Interest	2,600			
NCA	Motor vehicle (cost)	35,000			
NCA	Office equipment (cost)	7,500			
	Photographic expenses	3,100			
	Postage and stationery	1,150			
	Rent	6,500			
	Telephone expense	1,800			
	Wages	23,000			
		$123,850			$123,850

STEP 4

Prepare the statement of financial position

Super Snooper Detective Agency
Statement of Financial Position as at 31 March 2017

	$	$
ASSETS		
Non-current assets		
Property, plant and equipment		
Total carrying amount (Note 1)		45,400
Current assets		
Cash		3,400
Total assets		$48,800
EQUITY AND LIABILITIES		
Equity		
Capital at beginning of the year	45,950	
Profit for the year	11,850	
Drawings for the year	(30,000)	
Capital at end of the year		27,800
Non-current liabilities		
Loan (due 31 October 2024)	20,000	
Current liabilities		
GST payable	1,000	
Total liabilities		21,000
Total equity and liabilities		$48,800

> **Remember!**
> GST is a *current* liability.

Notes to the statement of financial position

1 *Property, plant and equipment*	$
Camera (cost)	1,700
Cellphone (cost)	1,200
Motor vehicle (cost)	35,000
Office equipment (cost)	7,500
	$45,400

Important!

- GST payable is always a current liability. For some businesses, it will be payable within 2 months. For others it will be payable within 6 months.

- The calculation of closing capital is shown in the *Equity* section of the statement.

ISBN: 9780170211055

Activities

1 The following trial balance was extracted from the accounting records of *Grubby Garbage Collection Service* as at 30 June 2018:

Grubby Garbage Collection Service Trial Balance as at 30 June 2018			
Cash	$ 7,750	Capital, 1 July 2017	$ 57,800
Computer (cost)	5,000	Fees	163,500
Drawings	30,000	Gain on sale of truck	1,500
General expenses	2,400	GST payable	800
Insurance	2,200	Loan (due 30 June 2025)	50,000
Interest on loan	5,200		
Petrol and oil	10,600		
Petty cash	250		
Repairs to trucks	200		
Trucks (cost)	150,000		
Wages	60,000		
	$273,600		$273,600

DO THIS!

a Classify the items in the trial balance according to the accounting equation, as in the example on pages 179 – 182. You should classify expenses as *Collection expenses*, *Administrative expenses* or *Finance costs*.

b Prepare the fully classified income statement and statement of financial position for *Grubby Garbage Collection Service*.

2 The following trial balance was extracted from the accounting records of *Deeper Drains and Sewers* as at 30 June 2017:

Deeper Drains and Sewers Trial Balance as at 30 June 2017			
Cash	$ 7,300	Capital, 1 July 2016	$182,000
Drawings	60,000	GST payable	3,500
Electricity	3,300	Hire fees	318,000
Insurance	18,000	Loan (due 31 July 2020)	200,000
Interest	14,800	Mortgage (12%, due	
Land and buildings (cost)	270,000	31 May 2025)	160,000
Machinery (cost)	240,000	Rent	10,400
Petrol and oil	23,200		
Petty cash	200		
Repairs to machinery	14,400		
Telephone and tolls	1,500		
Trucks (cost)	160,000		
Wages	61,200		
	$873,900		$873,900

DO THIS!

a Classify the items in the trial balance according to the accounting equation, as in the example on pages 179 – 182. You should classify expenses as *Drainage expenses*, *Administrative expenses* or *Finance costs*.

b Prepare the fully classified income statement and statement of financial position for *Deeper Drains and Sewers*.

3 The following trial balance was extracted from the accounting records of *Computa Whizz,* a mobile IT service business, as at 30 September 2019:

Computa Whizz Trial Balance as at 30 September 2019			
Cash	$ 9,100	Capital, 1 October 2018	$ 96,800
Computers (cost)	8,600	Fees	186,700
Drawings	41,000	GST payable	1,500
Electricity	2,400	Interest income	800
Insurance	2,200		
Interest expense	200		
Rent	18,000		
Repairs to computers	3,700		
Term deposit			
(due 31 May 2022)	20,000		
Vehicles (cost)	110,000		
Vehicle expenses	10,600		
Wages	60,000		
	$285,800		$285,800

DO THIS!

a Classify the items in the trial balance according to the accounting equation, as in the example on pages 179 – 182. You should classify expenses as *Servicing expenses, Administrative expenses* or *Finance costs.*

b Prepare the fully classified income statement and statement of financial position for *Computa Whizz.*

4 The following trial balance was extracted from the accounting records of *24/7 Vets,* a local veterinary emergency clinic, as at 31 March 2018:

24/7 Vets Trial Balance as at 31 March 2018			
Cellphone (cost)	$ 500	Bank overdraft	$ 2,400
Drawings	54,000	Capital, 1 April 2017	79,550
Electricity	1,800	Fees	195,000
GST receivable	3,000	Interest income	1,300
Insurance	1,650	Mortgage	
Interest on mortgage	6,000	(12%, due 30 June 2027)	50,000
Loss on sale of equipment	500		
Postage and stationery	1,650		
Premises (cost)	150,000		
Surgical equipment (cost)	15,000		
Surgery furniture (cost)	4,300		
Telephone expense	1,750		
Term deposit	20,000		
(due 30 June 2023)			
Vet supplies expense	3,600		
Wages (nurse)	64,500		
	$328,250		$328,250

24/7

HELP IN A HURRY

DO THIS!

a Classify the items in the trial balance according to the accounting equation, as in the example on pages 179 – 182. You should classify expenses as *Clinical expenses, Administrative expenses* or *Finance costs.*

b Prepare the fully classified income statement and statement of financial position for *24/7 Vets.*

ISBN: 9780170211055

The financial statements that Brad has prepared himself used cash-based accounting. This means that he had recorded only those transactions which involved the receipt or payment of cash.

In order to measure accurately the financial performance for the year and financial position at the end of the year, Brad's financial statements must be converted to the **accrual basis of accounting**. We first met this concept in Chapter 2.

DEFINITION

Accrual basis of accounting

The effects of transactions and other events are recognised when they occur (and not as cash or its equivalent is received or paid) and they are recorded in the accounting records and reported in the financial statements of the periods to which they relate.

Accrual accounting results in a number of additional entries in the accounting records of a business. In addition to the cash transactions, any credit transactions that have occurred in the reporting period must also be recorded and processed. Further, other events that do not involve the flow of cash will also be included. We will look at some of those later. For now, we will focus on credit transactions.

At the end of the reporting period, the following credit transactions that have not been recorded previously must be taken into account:

- Invoices for tour fees totalling $6,210 (including GST) had been sent but were unpaid
- Unpaid invoices on hand for tour food supplies totalled $1,150 (including GST)
- New kayaks costing $4,600 (including GST) were bought on credit during June and this invoice has not been paid.

We will consider each of these transactions separately below.

Invoices for tour fees totalling $6,210 (including GST) had been sent but were unpaid

Invoices sent to customers represent accounts receivable. The total amount of the invoices includes GST, so we must calculate the GST component:

$$\text{GST} = \$6,210 * {}^{3}/_{23}$$
$$= \$810$$

This information can be represented on the accounting equation as follows:

	A Accounts receivable	+	Ex	=	L GST payable	+	Eq	+	I Tour fees
Invoices of $6,210 for tour fees outstanding	+ 6,210			=	+ 810				+ 5,400

Important!

- The total amount of the invoices owing represents accounts receivable = $6,210.

- The GST payable on this transactions is a current liability = $810.

- Tour fees earned is the difference: $6,210 – 810 = $5,400.

This is an account payable. The total amount of the invoices includes GST, so we must calculate the GST component:

$$GST = \$1,150 * {}^{3}/_{23}$$
$$= \$150$$

This information can be represented on the accounting equation as follows:

	A	+	Ex	=		L		+	Eq	+	I
			Tour supplies			GST payable	Accounts payable				
Invoices on hand for tour supplies, $1,150			+ 1,000	=		− 150	+ 1,150				

Important!

- The total amount of the invoices owing for supplies represents accounts payable = $1,150.

- The GST refund due on this transaction = $150. This reduces the amount of GST payable overall, so is recorded as a reduction in a current liability.

- Tour supplies expense incurred is the difference: $1,150 − 150 = $1,000.

This transaction is the credit purchase of a non-current asset. It is therefore an account payable, similar to the previous transaction for tour supplies. The total amount of the invoices includes GST, so we must calculate the GST component:

$$GST = \$4,600 * {}^{3}/_{23}$$
$$= \$600$$

This information can be represented on the accounting equation as follows:

	A	+	Ex	=		L		+	Eq	+	I
	Outdoor equipment					GST payable	Accounts payable				
Invoices on hand for kayaks, $4,600	+ 4,000			=		− 600	+ 4,600				

Important!

- The amount of the invoice owing for kayaks represents accounts payable = $4,600.

- The GST refund due on this transaction = $600. Again, this is recorded as a reduction in a current liability.

- The cost of the kayaks is the difference: $4,600 − 600 = $4,000.

ISBN: 9780170211055

Activities

1 The following information has yet to be recorded at the end of the reporting period:

a Invoices outstanding for professional fees total $1,380 (including GST).
b Unpaid invoices on hand for supplies total $920 (including GST).
c At the end of the period an invoice was received for the credit purchase of machinery costing $2,760 (including GST).

 DO THIS!

Record the effect of these transactions on the accounting equation in the table below.

	A		+	Ex	=	L		+	Eq	+	I
	Accounts receivable	Machinery		Supplies expense		Accounts payable	GST payable				Fees
a											
b											
c											
d											

2 The following information has yet to be recorded at 30 June, the end of the reporting period:

a New carpet was installed during June at a cost of $2,300 (including GST). The invoice was received on 20 June but has not yet been paid.
b Invoices on hand for supplies used during June amount to $5,520 (including GST).
c Monthly invoices sent to customers on 30 June total $11,500 (including GST).
d Invoices totalling $920 (including GST) sent to customers in May remain unpaid.

 **DO THIS!**

Record the effect of these transactions on the accounting equation in the table below.

	A		+	Ex	=	L		+	Eq	+	I
	Accounts receivable	Carpet		Supplies expense		Accounts payable	GST payable				Fees
a											
b											
c											
d											

3 *Cheaper Computer Services* keeps cash-based accounting records during the year. The owner has asked you to record the following at the end of the reporting period:

- Invoices issued to customers but not yet paid total $13,800 (including GST)
- Unpaid invoices received from parts suppliers total $6,440 (including GST)
- A new printer costing $1,840 (including GST) has been purchased on credit but has not been recorded in the accounts.

Ledger balances before this information was recorded were: Service fees $160,000 Cr, Parts expense $72,000 Dr, Computer equipment $15,000 Dr and GST payable $1,800 Cr.

 **DO THIS!**

Calculate the updated balances of the following accounts after the above information has been recorded:

a Service fees **c** Computer equipment
b Parts expense **d** GST payable.

Accounting – A Beginning

ISBN: 9780170211055

Adjusting the Trial Balance

Aroha had prepared the trial balance below before the additional accrual transactions had been recorded.

Trendy Tourz
Trial Balance as at 30 June 2016

Account	$	Account	$
Accounting fees	200	Advertising income	600
Advertising	3,800	Capital, 1 July 2015	29,500
Cash	9,100	GST payable	6,400
Computer (cost)	3,000	Loan (due 30 June 2020)	17,000
Drawings	60,000	Tour fees	120,000
Electricity	1,000		
Insurance on van	1,500		
Interest on loan	1,800		
Outdoor equipment (cost)	22,000		
Petrol and oil	8,600		
Rent	10,400		
Shares in *Telecom*	10,000		
Telephone rental	600		
Tour supplies expense	6,800		
Van (cost)	30,000		
Van repairs	4,700		
	$173,500		$173,500

The table below summarises the effect of these three new transactions on the accounting equation:

	A		+	Ex	=	L		+	Eq	+	I
	Accounts receivable	Outdoor equipment		Tour supplies expense		GST payable	Accounts payable				Tour fees
Balance		22,000		6,800		6,400					120,000
Fees	6,210					810					5,400
Supplies				1,000		(150)	1,150				
Kayaks		4,000				(600)	4,600				
Total	6,210	26,000		7,800		6,460	5,750				125,400

We can use this information to update the trial balance. The adjusted trial balance (with changes highlighted) is shown on the next page.

Important!

There are two new accounts in the trial balance:

- **Accounts receivable** represents the amount owing from customers. This is a *current asset*.

- **Accounts payable** represents the amount owing to suppliers. This is a *current liability*.

Trendy Tourz
Adjusted Trial Balance as at 30 June 2016

Accounting fees	$ 200	Advertising income	$ 600
Advertising	3,800	Capital, 1 July 2015	29,500
Cash	9,100	GST payable	6,460
Computer (cost)	3,000	Loan (due 30 June 2020)	17,000
Drawings	60,000	Tour fees	125,400
Electricity	1,000	Accounts payable	5,750
Insurance on van	1,500		
Interest on loan	1,800		
Outdoor equipment (cost)	26,000		
Petrol and oil	8,600		
Rent	10,400		
Shares in *Telecom*	10,000		
Telephone rental	600		
Tour supplies expense	7,800		
Van (cost)	30,000		
Van repairs	4,700		
Accounts receivable	6,210		
	$184,710		$184,710

The trial balance can now be used to prepare the financial statements for the year, as in the previous section. The income statement is shown below.

Trendy Tourz
Income Statement for the year ended 30 June 2016

	$	$	$
Revenue			
Tour fees			125,400
Other income			
Advertising income			600
Total income			126,000
Less: **Expenses**			
Tour expenses			
Advertising	3,800		
Insurance on van	1,500		
Petrol and oil	8,600		
Tour supplies expense	7,800		
Van repairs	4,700		
		26,400	
Administrative expenses			
Accounting fees	200		
Electricity	1,000		
Rent	10,400		
Telephone rental	600		
		12,200	
Finance costs			
Interest on loan		1,800	
Total expenses			40,400
Profit for the year			$85,600

ISBN: 9780170211055

The statement of financial position is shown below.

Trendy Tourz
Statement of Financial Position as at 30 June 2016

	$	$	$
ASSETS			
Non-current assets			
Property, plant and equipment			
Total carrying amount (Note 1)		59,000	
Investments			
Shares in *Telecom*		10,000	
Total non-current assets			69,000
Current assets			
Cash		9,100	
Accounts receivable		6,210	
Total current assets			15,310
Total assets			$84,310
EQUITY AND LIABILITIES			
Equity			
Capital at beginning of the year		29,500	
Profit for the year		85,600	
Drawings for the year		(60,000)	
Capital at end of the year			55,100
Non-current liabilities			
Loan (due 30 June 2020)		17,000	
Current liabilities			
Accounts payable	5,750		
GST payable	6,460		
Total current liabilities		12,210	
Total liabilities			29,210
Total equity and liabilities			$84,310

Notes to the statement of financial position

1 *Property, plant and equipment*	$
Computer (cost)	3,000
Outdoor equipment (cost)	26,000
Van (cost)	30,000
	$59,000

Activities

1 The trial balance below is taken from *Straight Line Surveyors* as at 30 June 2017.

Straight Line Surveyors Trial Balance as at 30 June 2017			
Cash	$ 6,300	Capital, 1 July 2016	$ 13,300
Computer (cost)	5,000	Surveying fees	120,000
Drawings	65,000	GST payable	5,500
Equipment (cost)	22,000	Loan (due 30 April 2025)	20,000
Insurance (van)	1,700		
Interest	2,000		
Petrol and oil	8,000		
Rent	7,200		
Repairs (van)	1,300		
Surveying supplies	9,500		
Telephone expense	800		
Van (cost)	30,000		
	$158,800		$158,800

Additional information:
- Invoices unpaid for fees at the end of the period amount to $3,680 (including GST)
- Unpaid invoices on hand for supplies used during June are $1,150 (including GST)
- Equipment bought on credit in June for $2,760 (including GST) has not been recorded and the invoice remains unpaid.

DO THIS!

a Record the effect of these transactions on the accounting equation in the table below.

	A		+	Ex	=	L		+	Eq	+	I
	Accounts receivable	Equipment		Surveying supplies		Accounts payable	GST payable				Surveying fees
Balance		22,000		9,500			5,500				120,000
Total											

DO THIS!

b Classify the items in the trial balance according to the accounting equation, as in the example on pages 179 – 182. You should classify expenses as *Survey expenses*, *Administrative expenses* or *Finance costs*.

c Prepare the fully classified income statement and statement of financial position for *Straight Line Surveyors*.

ISBN: 9780170211055

2 The trial balance below is taken from *On Time Couriers* as at 31 March 2018.

On Time Couriers Trial Balance as at 31 March 2018			
Advertising	$ 7,500	Capital, 1 April 2017	$39,600
Cash	2,000	Courier fees	94,000
Courier vans (cost)	58,000	GST payable	800
Courier van repairs	4,000	Dividend income	200
Drawings	34,000	Loan (8%, due 2025)	25,000
General expenses	12,000		
Insurance	1,200		
Interest expense	2,250		
Office equipment (cost)	4,000		
Office wages	8,300		
Petrol and oil	7,000		
Petty cash	50		
Rent	9,000		
Shares in *The Warehouse*	10,000		
Van registration	300		
	$159,600		$159,600

Additional information:
- Invoices issued outstanding fees at the end of the period amount to $8,280 (including GST)
- Unpaid invoices on hand for petrol used during March are $920 (including GST)
- A new office printer bought on credit in March for $1,150 (including GST) has not been recorded and the invoice remains unpaid.

DO THIS!

a Record the effect of these transactions on the accounting equation in the table below.

	A		+	Ex	=	L		+	Eq	+	I
	Accounts receivable	Office equipment		Petrol and oil		Accounts payable	GST payable				Courier fees
Balance		4,000		7,000			800				94,000
Total											

DO THIS!

b Classify the items in the trial balance according to the accounting equation, as in the example on pages 179 – 182. You should classify expenses as *Courier expenses*, *Administrative expenses* or *Finance costs*.

c Prepare the fully classified income statement and statement of financial position for *On Time Couriers*.

3 The trial balance below is taken from *Smart's Shoe Repairs* as at 30 June 2020.

Smart's Shoe Repairs Trial Balance as at 30 June 2020			
Accountancy fees	$ 1,500	Bank overdraft	$ 2,900
Advertising	3,200	Capital, 1 July 2019	54,750
Cleaning expenses	1,100	GST payable	1,500
Computer (cost)	2,000	Commission income	750
Computer repairs	3,600	Loan (6%, due 2027)	15,000
Drawings	36,000	Repair income	53,500
Equipment (cost)	31,800		
General expenses	3,350		
Insurance	1,450		
Interest expense	1,600		
Petty cash	100		
Rent	22,000		
Stationery expense	250		
Supplies expense	18,700		
Telephone expense	1,750		
	$128,400		$128,400

Additional information:
- Invoices outstanding for repairs at the end of the period amount to $5,750 (including GST)
- Unpaid invoices on hand for supplies used during June are $1,150 (including GST)
- A new key cutting machine bought on credit in June for $9,200 (including GST) has not been recorded and the invoice remains unpaid.

DO THIS!

a Record the effect of these transactions on the accounting equation in the table below.

	A		+	Ex	=	L		+	Eq	+	I
	Accounts receivable	Equipment		Supplies expense		Accounts payable	GST payable				Repair income
Balance		31,800		18,700			1,500				53,500
Total											

DO THIS!

b Classify the items in the trial balance according to the accounting equation, as in the example on pages 179 – 182. You should classify expenses as *Workshop expenses*, *Administrative expenses* or *Finance costs*.

c Prepare the fully classified income statement and statement of financial position for *Smart's Shoe Repairs*.

Accounting – A Beginning

ISBN: 9780170211055

CHAPTER 7

More Financial Statements

- More Accruals
- Adjusting the Trial Balance
- Depreciation
- The Completed Financial Statements

More Accruals

In the previous chapter, some adjustments to the trial balance were made for transactions outstanding at the end of the reporting period. These adjustments were necessary in order to convert cash-based accounting records to the accrual basis so that the financial statements could be prepared.

At the end of the reporting period the assets and liabilities of the business must be measured accurately so that equity is calculated correctly. We recognised the accounts receivable asset resulting from outstanding payments from credit customers and the accounts payable liabilities resulting from credit purchases of either supplies or items of property, plant and equipment that remain unpaid.

Crossing Reporting Periods

Cash received or paid during a reporting period for income and expenses does not necessarily mean that the income or expense relates to that particular period. For example, an insurance policy may relate partly to the current reporting period and partly to the next period. A business may pay wages on one particular day of the week, for example, a Wednesday. If the reporting period ends on a Friday, there will still be two days' wages owing for the current period which will not be paid until the next reporting period.

Accounting for transactions which relate to more than one reporting period requires the use of **period-end adjustments**. These adjustments recognise assets and liabilities at the end of the period and adjust the income and expense balances accordingly. If we do not make these adjustments, the assets and liabilities will not be fairly stated in the statement of financial position. Thus the reported profit would be incorrect.

There are generally four types of period-end adjustments which arise in accounting for transactions that relate to more than one reporting period:

- Assets arising because expenses have been paid in advance (**prepayments**)
- Assets arising because income has been earned but not received at the end of the period (**accrued income**)
- Liabilities arising because there are expenses owing which have not been paid at the end of the period (**accrued expenses** or **expenses due**)
- Liabilities arising because there is income which has been received in advance at the end of the period (**income received in advance**).

We will now study the effect of each of these types of adjustment on the accounting equation.

Recognising New Assets

Prepayments

Prepayments are expenses which have been paid in advance at the end of the period. Insurance premiums will often relate to more than one reporting period. Any amount relating to the following period is a *current asset* since it has not been used up at the end of the period. Only that portion of the insurance expense relating to the current reporting period should appear in the income statement.

Consider the following example:

Insurance paid during the year ended 31 March was $600 (excluding GST). The insurance premium expires on 31 July. We can represent this situation with the following diagram:

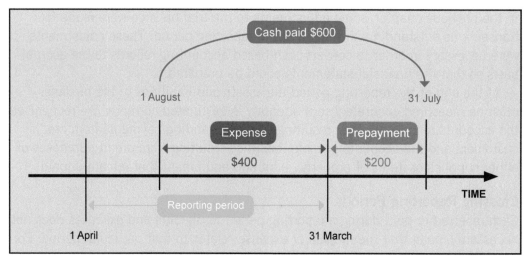

At 31 March, the insurance policy still has four months to run. Thus there is a current asset (a **prepayment**) at the end of the period equal to four months' insurance expense:

NO GST!

$$\text{Prepayment} = \frac{4}{12} \quad \text{x} \quad \$600 \qquad \text{Expense to 31 March} = \frac{8}{12} \quad \text{x} \quad \$600$$

$$= \$200 \qquad\qquad\qquad\qquad = \$400$$

No GST is involved because it was recorded when the insurance was first paid. This information can be presented on the accounting equation:

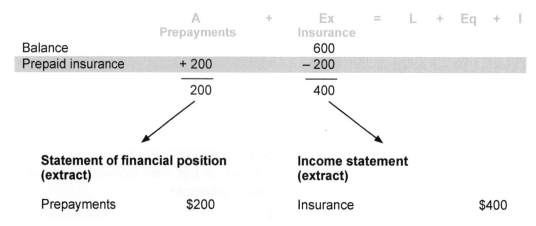

	A Prepayments	+	Ex Insurance	=	L	+	Eq	+	I
Balance			600						
Prepaid insurance	+ 200		– 200						
	200		400						

Statement of financial position (extract)		Income statement (extract)	
Prepayments	$200	Insurance	$400

Accounting – A Beginning
ISBN: 9780170211055

This adjustment means that the current asset, prepayments, is now shown at its correct amount of $200 in the statement of financial position and the insurance expense of $400 for the period is shown correctly in the income statement.

A prepayment does not strictly fit our traditional definition of a current asset because it is not likely to be received in cash. However, we still classify it as a current asset because we know that it will be consumed before the end of the next reporting period. If the premium had been cancelled on 31 March, there would be a refund of $200 due in cash from the insurance company.

Remember!

A prepayment is an expense paid in advance.

Income earned but not received (accrued income)

In the same way as all expenses for a reporting period had not been paid at the end of the period, all income earned in that reporting period may not have been recorded. This situation may arise where a business has earned income which it has not yet received, such as interest on a term deposit.

At the end of the reporting period, the term deposit has earned interest which may not be received in cash until the following reporting period. This interest is owing to the business, which means it is a current asset, just like an account receivable. We call this type of asset **accrued income**.

Consider the following example:

On 1 July a firm invested $20,000 cash in a term deposit at the rate of 6% interest per annum. The interest is payable six-monthly and the end of the reporting period is on 31 March.

This situation can be represented by the following diagram:

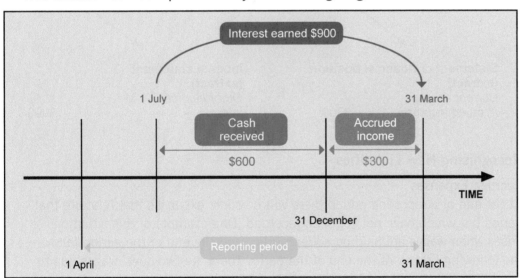

The first payment of interest was received by the firm on 31 December. The amount of this payment was calculated as follows:

$$\text{Annual interest} = 6\% \times \$20,000$$
$$= \$1,200$$

$$\text{Interest received} = \frac{6}{12} \times \$1,200$$

$$= \$600$$

NO GST!

At the end of the reporting period, the bank owes a further three months' interest which will not be paid until the next six-monthly payment is due on 30 June. This interest is a current asset, called **accrued income**.

$$\text{Accrued income} = \frac{3}{12} \times \$1{,}200$$

$$= \$300$$

The amount of interest earned for the reporting period to 31 March is thus the $600 which has been received plus the $300 which is still owing, giving a total of $900. This is the amount which should be shown as interest income in the income statement. There is no GST involved since interest is exempt from GST. Another way of calculating the income earned is simply to multiply the annual interest by the proportion of the year for which the money has been invested. The term deposit was made nine months before the end of the reporting period, hence

$$\text{Interest earned} = \frac{9}{12} \times \$1{,}200$$

$$= \$900$$

The interest received is $600. Thus interest earned of $900 – 600 = $300 is still owing to the business. This is the amount of the accrued income.

This information can be presented on the accounting equation:

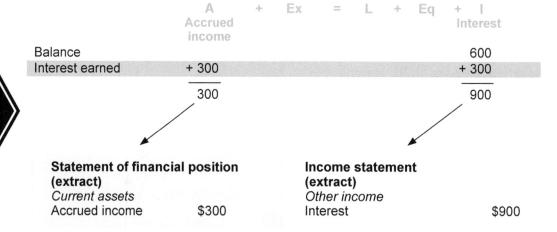

	A Accrued income	+	Ex	=	L	+	Eq	+	I Interest
Balance									600
Interest earned	+ 300								+ 300
	300								900

Statement of financial position (extract)
Current assets
Accrued income $300

Income statement (extract)
Other income
Interest $900

NO GST!

<aside>
Remember!

Accrued income is income owing to the business.
</aside>

Recognising New Liabilities

Accrued Expenses

At the end of a reporting period there will be some expenses that relate to that period but which have not yet been recorded. One example of this situation arises when wages are paid on a Wednesday, and the end of the period falls on the following Friday. At the end of the period there are two days' wages due to employees which will not be paid until the following reporting period. However, since the employees have worked those two days, the wages owing at the end of the period represent a current liability of the firm. We call this liability an **accrued expense**. These additional wages are an expense of the current reporting period and should therefore be added to the wages expense in the income statement. The current liability will be extinguished on the first pay day of the next period.

Consider the following example:

A wages expense account showed that $51,600 had been paid in wages during the year. At the end of the period a further two days of wages had been earned by employees but would not be paid until the following pay day. The weekly wages expense is $1,000 for a five-day working week. This situation is represented in the diagram on the next page.

NO GST!

Wages are exempt from GST. The liability for wages at the end of the period is:

$$\text{Liability} = \frac{2}{5} \times \$1,000 \qquad\qquad \text{Expense to 31 March} = \frac{6}{100} \times \$20,000$$

$$= \$400 \qquad\qquad\qquad\qquad\qquad = \$1,200$$

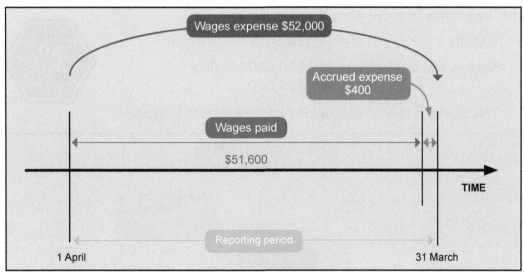

The $400 outstanding is a current liability and will be shown in the statement of financial position. It will be paid in the first week of the next reporting period. The $400 is also an expense of the current reporting period and must be included in the wages expense shown in the income statement.

This information can be presented on the accounting equation:

	A	+	Ex Wages	=	L Accrued expenses	+	Eq	+	I
Balance			51,600						
Wages owing			+ 400		+ 400				
			52,000		400				

Remember!

Accrued expenses are expenses owed by the business.

Income statement (extract)
Administrative expenses
Wages $52,000

Statement of financial position (extract)
Current liabilities
Accrued expenses $400

Income received in advance

In some situations income will be received in cash before it has actually been earned. This may arise if a business owns premises which are let in return for rental payments. Most rent is paid in advance. At the end of a reporting period, the business will have received rent in cash which applies to the following period. These rental payments represent a current liability since the firm is obliged to allow the tenant to occupy the building for the period for which the rent has been paid. We call this current liability **income received in advance**.

Consider the following example:
A business has received $30,000 (excluding GST) in rental payments during a reporting period. Of this, $4,000 is rent which has been received in advance for the next reporting period.

ISBN: 9780170211055

The $4,000 represents income received in advance, a current liability of the business. Since rent has been received, the business has an obligation to provide rental accommodation to the tenant or else refund the rent. The $4,000 has not yet been earned and should therefore be deducted from the amount of rent received before the income statement is prepared. There is no GST involved because it was recorded when the cash was received.

Liability   = $4,000

Rent earned to 31 March   = $30,000 – 4,000
                                  = $26,000

NO GST!

This situation may be represented by the following diagram:

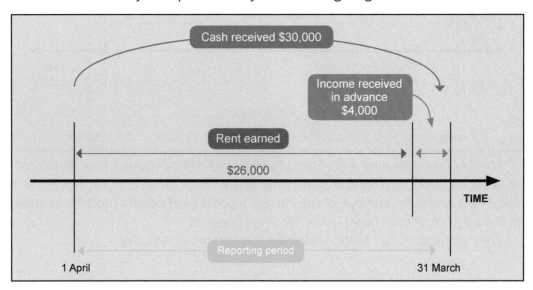

It may not seem obvious at first that income received in advance is a liability, since no cash will have to be paid. However, it does represent an obligation to provide a service that will requires a sacrifice by the business in the future. We recognise this obligation as a liability in the financial statements. Should our business decide to sell the building at the end of the reporting period, it would be liable to refund $4,000 cash to the tenant. When the period of time has passed during which the $4,000 rent has been earned by the business, the current liability will be extinguished.

This information can be presented on the accounting equation:

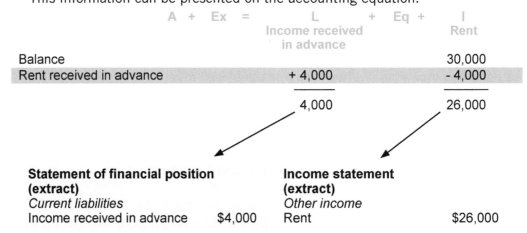

	A + Ex =	L Income received in advance	+ Eq +	I Rent
Balance				30,000
Rent received in advance		+ 4,000		- 4,000
		4,000		26,000

Statement of financial position (extract)
Current liabilities
Income received in advance $4,000

Income statement (extract)
Other income
Rent $26,000

Activities

1 Each of the situations below has occurred at the end of the reporting period.

a Rates paid in the year ended 31 December 2016 apply partly to the period ending 30 June 2017.

b A magazine publisher has received subscriptions for nine months relating to the following reporting period. These may be cancelled by subscribers at any time.

c A firm which sells goods on commission has not received the last $100 of commission due for this reporting period.

d At the end of the reporting period, wages of $900 had been earned by employees. These wages will be paid next week.

e A full year's premium on an insurance policy for the buildings was paid on 15 January. The end of the reporting period is on 31 March.

f Rent for part of the premises which is let to another business has been received for the three months beginning on 1 March. The end of the reporting period is on 31 March. Unused rent is refundable at one month's notice.

DO THIS!

Classify each situation using one of the following terms: *prepayment, accrued expense, income received in advance, accrued income.*

2 Copy and complete the following table. (The first example has been done for you.)

		Type of account (income or expense?)	Name of account	Amount of adjustment $	Type of account created (asset or liability?)	Name
a	Insurance paid in advance, $200	Expense	Insurance	– 200	Asset	Prepayments
b	Interest due but not received, $50					
c	Wages due but unpaid, $450					
d	Rent received in advance, $150					
e	Rates paid in advance, $250					
f	Interest on loan due but unpaid, $260					
g	Dividends due but not received, $100					
h	Rent of $500 paid in advance					
i	Commission of $250 earned but not received					
j	Fees of $250 received in advance					
k	Interest of $280 on a mortgage due but unpaid					

ISBN: 9780170211055

3 The following matters are outstanding at the end of the reporting period, 31 March 2016. Each item refers to a separate business.

i Wages of $400 are owing to employees. During the year $20,000 has already been paid for wages.

ii The balance in the Rent expense account at the end of the reporting period was $55,000 Dr. Of this, $3,000 has been paid for the next reporting period.

iii Dividends of $2,000 have been received during the year. At the end of the reporting period a further $250 was due but had not been received.

iv Purchases of $3,680 (including GST) were made on credit on the last day of the reporting period but these have not been recorded. The balance of the Purchases account to date was $120,000 Dr. The GST payable account had a balance of $1,200 Cr.

v The balance in the Magazine subscriptions revenue account at the end of the reporting period was $90,000 Cr. Of this, $20,000 relates to magazines to be published in the next reporting period. Subscribers may cancel their subscriptions and receive a refund at any time.

vi During the year interest of $7,700 had been paid on the mortgage. A further $700 is due but unpaid at the end of the reporting period.

vii The balance in the Insurance expense account at 31 March was $1,300. Of this, $220 relates to the following reporting period.

viii Sales of $46,000 (including GST) have been invoiced but are unpaid at the end of the reporting period. The Sales account has a balance of $498,000 Cr, and the GST payable account has a balance of $700 Cr.

ix Office furniture costing $2,760 (including GST) was purchased on credit during March but the invoice has not been recorded. The Office furniture account had a balance of $12,000 Dr and the GST payable account had a balance of $1,500 Cr.

DO THIS!

For each of **i – ix** above:

a Calculate the amount of the income or expense which would be shown in the income statement prepared for the year ended 31 March 2016.

b Prepare an extract from the statement of financial position prepared at 31 March 2016 to show the relevant asset or liability.

4 The following are some reasons that explain the treatment of GST when period-end adjustments are carried out:

A The cash has changed hands so the GST has already been taken into account.
B The item is exempt from GST.
C GST must be taken into account because the transaction occurred before the end of the reporting period but no cash has changed hands.

The following are the period-end adjustments for *Priceless Products*:

a Part of the car insurance has been paid for the following period.
b Subscriptions to staff magazines that will be published in the following reporting period have been received.
c A new computer has been purchased on credit and has not been recorded.
d Wages and interest on a loan are owing but have not been paid.
e Interest on a term deposit is due but has not been received.
f Sales were invoiced but remain unpaid and have not been recorded.

DO THIS!

For each of **a – f** above, identify the reason for the treatment of GST at the end of the reporting period. Choose between A, B and C.

 ISBN: 9780170211055

Adjusting the Trial Balance

The period-end adjustments that we met in the previous section created a number of new accounts which will need to be added to the ledger so that they will appear in the trial balance. They will then be included in the financial statements.

At the end of the reporting period, Brad has the following information which must be included in the financial statements of *Trendy Tourz*:

- Interest on the bank loan of $150 is due but unpaid
- Rent of $800 has been paid in advance for the following year
- A dividend on the *Telecom* shares of $200 has been announced but not paid
- Advertising income of $400 earned from painting the van with advertising for a local adventure park has been received in advance for the following year.

We will examine the effect of each of these transactions on the accounting equation individually.

Interest on the bank loan of $150 is due but unpaid

This is an *accrued expense*. The interest expense for the year will increase. We create a new liability account for **accrued expenses**:

	A	+	Ex Interest	=	L Accrued expenses		+ Eq + I
Balance			1,800				
Interest owing			+ 150		+ 150		
			1,950		150		

Rent of $800 has been paid in advance for the following year

This is a *prepayment*. The amount shown for rent in the trial balance will decrease. We create a new asset account for **prepayments**.

	A Prepayments	+	Ex Rent	=	L + Eq + I
Balance			10,400		
Prepaid rent	+ 800		– 800		
	800		9,600		

ISBN: 9780170211055

A dividend on the Telecom shares of $200 has been announced but not paid

This is *accrued income*. The dividend has been announced and will be paid by *Telecom* in the next reporting period. However, it has been earned in the current period so must be reported as part of this period's income.

Since there has been no other dividend income received during the year, we must create two new accounts in this case: one for **accrued income** (an asset account) and one for **dividend income** (an income account). The effect on the accounting equation is as follows:

	A Accrued income	+ Ex	= L	+ Eq	+ I Dividend income
Dividends earned	+ 200				+ 200
	200				200

Advertising income of $300 has been received in advance for the following year

This is income received in advance. The firm had paid Brad $600 for six months' advertising in advance. At the end of the period, he was still obliged to carry the advertising for a further three months. The effect on the accounting equation is:

	A + Ex	= L Income received in advance	+ Eq +	I Advertising
Balance				600
Advertising received in advance		+ 300		– 300
		300		300

The adjusted trial balance below shows the effect of all the period-end adjustments for *Trendy Tourz*. This is a convenient way to update a trial balance with additional information at the end of the period. The highlighted cells show the new accounts, adjustments and revised balances. The adjustments we did earlier are also shown.

Trendy Tourz
Trial Balance as at 30 June 2016

	Trial balance	Adjust-ments	Adjusted trial balance		Trial balance	Adjust-ments	Adjusted trial balance
Accounting fees	200		200	Advertising income	600	(300)	300
Advertising	3,800		3,800	Capital, 1 July 2015	29,500		29,500
Cash	9,100		9,100	GST payable	6,400	60	6,460
Computer (cost)	3,000		3,000	Loan (due 30 June 2020)	17,000		17,000
Drawings	60,000		60,000	Tour fees	120,000	5,400	125,400
Electricity	1,000		1,000	Accounts payable		5,750	5,750
Insurance on van	1,500		1,500	Accrued expenses		150	150
Interest on loan	1,800	150	1,950	Income received in advance		300	300
Outdoor equipment (cost)	22,000	4,000	26,000	Dividend income		200	200
Petrol and oil	8,600		8,600				
Rent	10,400	(800)	9,600				
Shares in *Telecom*	10,000		10,000				
Telephone rental	600		600				
Tour supplies expense	6,800	1,000	7,800				
Van (cost)	30,000		30,000				
Van repairs	4,700		4,700				
Accounts receivable		6,210	6,210				
Accrued income		200	200				
Prepayments		800	800				
	$173,500	11,560	185,060		$173,500	11,560	185,060

Accounting – A Beginning   ISBN: 9780170211055

More Financial Statements

The trial balance that we prepared on the previous page can be used to prepare the financial statements for *Trendy Tourz* in exactly the same way as before. The financial statements will look very similar, but the amounts of some income and expense items will be different. The income statement will have an extra line for dividend income. The statement of financial position will have additional current asset and current liability accounts.

The changes from the financial statements that we prepared on pages 190-1 are highlighted in the following adjusted financial statements:

Trendy Tourz
Income Statement for the year ended 30 June 2016

	$	$	$
Revenue			
Tour fees			125,400
Other income			
Advertising income		300	
Dividend income		200	
Total other income			500
Total income			125,900
Less: **Expenses**			
Tour expenses			
Advertising	3,800		
Insurance on van	1,500		
Petrol and oil	8,600		
Tour supplies expense	7,800		
Van repairs	4,700		
		26,400	
Administrative expenses			
Accounting fees	200		
Electricity	1,000		
Rent	9,600		
Telephone rental	600		
		11,400	
Finance costs			
Interest on loan		1,950	
Total expenses			39,750
Profit for the year			$86,150

Important!

- The line items highlighted above are those that have been affected by the period-end adjustments.

- Since items of income and expenses have changed, the subtotals are affected and the overall profit has therefore changed.

Trendy Tourz
Statement of Financial Position as at 30 June 2016

	$	$	$
ASSETS			
Non-current assets			
Property, plant and equipment			
Total carrying amount (Note 1)		59,000	
Investments			
Shares in *Telecom*		10,000	
Total non-current assets			69,000
Current assets			
Cash		9,100	
Accounts receivable		6,210	
Accrued income		200	
Prepayments		800	
Total current assets			16,310
Total assets			$85,310
EQUITY AND LIABILITIES			
Equity			
Capital at beginning of the year		29,500	
Profit for the year		86,150	
Drawings for the year		(60,000)	
Capital at end of the year			55,650
Non-current liabilities			
Loan (due 30 June 2020)		17,000	
Current liabilities			
Accounts payable	5,750		
GST payable	6,460		
Accrued expenses	150		
Income received in advance	300		
Total current liabilities		12,660	
Total liabilities			29,660
Total equity and liabilities			$85,310

Notes to the statement of financial position

1 *Property, plant and equipment*	$
Computer (cost)	3,000
Outdoor equipment (cost)	26,000
Van (cost)	30,000
	$59,000

ISBN: 9780170211055

Activities

1 Molly Coddle runs *Kare for Kiddies*, caring for sick children in their own homes while their parents work. The following financial statements were prepared for the year ended 31 March 2016:

Kare for Kiddies Income Statement for the year ended 31 March 2016			
	$	$	$
Revenue			
Fees			160,000
Less: Expenses			
Care expenses			
Advertising	3,600		
Laundry	2,700		
Wages	75,000		
		81,300	
Administrative expenses			
Motor vehicle lease	18,000		
Petrol and oil	9,300		
Telephone	1,300		
		28,600	
Finance costs			
Interest		100	
Total expenses			110,000
Profit for the year			$50,000

Kare for Kiddies Statement of Financial Position as at 31 March 2016		
	$	$
Assets		
Non-current assets		
Property, plant and equipment (cost)		15,000
Current assets		
Cash		18,000
Total assets		$33,000
Equity and liabilities		
Equity		
Capital at beginning of the year	20,000	
Profit for the year	50,000	
Drawings for the year	(40,000)	
Capital at end of the year		30,000
Current liabilities		
GST payable		3,000
Total equity and liabilities		$33,000

Additional information:
- Wages due but unpaid, $450
- Vehicle lease paid in advance, $1,500
- Fees received in advance, $2,500.

Molly is unsure about the accuracy of these statements because she has found some extra information (shown in the box) which has not been included.

DO THIS!

Re-prepare the financial statements of *Kare for Kiddies* to include the additional information.

2

The following trial balance was prepared from the accounting records of *Boney Stretch*, a physiotherapist, as at 30 June 2018:

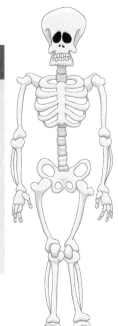

Boney Stretch			
Trial Balance as at 30 June 2018			
Cash	$3,000	Capital, 1 July 2017	$21,000
Drawings	30,000	Fees	63,500
Electricity	2,900	GST payable	1,700
Equipment (cost)	18,000	Loan (due 31 July 2025)	12,000
Fixtures and fittings (cost)	14,000		
General expenses	1,600		
Interest on loan	1,500		
Rent	5,400		
Telephone expense	1,200		
Wages	20,600		
	$98,200		$98,200

The following adjustments are required at the end of the reporting period:

- Rent paid in advance, $400
- Wages due but unpaid, $300
- Interest due on loan, $200
- Fees received in advance, $1,000.

DO THIS!

a Prepare the adjusted trial balance.
b Prepare the fully classified income statement and statement of financial position for *Boney Stretch*. You should classify expenses as *Clinic expenses*, *Administrative expenses* or *Finance costs*.

3

The following trial balance was prepared from the accounting records of *Leave it 2Us*, private investigators, as at 31 March 2017:

Leave it 2Us			
Trial Balance as at 31 March 2017			
Advertising	$ 650	Capital, 1 April 2016	$34,500
Cash	13,500	Commission	3,600
Drawings	15,000	Fees	262,300
Electricity	2,200	GST payable	300
Equipment (cost)	27,000	Loan (due 31 July 2021)	25,000
Insurance	2,600		
Interest	1,700		
Office expenses	7,850		
Phone expenses	12,900		
Vehicle expenses	8,700		
Vehicles (cost)	48,000		
Wages	185,600		
	$325,700		$325,700

ISBN: 9780170211055

The following adjustments are required at the end of the reporting period:

- Insurance paid in advance, $400
- Wages due but unpaid, $450
- Interest due on bank loan, $300
- Commission due but not received, $100.

a Prepare the adjusted trial balance.
b Prepare the fully classified income statement and statement of financial position for *Leave it 2Us*. You should classify expenses as *Investigative expenses*, *Administrative expenses* or *Finance costs*.

4 The trial balance below is taken from the accounting records of *Hospitality Inn*, which is a local boarding house.

Hospitality Inn Trial Balance as at 30 September 2019			
Drawings	$ 25,000	Bank overdraft	$ 950
Electricity	1,900	Boarding fees	76,500
Furniture and fittings (cost)	45,600	Capital, 1 October 2018	153,000
General expenses	3,400	Dividend income	450
GST receivable	1,000	Mortgage (due 31 May 2030)	50,000
Interest on mortgage	3,700		
Laundry expenses	5,300		
Meal expenses	16,400		
Premises (cost)	120,000		
Rates	2,400		
Repairs	5,900		
Shares in *The Warehouse*	10,000		
Telephone expense	1,300		
Van (cost)	15,000		
Wages	24,000		
	$280,900		$280,900

Adjustments for the following are required at the end of the reporting period:

- Rates paid in advance, $400
- Interest due on mortgage, $250
- Wages due but unpaid, $300
- Boarding fees received in advance, $2,500
- Dividends due but not received, $150.

a Prepare the adjusted trial balance.
b Prepare the fully classified income statement and statement of financial position for *Hospitality Inn*. You should classify expenses as *Boarding expenses*, *Administrative expenses* or *Finance costs*.

ISBN: 9780170211055

Depreciation

Over a period of time, property, plant and equipment wear out or become obsolete (out-of-date). This means that these assets lose their future economic benefit to the business. This loss is called **depreciation**.

Depreciation is charged in order to allocate the cost of using an asset over its useful economic lifetime. Thus the asset is gradually converted to an expense as it wears out or becomes obsolete. If depreciation is not charged, the amount stated for the asset in the statement of financial position will be too high, because the loss of future economic benefit will not have been recognised. The expenses of the business will be understated, which means that the profit will be overstated.

At the end of its useful economic life, an item of property, plant or equipment is likely to be sold. The amount which is expected to be received on the sale is called the **residual value** (or salvage value).

Some formal definitions relating to depreciation are:

DEFINITION

Depreciation

Depreciation is the systematic allocation of the depreciable amount of an asset over its useful life.

Depreciable amount is the cost of an asset (excluding GST) less its residual value.

The *residual value* of an asset is the estimated amount that an entity would currently obtain from disposal of the asset, after deducting the estimated costs of disposal, if the asset were already of the age and in the condition expected at the end of its useful life.

Calculating Depreciation

In order to calculate the depreciation expense, we need three pieces of information about the asset:

- Historical cost
- Residual value
- Useful economic life.

Of these, only the historical cost is known. Both the residual value and the useful economic life must be estimated when the asset is purchased because they will not be known until some future time.

Consider the following example:

A car which cost $12,000 (excluding GST) is estimated to last for three years. At the end of the three-year period it is expected that the car will be sold for $3,300.

The total amount of depreciation expense over the three-year period is estimated to be $8,700 ($12,000 − $3,300). If we estimate that the future services offered by the car reduce by the same amount each year, then $2,900 must be charged to expenses each year. The calculation is:

NO GST!

$$\text{Annual depreciation expense} = \frac{\text{Cost} - \text{Residual Value}}{\text{Economic life}}$$

$$= \frac{\$12,000 - 3,300}{3}$$

$$= \$2,900$$

ISBN: 9780170211055

We can represent this situation by the following diagram:

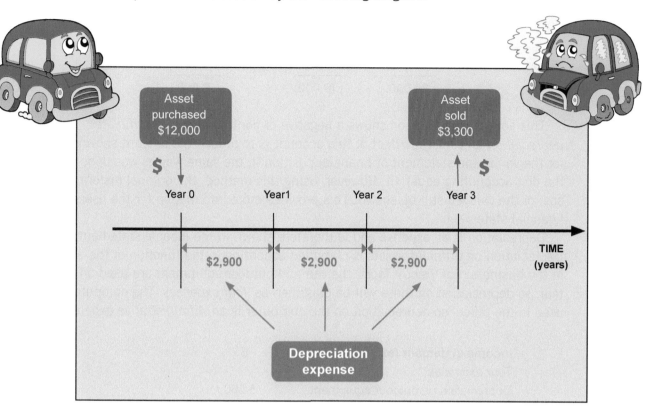

Recording Depreciation in the Accounts

Let's return to *Trendy Tourz*. Depreciation for the period up until 30 June has been calculated as:

- Computer $1,200   ▪ Outdoor equipment $5,500   ▪ Van $6,000.

(No depreciation is to be charged on the new kayaks because they have only just been purchased and have not been used.)

It is possible to represent the depreciation expense on the accounting equation as shown below. (We will use the van in our example.)

	A Van	+	Ex Depreciation on van	=	L	+	Eq	+	I
Balance	30,000								
Depreciation on van	− 6,000		+ 6,000						
	6,000		6,000						

The carrying amount of the van has been reduced by $6,000. This is the amount which has been charged to the depreciation expense account.

This method of representing the depreciation of an item of property, plant and equipment on the accounting equation is not particularly satisfactory because the original cost of the van would no longer appear in the statement of financial position.

A better method of showing the depreciation expense is represented on the accounting equation below:

	Van	A Accumulated depreciation on van	+	Ex Depreciation on van	= L + Eq + I
Balance	30,000				
Depreciation on van		− 6,000		+ 6,000	
	30,000	(6,000)		6,000	

This accounting equation shows a negative or **contra** asset – *Accumulated depreciation on van*. The effect of this account is to reduce the amount shown for the van in the statement of financial position in the same way as was done in the first accounting equation. However, using this method, the original historical cost of the van will still be shown. This provides more information for the users of financial statements.

Depreciation is an **expense** and is therefore shown in the income statement. Depreciation on different assets is classified according to the function of the asset in the business. For *Trendy Tourz*, the van and outdoor equipment are used on tour, so depreciation on these will be classified as *Tour expenses*. The computer is used in the office, so depreciation on the computer is an *Administrative expense*:

Income statement (extract)	$
Tour expenses	
Depreciation on outdoor equipment	5,500
Depreciation on van	6,000
Administrative expenses	
Depreciation on computer	1,200

The accumulated depreciation accounts, which are contra asset accounts, are shown in the notes to the statement of financial position where they are deducted from the historical cost of the relevant asset to obtain its carrying amount:

Notes to the statement of financial position

1 *Property, plant and equipment*

	Computer	Outdoor equipment	Van	Total
	$	$	$	$
Cost	3,000	26,000	30,000	59,000
Accumulated depreciation	(1,200)	(5,500)	(6,000)	(12,700)
Carrying amount	1,800	20,500	24,000	46,300

The total amount for property, plant and equipment is shown in the body of the statement of financial position:

Statement of financial position (extract)	
Non-current assets	$
Property, plant and equipment	
Total carrying amount (Note 1)	46,300

ISBN: 9780170211055

The difference between the historical cost and the accumulated depreciation is the **carrying amount** (or book value) of the asset. The carrying amount of the computer is $1,800, of the outdoor equipment is $20,500 and of the van is $24,000.

The accumulated depreciation account for each asset shows the total depreciation on the asset that has been charged to expenses since that asset was purchased. Suppose that, in the following reporting period, to 30 June 2017, Brad bought no additional assets and the depreciation expense was:

- Computer $1,200
- Outdoor equipment $6,500
- Van $6,000.

The depreciation on outdoor equipment has changed because Brad bought new kayaks right at the end of the previous year. Now that they have been used in the business for a year, they must be depreciated.

The depreciation expense in the income statement would be:

Income statement (extract)	$
Tour expenses	
Depreciation on outdoor equipment	6,500
Depreciation on van	6,000
Administrative expenses	
Depreciation on computer	1,200

The note to the statement of financial position would be:

Notes to the statement of financial position

1 *Property, plant and equipment*

	Computer	Outdoor equipment	Van	Total
	$	$	$	$
Cost	3,000	26,000	30,000	59,000
Accumulated depreciation	(2,400)	(12,000)	(12,000)	(26,400)
Carrying amount	600	14,000	18,000	32,600

The accumulated depreciation on the computer is now $2,400, which represents the $1,200 for each year. The carrying amount is now $600 ($3,000 – 2,400). Each year, the accumulated depreciation increases and the carrying amount of the asset decreases correspondingly. Eventually the asset will be fully depreciated and have no carrying amount. If the original estimates of useful economic life and residual value were correct, the asset's economic benefit will have expired and it will be sold or dumped.

The carrying amount for property, plant and equipment in the non-current assets section of the statement of financial position would now be $32,600:

Statement of financial position (extract)	
Non-current assets	$
Property, plant and equipment	
Total carrying amount (Note 1)	32,600

Important!

- **Depreciation** is an *expense*. It is classified in the income statement according to the way the asset is used.

- **Accumulated depreciation** is a *contra asset*. It reduces the carrying amount of the asset in the statement of financial position.

The Depreciation Schedule

The pattern of depreciation charges over the useful life of an asset is often summarised in a **depreciation schedule**.

The van for *Trendy Tourz* cost $30,000 and is to be depreciated at 20% per annum based on cost. This represents a depreciation expense of $6,000 per annum. After five years, the total cost of the van will have been depreciated and the van's carrying amount will be zero. This information can be presented in a depreciation schedule such as this:

Year	Cost	Carrying amount (beginning)	Depreciation expense	Accumulated depreciation (end)	Carrying amount (end)
	$	$	$	$	$
1	30,000	30,000	6,000	6,000	24,000
2		24,000	6,000	12,000	18,000
3		18,000	6,000	18,000	12,000
4		12,000	6,000	24,000	6,000
5		6,000	6,000	30,000	—

If an asset is sold before the end of its expected useful economic life, the amount of any gain or loss on sale is calculated by taking the difference between the asset's carrying amount and the selling price. For example, if the van above was sold for $15,000 after two years, there would be a loss on sale of $18,000 – 15,000 = $3,000. If it was sold for $20,000 there would be a gain on sale of $20,000 – 18,000 = $2,000.

Gee Aroha, this end of year business gets a bit complicated!

Hmmm...I suppose it seems that way but it's really just a matter of getting things into the right reporting periods.

KiWi KRAFTZ

Yes I can see that you need to have the correct amounts for assets and liabilities so that you get the equity right.

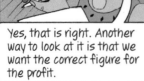

Yes, that is right. Another way to look at it is that we want the correct figure for the profit.

You can't ever be totally exact though, can you? I mean, the depreciation is only an estimate for a start.

Yes you are right there. The only way we really know how a business has performed is to wait until the end of its lifetime. That's not a lot of use to us when we are trying to make day-to-day decisions.

That's why we use reporting periods, right?

Yep!

Accounting – A Beginning   ISBN: 9780170211055

Activities

1 A motor vehicle was purchased on 1 April 2017 for $40,000 (excluding GST). It was expected to last for five years, after which it would be sold for $5,000.

DO THIS!

a Calculate the annual depreciation expense for the motor vehicle.
b Prepare a depreciation schedule for the five-year period.
c Calculate the gain or loss on sale if the vehicle was sold for $16,000
   i at the end of year 1
   ii at the end of year 3
   iii at the end of year 5.

2 An item of plant was purchased for $100,000 (excluding GST) on 1 April 2016. It is expected have an economic life of six years and then it will be sold for $10,000.

DO THIS!

a Calculate the annual depreciation expense for the plant.
b Prepare a depreciation schedule for the six-year period.
c Calculate the gain or loss on sale if the plant was sold for $50,000
   i at the end of year 2
   ii at the end of year 4
   iii at the end of year 6.

3 The following information was extracted from the trial balance of *Wild and Woolly* at 30 June 2017, before the current year's depreciation had been recorded.

Wild and Woolly			
Trial balance (extract) as at 30 June 2017			
Motor vehicle (cost)	$20,000	Accumulated depreciation – motor vehicle	$6,000
Shop fittings (cost)	10,000	Accumulated depreciation – shop fittings	5,000

The firm has a policy of charging depreciation on the motor vehicle on the basis of 20% per annum based on cost and on shop fittings on the basis of 10% per annum based on cost.

DO THIS!

Complete the note to the statement of financial position below at 30 June 2017.

Notes to the Statement of Financial Position			
1 *Property, plant and equipment*			
	Motor vehicle $	Shop fittings $	Total $
Cost			
Accumulated depreciation			
Carrying amount			

4 The following information was extracted from the trial balance of *Auto Repairs* at 31 March 2016, before the current year's depreciation had been recorded:

Auto Repairs			
Trial balance (extract) as at 31 March 2016			
Van (cost)	$45,000	Accumulated depreciation – van	$15,000
Equipment (cost)	30,000	Accumulated depreciation – equipment	12,000
Computer (cost)	1,800	Accumulated depreciation – computer	900

Depreciation is calculated on the straight line basis using the following expected useful lives and residual values:

Asset	Useful life (years)	Residual value $
Van	5	5,000
Equipment	10	2,000
Computer	3	nil

DO THIS! Complete the extract from, and note to, the statement of financial position below at 31 March 2016.

Statement of Financial Position (extract) as at 31 March 2016	
Non-current assets	$
Property, plant and equipment (Note 1)	

Notes to the Statement of Financial Position				
1 *Property, plant and equipment*				
	Van $	Equipment $	Computer $	Total $
Cost				
Accumulated depreciation				
Carrying amount				

5 The following information was extracted from the trial balance of *Drills' Dentistry* at 31 March 2018, before the current year's depreciation had been recorded.

Drill's Dentistry			
Trial balance (extract) as at 31 March 2018			
Furniture (cost)	$130,000	Accumulated depreciation – furniture	$23,000
Dental equipment (cost)	80,000	Accumulated depreciation – dental equipment	14,000
Computer (cost)	2,400	Accumulated depreciation – computer	600

Depreciation is calculated on the straight line basis using the following expected useful lives and residual values:

Asset	Useful life (years)	Residual value $
Furniture	10	15,000
Dental equipment	4	10,000
Computer	2	nil

DO THIS! Complete the extract from, and note to, the statement of financial position on the next page at 31 March 2018.

Statement of Financial Position (extract) as at 31 March 2018				
Non-current assets			$	
Property, plant and equipment (Note 1)				

Notes to the Statement of Financial Position

1 *Property, plant and equipment*

	Furniture	Dental equipment	Computer	Total
	$	$	$	$
Cost				
Accumulated depreciation				
Carrying amount				

6 The following information was extracted from the trial balance of *Megan's Mowing* at 30 June 2019, before the current year's depreciation had been recorded.

Megan's Mowing Trial balance (extract) as at 30 June 2019			
Van (cost)	$25,000	Accumulated depreciation – van	$10,000
Mowers (cost)	12,500	Accumulated depreciation – mowers	6,000
Mulcher (cost)	1,400	Accumulated depreciation – mulcher	800

Depreciation is calculated on the straight line basis using the following expected useful lives and residual values:

Asset	Useful life (years)	Residual value $
Van	5	3,000
Mowers	3	500
Mulcher	5	200

DO THIS!

Complete the extract from, and note to, the statement of financial position below at 30 June 2019.

Statement of Financial Position (extract) as at 30 June 2019				
Non-current assets			$	
Property, plant and equipment (Note 1)				

Notes to the Statement of Financial Position

1 *Property, plant and equipment*

	Van	Mowers	Mulcher	Total
	$	$	$	$
Cost				
Accumulated depreciation				
Carrying amount				

The Completed Financial Statements

The depreciation entries that were recorded in the previous section can be added to the adjusted trial balance. This provides the updated balances for all the accounts in the ledger and can be used to prepare the final financial statements.

The completed adjusted trial balance for *Trendy Tourz* is shown below, with the depreciation entries highlighted.

Trendy Tourz
Trial Balance as at 30 June 2016

	Trial balance	Adjust-ments	Adjusted trial balance		Trial balance	Adjust-ments	Adjusted trial balance
Accounting fees	200		200	Advertising income	600	(300)	300
Advertising	3,800		3,800	Capital, 1 July 2015	29,500		29,500
Cash	9,100		9,100	GST payable	6,400	60	6,460
Computer (cost)	3,000		3,000	Loan (due 30 June 2020)	17,000		17,000
Drawings	60,000		60,000	Tour fees	120,000	5,400	125,400
Electricity	1,000		1,000	Accounts payable		5,750	5,750
Insurance on van	1,500		1,500	Accrued expenses		150	150
Interest on loan	1,800	150	1,950	Income received in advance		300	300
Outdoor equipment (cost)	22,000	4,000	26,000	Dividend income		200	200
Petrol and oil	8,600		8,600	*Accumulated depreciation:*			
Rent	10,400	(800)	9,600	Computer		1,200	1,200
Shares in Telecom	10,000		10,000	Outdoor equipment		5,500	5,500
Telephone rental	600		600	Van		6,000	6,000
Tour supplies expense	6,800	1,000	7,800				
Van (cost)	30,000		30,000				
Van repairs	4,700		4,700				
Accounts receivable		6,210	6,210				
Accrued income		200	200				
Prepayments		800	800				
Depreciation on computer		1,200	1,200				
Depreciation on outdoor equipment		5,500	5,500				
Depreciation on van		6,000	6,000				
	$173,500	24,260	197,760		$173,500	24,260	197,760

Important!

- The line items highlighted above are those that have been affected by the depreciation adjustments.

- Since depreciation is usually only calculated at the end of the reporting period, we have created new accounts in the ledger for depreciation expenses.

- We have also created new accounts for accumulated depreciation on each of the asset classes. This is because the business is in its first year of operation. In later years the accumulated depreciation accounts will already be in the trial balance.

Remember!

Accumulated depreciation represents the total depreciation charged on an asset since it was first purchased.

Accounting – A Beginning

ISBN: 9780170211055

The revised income statement is shown below. Highlighted changes show the effect of depreciation on the various expense groups and the profit for the year.

Trendy Tourz
Income Statement for the year ended 30 June 2016

	$	$	$
Revenue			
Tour fees			125,400
Other income			
Advertising income		300	
Dividend income		200	
Total other income			500
Total income			125,900
Less: **Expenses**			
Tour expenses			
Advertising	3,800		
Depreciation on outdoor equipment	5,500		
Depreciation on van	6,000		
Insurance on van	1,500		
Petrol and oil	8,600		
Tour supplies expense	7,800		
Van repairs	4,700		
		37,900	
Administrative expenses			
Accounting fees	200		
Depreciation on computer	1,200		
Electricity	1,000		
Rent	9,600		
Telephone rental	600		
		12,600	
Finance costs			
Interest on loan		1,950	
Total expenses			52,450
Profit for the year			$73,450

The updated statement of financial position is shown on the next page. Highlighted changes show the effect of depreciation on the various assets in the both the property, plant and equipment note and the non-current assets section of the statement itself. The revised profit for the year is shown in the equity section.

Trendy Tourz
Statement of Financial Position as at 30 June 2016

	$	$	$
ASSETS			
Non-current assets			
Property, plant and equipment			
Total carrying amount (Note 1)		46,300	
Investments			
Shares in *Telecom*		10,000	
Total non-current assets			56,300
Current assets			
Cash		9,100	
Accounts receivable		6,210	
Accrued income		200	
Prepayments		800	
Total current assets			16,310
Total assets			$72,610
EQUITY AND LIABILITIES			
Equity			
Capital at beginning of the year		29,500	
Profit for the year		73,450	
Drawings for the year		(60,000)	
Capital at end of the year			42,950
Non-current liabilities			
Loan (due 30 June 2020)		17,000	
Current liabilities			
Accounts payable	5,750		
GST payable	6,460		
Accrued expenses	150		
Income received in advance	300		
Total current liabilities		12,660	
Total liabilities			29,660
Total equity and liabilities			$72,610

Notes to the statement of financial position

1 *Property, plant and equipment*

	Computer	Outdoor equipment	Van	Total
	$	$	$	$
Cost	3,000	26,000	30,000	59,000
Accumulated depreciation	(1,200)	(5,500)	(6,000)	(12,700)
Carrying amount	1,800	20,500	24,000	46,300

Accounting – A Beginning

ISBN: 9780170211055

Activities

1 Basil Tutu, a freelance wildlife photographer, had the trial balance below as at 31 March 2019:

Basil Tutu Trial Balance as at 31 March 2019			
Cameras (cost)	$ 4,500	Capital, 1 April 2018	$36,000
Cash	7,900	Fees	74,500
Drawings	35,000	GST payable	4,000
Insurance	800	Interest	1,500
Materials expense	12,500		
Motor vehicle lease	8,500		
Outdoor equipment (cost)	10,000		
Rent	4,700		
Telephone expense	1,700		
Term deposit	25,000		
Travelling expenses	5,400		
	$116,000		$116,000

Additional information:
- Rent of $600 has been paid in advance
- Interest of $500 on the term deposit (8%, due 31 July 2020) has not been received
- Fees of $800 have been received in advance
- Invoices on hand for photographic materials total $1,380 (including GST)
- Invoices issued to customers for fees unpaid amount to $2,760 (including GST)
- Depreciation to be charged based on cost: cameras, 20% per annum, outdoor equipment 10% per annum.

DO THIS!

a Prepare the adjusted trial balance.
b Prepare the fully classified income statement and statement of financial position for Basil Tutu. Classify expenses as *Field expenses*, *Administrative expenses* or *Finance costs*.

2 The following is the trial balance of *Ban Bugs Control Services* as at 31 March 2019:

Ban Bugs Control Services Trial Balance as at 31 March 2019			
Cash	$ 9,850	Capital, 1 April 2018	$15,800
Computer (cost)	5,000	Fees	65,000
Drawings	30,000	GST payable	1,850
Equipment (cost)	6,000	Loan (due 30 June 2023)	10,000
Insurance	1,400		
Interest	1,000		
Motor vehicle (cost)	25,000		
Petrol and oil	6,500		
Rent	5,600		
Repairs (motor vehicle)	1,200		
Telephone expense	1,100		
	$92,650		$92,650

Additional information:

- Rent of $400 has been paid in advance
- There is $200 owing for loan interest
- Depreciation is as follows: $5,000 on the motor vehicle, $2,000 on the computer and $600 on the equipment
- Invoices outstanding from customers for fees amount to $2,300 (including GST).

BAN BUGS

DO THIS!

a Prepare the adjusted trial balance.
b Prepare the fully classified income statement and statement of financial position for *Ban Bugs Control Services*. Classify expenses as *Service expenses*, *Administrative expenses* or *Finance costs*.

3

John Raki is the owner of *Fixit Appliance Repairs*, a mobile appliance repair business operating from Thames. He operates from a van responding to customers covering the Coromandel region. John rents premises where he has a workshop and a small office.
    The trial balance of the firm as at 31 December 2016 is shown below.

Fixit Appliance Repairs Trial Balance as at 31 December 2016			
Accounting fees	$ 800	Accumulated depreciation	
Advertising	6,000	– Office equipment	$ 1,000
Drawings	35,000	– Van	4,500
Electricity	2,200	Bank overdraft	600
Interest – loan	1,200	Capital, 1 January 2016	39,500
Office equipment (cost)	16,000	Dividend income	1,200
Office salaries	24,000	Fees	95,000
Petty cash	100	GST payable	800
Rent	11,200	Loan (8%, due 2020)	20,000
Shares in *Alpha Limited* (cost)	14,000		
Telephone expense	1,600		
Van (cost)	45,000		
Van expenses	5,500		
	$162,600		$162,600

Additional information:

- Rent of $800 has been paid in advance
- Office salaries of $500 are outstanding
- Three months' interest on the loan is due but unpaid
- Dividends of $300 from *Alpha Limited* are due but not received
- Depreciation of $1,500 is to be charged on office equipment
- Depreciation on the van is to be charged on the basis of a five-year economic life with no residual value
- Invoices of $4,600 (including GST) for fees are outstanding at the end of the reporting period.

DO THIS!

a Prepare the adjusted trial balance.
b Prepare the fully classified income statement and statement of financial position for *Fixit Appliance Repairs*. Classify expenses as *Service expenses*, *Administrative expenses* or *Finance costs*.

ISBN: 9780170211055

Trading Organisations and Cash Budgets

- The Trading Statement
- Preparing the Income Statement
- More Accruals
- Cash Budgets

A trading organisation is one that buys goods from a supplier and sells them to customers at a profit. The most common form of trading organisation is a retail store. The local dairy, supermarket and appliance store are all examples of trading organisations.

There are other types of organisations which engage in trading activities. Clubs and societies may sell refreshments, run a bar, or perhaps buy and sell sports equipment or uniforms. Farms are also trading organisations. They sell livestock which have been bred or crops which have been grown on the farm. For now, we will concern ourselves with retailers and wholesalers.

Manufacturer ⟶ **Wholesaler** ⟶ **Retailer**

sells goods to   sells goods to

When a firm sells goods, it must earn a profit if the owner is to receive a return on his or her investment in the business. This means that the selling price of the goods must be higher than the price that was paid for them. A manufacturer must sell goods to the wholesaler at a price which is higher than the cost of manufacturing them. A retailer must sell the same goods at a price which is higher than was paid to the wholesaler. Thus, by the time goods are sold to the public, the original cost has been increased by two lots of markup.

Remember!

The markup is the difference between the cost price and the selling price.

The markup (excess of selling price over cost price) must also be sufficient to cover the other expenses of the business. The difference between the selling price of the goods and the cost price is thus extremely important. If this does not cover all of the expenses, the business will make a loss and the owner will not receive a return on his or her investment.

The Trading Statement

The difference between the sales revenue and the cost of those sales is called the **gross profit**. It is calculated from the formula:

Gross profit = Sales − Cost of sales

For now, we will say that the cost of sales is equal to the cost of the goods that were sold. In the next section we will look at other factors that affect the cost of sales.

We can show the gross profit for a period in a trading statement such as this:

Trading Statement for the year ended . . .

	$
Sales	2,000
Less: Cost of goods sold	800
Gross profit	$1,200

However, we must know the cost of goods sold in order to prepare this statement. The cost of goods sold could be recorded as each item is sold if we have a computerised sales system, or if we sell only a few items. However, this is not practical when a manual system is being used and there are many transactions – for example in a small dairy. In such cases we need the following information to calculate the cost of the goods that have been sold:

- the cost of the opening inventory
- the cost of purchases during the period
- the cost of the closing inventory.

An example of the calculation of the cost of goods sold, where each item of inventory costs $100, is shown below.

> **Remember!**
>
> Goods held for resale to customers are called *stock* or *inventory*.

Calculation of the Cost of Goods Sold

Number		Cost $
Opening inventory (4)		400
Plus: Purchases (6)		600
Goods available for sale (10)		1,000
Less: Closing inventory (2)		200
Goods sold (8)		800

The trading statement above shows the cost of goods sold that had already been calculated. The following information was used:

- The total sales were $2,000
- The cost of the inventory at the beginning of the period was $400
- Goods purchased during the period cost $600
- The cost of the inventory on hand at the end of the period was $200.

The full version of the trading statement is shown opposite.

These trading statements show sales, the cost of goods sold and the gross profit. There are, however, some other items which may arise and will need to be included to calculate the gross profit.

ISBN: 9780170211055

Trading Statement for the year ended . . .

	$	$
Revenue		
Sales		2,000
Less: Cost of goods sold		
Inventory, beginning of year	400	
Plus: Purchases	600	
Cost of goods available for sale	1,000	
Less: Inventory, end of year	(200)	
Cost of goods sold		800
Gross profit		$1,200

> **Remember!**
>
> Sales are *revenue* for a trading organisation.

For example, there are occasions when customers may return goods which they have previously purchased (sales returns), or be given some credit because the goods were damaged (allowances). These sales returns and allowances must be deducted from the sales which have been recorded in the trading statement.

In the same way, a business may return goods to suppliers or receive allowances from them. These purchases returns and allowances must be deducted from the purchases recorded in the trading statement.

The information below has been extracted from the trial balance of *Kiwi Krafts* as at 30 June 2016:

- Sales $124,000
- Sales returns $1,150
- Inventory at 1 July 2015 $12,000.

- Purchases $49,500
- Purchases returns $900

The stocktake at the end of the reporting period showed that inventory on hand had cost $12,700 (excluding GST).

We can use this information to prepare the trading statement for *Kiwi Krafts* that is shown below. (Later in the chapter we will extend this trading statement to the full income statement which shows the profit for the year.)

Kiwi Krafts
Trading Statement for the year ended 30 June 2016

	$	$
Revenue		
Sales		124,000
Less: Sales returns		1,150
Net sales		122,850
Less: Cost of goods sold		
Inventory, beginning of year	12,000	
Plus: Purchases	49,500	
Less: Purchases returns	(900)	
Cost of goods available for sale	60,600	
Less: Inventory, end of year	(12,700)	
Cost of goods sold		47,900
Gross profit		$74,950

Activities

1 The table below shows the relationship between sales, cost of goods sold and gross profit for a number of businesses. Some of the information is missing.

	Sales	–	Cost of goods sold	=	Gross profit
a	$100,000		$65,000		
b	35,000				23,000
c			45,000		15,000
d	320,000		230,000		
e	135,000				25,000
f			12,000		4,500

Calculate the missing information and complete the table.

2 The following information has been taken from the accounting records of *Betta Bikes* for the year ended 31 December 2019:

- Sales, $250,000
- Inventory at 1 January 2019, $30,000
- Inventory at 31 December 2019, $45,000
- Purchases during the year, $175,000.

Prepare the trading statement to show the gross profit of *Betta Bikes* for the year.

3 The following information has been taken from the accounting records of *Gary's Groceries* for the year ended 30 June 2017:

- Sales, $120,000
- Inventory at 1 July 2016, $7,500
- Purchases during the year, $83,500
- Inventory on hand at 30 June 2017, $6,000.

Prepare the trading statement to show the gross profit of *Gary's Groceries* for the year.

4 Peta Taka has come to you for help because he has lost the stocktaking sheets which he prepared on 31 March 2018. He has brought a set of notes which he took from the accounts prepared by his accountant. However, he is very keen to find out the cost of his closing inventory. You have established that:

- Sales for the year were $95,000
- The inventory on hand at 1 April 2017 had cost $12,500
- Purchases during the year amounted to $60,800
- The gross profit for the year was $36,700.

Prepare a trading statement which shows the cost of the closing inventory on hand.

ISBN: 9780170211055

More Complex Trading Statements

There are other expenses, apart from purchases, which may form part of the cost of sales. Any other expenses which are incurred in getting the goods into the location and condition where they can be sold must also be included in the cost of sales calculation. Such expenses may include:

- Customs duty
- Cartage inwards
- Freight inwards
- Packaging materials.

Customs duty is payable when goods are imported from overseas. This duty must be paid before the Customs Department will release the goods. It is an expense incurred to get the goods into the location where they can be sold.

Cartage or freight paid to get the goods to the location of sale is also part of the cost of sales. Cartage is a term used to describe the cost of local delivery, for example from the railway station to the warehouse. Freight is the term used to describe long-distance carriage such as between cities or from overseas.

Packaging materials are sometimes used where a trader buys bulk supplies and packages them into smaller amounts. An example of this may be a supermarket which purchases a large quantity of rice, and later packages this rice into small saleable packets. The cost of packaging the rice is part of the cost of getting the goods into the condition in which they will finally be sold.

Cost of sales = Cost of goods sold + other trading expenses

Consider the following example:

Golden Dragon Foods is a wholesaler that imports foodstuffs in bulk, repackages them and sells them to supermarkets and grocery shops. The following information relates to the year ended 31 March 2017:

- Sales for the year amounted to $760,000
- Sales returns made by customers were $10,000
- Purchases for the year were $555,000
- Purchases returns to suppliers amounted to $5,000
- Customs duty paid was $20,000
- Packaging costs were $40,000
- Inventory on hand at the beginning of the year had cost $50,000
- Inventory on hand at the end of the year had cost $60,000.

The trading statement is shown below.

Golden Dragon Foods
Trading Statement for the year ended 31 March 2017

	$	$	$
Revenue			
Sales			760,000
Less: Sales returns			(10,000)
Net sales			750,000
Less: Cost of sales			
Inventory, beginning of year		50,000	
Plus: Purchases	555,000		
Less: Purchases returns	(5,000)		
		550,000	
Cost of goods available for sale		600,000	
Less: Inventory, end of year		(60,000)	
Cost of goods sold		540,000	
Plus: Customs duty		20,000	
Packaging costs		40,000	
Cost of sales			600,000
Gross profit			$150,000

Remember!

The cost of sales includes:

- cost of goods sold
- any other expenses which are incurred in getting the goods into the location and condition where they can be sold.

Important!

- The sales returns have been deducted from the gross sales in the trading statement.
- The purchases returns have been deducted from purchases to produce a figure for net purchases in the cost of goods sold section.
- Customs duty and packaging costs have been added to the cost of goods sold since they form part of the cost of sales.

ISBN: 9780170211055

Activities

1 The following information was extracted from the accounting records of *Foreign Traders* at 30 September 2019:

- Sales $200,000
- Purchases $51,900
- Cartage inwards $3,600.

- Sales returns $5,000
- Purchases returns $1,300

The inventory at 1 October 2018 was $2,500 and the inventory at 30 September 2019 was $1,900.

Prepare the trading statement to show the gross profit of *Foreign Traders* for the year.

2 The following information was extracted from the accounting records of *Import Specialities* on 31 December 2016:

- Sales $495,000
- Purchases $289,000
- Freight inwards $5,500

- Sales returns $15,000
- Purchases returns $1,300
- Customs duty $2,000.

Inventory as at 1 January 2016 was $64,000 and on 31 December 2016 the inventory was $72,500.

Prepare the trading statement to show the gross profit of *Import Specialties* for the year.

3 *Daisy's Dollies* had the following balances in its accounting records as at 31 March 2020:

- Sales $700,000
- Purchases $495,000
- Cartage inwards $27,000

- Sales returns $10,000
- Purchases returns $4,500
- Packaging costs $13,000.

Inventory on hand was $50,000 on 1 April 2019 and $63,000 on 31 March 2020.

Prepare the trading statement to show the gross profit of *Daisy's Dollies* for the year.

4 *Tala's Takeaways* had a fire in early July 2017 and all the invoices for the year ended 30 June were destroyed. Fortunately Tala had kept his stock records at home and was able to tell you that the inventory at 1 July 2016 had cost $2,600 and at 30 June 2017 inventory which had cost $3,200 was on hand. The sales for the year were $250,000. Previous history shows that the gross profit for the business should be 25% of sales.

Prepare the trading statement to show the gross profit of *Tala's Takeaways* and hence calculate the cost of purchases for the year.

Hint

Work backwards!

Preparing the Income Statement

The income statement for a trading organisation is an extension of the trading statement. In general, it is arranged according to the formula:

$$\text{Profit} = \text{Gross profit} - \text{Expenses}$$

Sometimes businesses earn other income in addition to sales. If this is the case, the other income is added to the gross profit before the expenses are deducted to calculate profit.

Let's return to *Kiwi Krafts*. At the end of June 2016, after the cash journals had been posted to the ledger and the adjustments for accounts receivable and accounts payable had been processed, *Kiwi Krafts* had the following trial balance:

Kiwi Krafts Trial Balance as at 30 June 2016			
Advertising	1,800	Capital, 1 July 2015	$ 28,375
Cash	8,195	Commission	7,200
Cash register (cost)	800	GST payable	3,000
Drawings	43,200	Interest income	120
Interest on loan	2,100	Loan (due 31 July 2019)	25,000
Inventory, 1 July 2015	12,000	Purchases returns	900
Purchases	49,500	Sales	124,000
Rent	13,000	Accounts payable	3,450
Sales returns	1,150		
Shop fittings (cost)	8,000		
Van (cost)	20,000		
Van expenses	1,950		
Wages	24,600		
Accounts receivable	5,750		
	$192,045		$192,045

The highlighted items will all appear in the income statement. The colour coding relates to the part of the statement where they will appear – the trading section or the remainder of the statement.

Important!

- Sales returns reduce the income from sales. Sales have a **credit** balance and appear on the *right hand side* of the trial balance. Sales returns thus have a **debit** balance and appear on the *left hand side* of the trial balance.

- Purchases returns reduce the purchases expense. Purchases have a **debit** balance and appear on the *left hand side* of the trial balance. Purchases returns thus have a **credit** balance and appear on the *right hand side* of the trial balance.

We prepared the trading statement earlier (page 225). Now we will extend that trading statement into the full income statement.

Accounting – A Beginning   ISBN: 9780170211055

Kiwi Krafts
Income Statement for the year ended 30 June 2016

	$	$	$
Revenue			
Sales			124,000
Less: Sales returns			1,150
Net sales			122,850
Less: Cost of goods sold			
Inventory, beginning of year		12,000	
Plus: Purchases		49,500	
Less: Purchases returns		(900)	
Cost of goods available for sale		60,600	
Less: Inventory, end of year		(12,700)	
Cost of goods sold			47,900
Gross profit			74,950
Plus: **Other income**			
Commission		7,200	
Interest income		120	
			7,320
			82,270
Less: **Expenses**			
Distribution costs			
Advertising	1,800		
Wages	24,600		
		26,400	
Administrative expenses			
Rent	13,000		
Van expenses	1,950		
		14,950	
Finance costs			
Interest on loan		2,100	
Total expenses			43,450
Profit for the year			$38,820

Important!

- The opening inventory for the period appears in the trial balance. This becomes an expense (part of cost of goods sold) because it has been sold by the end of the period.

- The closing inventory is an asset at the end of the period. It reduces the cost of goods sold expense and appears as a current asset in the statement of financial position.

Statement of financial position (extract)

	$	$
Current assets		
Cash	8,195	
Accounts receivable	5,750	
Inventory	12,700	
Total current assets		26,645

Trading Organisations
Summary of Income and Expense Classifications

INCOME

Revenue
- Sales
- Fees

Other income
- Commission income
- Interest income
- Rental income
- Dividend income
- Gain on sale of property, plant and equipment

EXPENSES

Trading expenses
(Shown in the Trading Statement, or the Trading section of the Income Statement)

- Cartage inwards
- Customs duty
- Freight inwards
- Packaging costs
- Purchases

Distribution costs
- Advertising
- Cartage outwards
- Commission
- Delivery expenses
- Depreciation on shop fittings
- Depreciation on delivery vehicles
- Freight outwards
- Repairs to delivery vehicles
- Repairs and maintenance (shop fittings)
- Sales wages and salaries
- Travelling expenses

Finance costs
- Interest

Administrative expenses
- Accounting fees
- Audit fees
- Bad debts
- Depreciation (other than shop fittings or delivery vehicles)
- Donations
- Electricity
- General expenses
- Insurance
- Loss on sale of property, plant and equipment
- Office expenses
- Postage
- Printing
- Rates
- Rent
- Repairs and maintenance (other than to shop fittings or delivery vehicles)
- Salaries (office or other administration)
- Stationery
- Telephone, tolls and internet
- Vehicle expenses (other than delivery vehicles)
- Wages (office or other administration)

ISBN: 9780170211055

Activities

1 The following is the trial balance of *Mexican Food Supplies* as at 30 June 2017:

Mexican Food Supplies Trial Balance as at 30 June 2017			
Advertising	$ 3,000	Bank overdraft	$ 2,000
Drawings	40,000	Capital, 1 July 2016	33,600
Electricity	1,800	GST payable	1,250
Equipment (cost)	16,000	Sales	200,000
Insurance	1,000		
Interest on overdraft	750		
Inventory, 1 July 2016	21,000		
Lease of delivery van	12,000		
Office supplies expense	3,600		
Postage and stationery	1,200		
Purchases	90,000		
Salaries (office)	15,000		
Telephone expense	800		
Van expenses	2,200		
Wages (sales)	28,500		
	$236,850		$236,850

The items below have yet to be recorded on 30 June 2017:
- Invoices totalling $23,000 (including GST) have been sent to customers but remain unpaid
- Unpaid invoices from suppliers for goods purchased total $17,250 (including GST).

DO THIS!

a Record the accruals for accounts receivable and accounts payable on the accounting equation in the table below.

	A +	Ex =	L		+ Eq +	I
	Accounts receivable	Purchases	Accounts payable	GST payable		Sales
Balance						
Sales						
Purchases						
Total						

Inventory on hand at 30 June 2017 had cost $25,000.

DO THIS!

b Prepare the fully classified income statement and statement of financial position for *Mexican Food Supplies*.

Remember!

Closing inventory is a *current asset*.

2 The following is the trial balance of *Action Appliance Store* as at 31 March 2018:

Action Appliance Store Trial Balance as at 31 March 2018			
Accountancy fees	$ 2,400	Capital, 1 April 2017	$239,400
Advertising	5,500	GST payable	5,000
Cash at bank	14,700	Mortgage (10%, due	
Cash on hand	500	31 July 2025)	100,000
Delivery van (cost)	35,000	Rent	22,000
Drawings	45,000	Sales	412,000
Electricity	6,200		
Fittings (cost)	23,400		
Insurance	6,700		
Interest on mortgage	10,000		
Inventory, 1 April 2017	150,000		
Land and buildings (cost)	140,000		
Office expenses	22,500		
Purchases	258,000		
Sales commissions	55,000		
Van expenses	3,500		
	$778,400		$778,400

The items below have yet to be recorded on 31 March 2018:
- Invoices on hand for appliances purchased which have yet to be paid total $11,500 (including GST)
- Invoices totalling $18,400 (including GST) have been sent to customers but remain unpaid.

DO THIS!

a Record the accruals for accounts receivable and accounts payable on the accounting equation in the table below.

	A	+	Ex	=	L		+	Eq	+	I
	Accounts receivable		Purchases		Accounts payable	GST payable				Sales
Balance										
Sales										
Purchases										
Total										

Inventory on hand at 31 March 2018 had cost $165,000.

DO THIS!

b Prepare the fully classified income statement and statement of financial position for *Action Appliance Store*.

3 The trial balance opposite was prepared for *Petvet Supplies* as at 31 March 2016:

The items below have yet to be recorded on 31 March 2016:
- Local veterinarians have been invoiced a total of $46,000 (including GST) but their accounts remain unpaid
- Invoices on hand for pet food supplies purchased totalling $9,200 (including GST) have yet to be paid.

ISBN: 9780170211055

Petvet Supplies			
Trial Balance as at 31 March 2016			
Advertising	$ 1,600	Capital, 1 April 2015	$172,500
Cash	5,500	Commission income	10,300
Car (cost)	30,000	GST payable	7,500
Delivery van (cost)	15,500	Mortgage	
Drawings	61,000	(due 31 May 2040)	248,000
Electricity	1,900	Rental income	10,400
General expenses	700	Sales	400,000
Interest	19,400		
Inventory, 1 April 2015	23,500		
Land (cost)	125,000		
Premises (cost)	360,000		
Purchases	156,800		
Rates	2,000		
Salaries – office	22,500		
Telephone expense	900		
Van expenses	8,900		
Wages – shop	13,500		
	$848,700		$848,700

DO THIS!

a Record the accruals for accounts receivable and accounts payable on the accounting equation in the table below.

	A	+	Ex	=	L		+	Eq	+	I
	Accounts receivable		Purchases		Accounts payable	GST payable				Sales
Balance										
Sales										
Purchases										
Total										

Inventory on hand at 31 March 2016 had cost $20,300.

DO THIS!

b Prepare the fully classified income statement and statement of financial position for *Petvet Supplies*.

4 The following is the trial balance of *Gardener's Delight* as at 30 June 2019, after period-end accruals for accounts receivable and payable had been recorded:

Gardener's Delight Trial Balance as at 30 June 2019			
Accounts receivable	$32,000	Accounts payable	$25,600
Cartage inwards	500	Bank overdraft	2,500
Cartage outwards	4,050	Capital, 1 July 2018	141,200
Drawings	34,000	GST payable	3,000
Electricity	3,500	Mortgage	
General expenses	800	(due 31 May 2028)	135,000
Goodwill (cost)	10,000	Purchases returns	2,300
Insurance	1,400	Sales	395,000
Interest	6,300		
Inventory, 1 July 2018	76,000		
Land and buildings (cost)	260,000		
Purchases	199,700		
Sales returns	4,750		
Sales commissions	6,800		
Shop fittings (cost)	25,000		
Travelling expenses	8,300		
Wages – office	31,500		
	$704,600		$704,600

Inventory on hand at 30 June 2019 had cost $63,200.

DO THIS!

Prepare the fully classified income statement and statement of financial position for *Gardener's Delight.*

ISBN: 9780170211055

More Accruals

In the previous section, we recorded the accrual adjustments necessary to prepare the trading section of the income statement for *Kiwi Krafts*. However, at the end of the period there will be other period-end adjustments required and the depreciation expense for the period must also be recorded. Suppose the following items are still outstanding at 30 June 2016:

- Interest due but not received on the bank account is $25
- Wages due but not paid amount to $200
- Commission income of $350 has been received in advance
- Rent of $1,000 has been paid for the following reporting period.

Additional adjustments are required for depreciation:

- The cash register is depreciated at $160 per annum
- Shop fittings are depreciated at the rate of 10% per annum based on cost
- The van is expected to have a useful economic life of five years and residual value of $2,000.

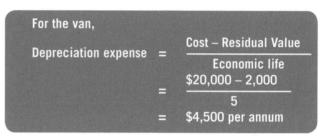

For the van,

$$\text{Depreciation expense} = \frac{\text{Cost} - \text{Residual Value}}{\text{Economic life}}$$
$$= \frac{\$20,000 - 2,000}{5}$$
$$= \$4,500 \text{ per annum}$$

The adjusted trial balance is shown below. Note that the adjustments for accounts receivable and accounts payable that we covered in the previous section are also shown on this adjusted trial balance.

Kiwi Krafts
Adjusted Trial Balance as at 30 June 2016

Advertising	1,800		1,800	Capital, 1 July 2015	28,375		28,375
Cash	8,195		8,195	Commission	7,200	(350)	6,850
Cash register (cost)	800		800	GST payable	2,700	300	3,000
Drawings	43,200		43,200	Interest income	120	25	145
Interest on loan	2,100		2,100	Loan (due 31 July 2019)	25,000		25,000
Inventory, 1 July 2015	12,000		12,000	Purchases returns	900		900
Purchases	46,500	3,000	49,500	Sales	119,000	5,000	124,000
Rent	13,000	(1,000)	12,000	Accounts payable		3,450	3,450
Sales returns	1,150		1,150	Accrued expenses		200	200
Shop fittings (cost)	8,000		8,000	Income received in advance		350	350
Van (cost)	20,000		20,000	*Accumulated depreciation:*			
Van expenses	1,950		1,950	– Cash register		160	160
Wages	24,600	200	24,800	– Shop fittings		800	800
Accounts receivable		5,750	5,750	– Van		4,500	4,500
Prepayments		1,000	1,000				
Accrued income		25	25				
Depreciation:							
– Cash register		160	160				
– Shop fittings		800	800				
– Van		4,500	4,500				
	183,295	14,435	197,730		183,295	14,435	197,730

The financial statements prepared from the adjusted trial balance are shown below. The items that were adjusted in this section of the chapter are highlighted in the statements.

Kiwi Krafts
Income Statement for the year ended 30 June 2016

	$	$	$
Revenue			
Sales			124,000
Less: Sales returns			1,150
Net sales			122,850
Less: Cost of goods sold			
Inventory, beginning of year		12,000	
Plus: Purchases		49,500	
Less: Purchases returns		(900)	
Cost of goods available for sale		60,600	
Less: Inventory, end of year		(12,700)	
Cost of goods sold			47,900
Gross profit			74,950
Plus: **Other income**			
Commission		6,850	
Interest income		145	
			6,995
			81,945
Less: **Expenses**			
Distribution costs			
Advertising	1,800		
Depreciation on cash register	160		
Depreciation on shop fittings	800		
Wages	24,800		
		27,560	
Administrative expenses			
Depreciation on van	4,500		
Rent	12,000		
Van expenses	1,950		
		18,450	
Finance costs			
Interest on loan		2,100	
Total expenses			48,110
Profit for the year			$33,835

Accounting – A Beginning

ISBN: 9780170211055

Kiwi Krafts
Statement of Financial Position as at 30 June 2016

	$	$	$
ASSETS			
Non-current assets			
Property, plant and equipment			
Total carrying amount (Note 1)			23,340
Current assets			
Cash		8,195	
Accounts receivable		5,750	
Inventory		12,700	
Accrued income		25	
Prepayments		1,000	
Total current assets			27,670
Total assets			$51,010
EQUITY AND LIABILITIES			
Equity			
Capital at beginning of the year		28,375	
Profit for the year		33,835	
Drawings for the year		(43,200)	
Capital at end of the year			19,010
Non-current liabilities			
Loan (due 31 July 2019)		25,000	
Current liabilities			
Accounts payable	3,450		
GST payable	3,000		
Accrued expenses	200		
Income received in advance	350		
Total current liabilities		7,000	
Total liabilities			32,000
Total equity and liabilities			$51,010

Notes to the statement of financial position

1 *Property, plant and equipment*

	Cash register $	Shop fittings $	Van $	Total $
Cost	800	8,000	20,000	28,800
Accumulated depreciation	(160)	(800)	(4,500)	(5,460)
Carrying amount	640	7,200	15,500	23,340

Activities

1 The following trial balance was prepared for *Sally's Superette* as at 31 March 2016:

Sally's Superette Trial Balance as at 31 March 2016			
Cartage outwards	$ 2,590	Accumulated depreciation	
Cash	2,460	– Delivery van	$ 8,400
Delivery van (cost)	21,000	– Fixtures and fittings	1,400
Drawings	25,000	Capital, 1 April 2015	62,590
Electricity	2,200	Commission	3,600
Fixtures and fittings (cost)	7,000	GST payable	3,000
Insurance	2,550	Mortgage	
Interest	4,700	(due 31 October 2022)	80,000
Inventory, 1 April 2015	10,800	Sales	240,000
Petrol and oil	3,640		
Petty cash	50		
Premises (cost)	120,000		
Purchases	176,000		
Wages – shop	21,000		
	$398,990		$398,990

Inventory on hand at 31 March 2016 had cost $26,600.

Additional information:
- Interest due on mortgage, $500
- Invoices on hand for purchases amount to $3,680 (including GST)
- Some shelving was purchased on credit for $1,840 (including GST) in March and this invoice has not been paid
- Depreciation of $700 is to be charged on fixtures and fittings
- Depreciation is to be charged on the delivery van based on an economic life of five years with no residual value.

> **Remember!**
> Closing inventory is a *current asset*.

DO THIS!

a Prepare the adjusted trial balance.
b Prepare the fully classified income statement and statement of financial position for *Sally's Superette*.

2 The trial balance on the next page was prepared for *Impact Interiors* as at 31 March 2018.

Inventory on hand at 31 March 2018 had cost $58,500.

Additional information:
- Rates of $250 and rent of $2,500 have been paid in advance
- Wages of $500 are due but unpaid
- Accounts are owing for purchases, $17,020 (including GST)
- Outstanding invoices owed by customers total $4,600 (including GST)
- Interest has not been received on the term deposit which has been invested for the past six months at 8% per annum. It will mature on 30 September this year.
- Depreciation of $1,400 is to be charged on fittings.

Accounting – A Beginning

ISBN: 9780170211055

Impact Interiors Trial Balance as at 31 March 2018			
Accountancy fees	$ 1,200	Accumulated depreciation	
Advertising	2,950	– Fittings	$ 2,800
Cartage inwards	1,000	Bank overdraft	1,400
Customs duty	1,800	Capital, 1 April 2017	82,100
Drawings	45,000	Gain on sale of fittings	1,500
Electricity	2,900	GST payable	4,500
Fittings (cost)	14,000	Purchases returns	1,600
Insurance	950	Sales	320,000
Interest on overdraft	100		
Inventory, 1 April 2017	65,000		
Petty cash	100		
Purchases	219,000		
Rates	1,200		
Rent	17,500		
Repairs	800		
Sales returns	2,000		
Telephone and tolls	1,900		
Term deposit	10,000		
Wages – shop	26,500		
	$413,900		$413,900

IMPACT INTERIORS

DO THIS!

a Prepare the adjusted trial balance.
b Prepare the fully classified income statement and statement of financial position for *Impact Interiors.*

 3 The following trial balance was prepared for *Kool Klothing*, a clothing retailer, as at 31 December 2018:

Kool Klothing Trial Balance as at 31 December 2018			
Accountancy fees	$ 1,500	*Accumulated depreciation*	
Cash	400	– Fixtures and fittings	$ 3,600
Drawings	42,000	– Van	4,400
Fixtures and fittings (cost)	18,000	Capital, 1 January 2018	111,350
General expenses	3,850	GST payable	6,000
Goodwill (cost)	40,000	Loan (due 30 April 2023)	20,000
Insurance	2,400	Sales	300,000
Interest	2,200		
Inventory, 1 January 2018	66,600		
Light and power	3,000		
Petty cash	200		
Purchases	204,000		
Rent and rates	8,300		
Stationery expense	2,750		
Telephone expense	1,950		
Van (cost)	22,000		
Van expenses	3,300		
Wages (shop)	22,900		
	$445,350		$445,350

Inventory on hand at 31 December 2018 was $64,600.

Additional information:

- Unpaid invoices on hand for purchases totalled $46,000 (including GST)
- Sales invoices outstanding totalled $25,760 (including GST)
- Interest of $200 on the loan is due but not paid
- Insurance of $300 has been paid in advance
- Rent and rates of $450 have been paid in advance
- Wages of $600 are due but unpaid
- Depreciation is to be charged on the straight line basis. Economic lives are: fixtures and fittings 10 years and the van 5 years. No residual value is expected.

DO THIS!

a Prepare the adjusted trial balance.
b Prepare the fully classified income statement for *Kool Klothing*.
c Prepare the following extracts from statement of financial position:
  i Current assets
  ii Current liabilities
  iii Non-current assets (including a note for property, plant and equipment).

4 The following trial balance was taken from the accounting records of *Barry's Bargain Basement* as at 30 June 2017:

Barry's Bargain Basement Trial Balance as at 30 June 2017			
Accountancy fees	$ 1,000	*Accumulated depreciation*	
Advertising	2,300	– Cellphones	$ 300
Cellphones (cost)	1,500	– Shop fittings	2,200
Customs duty	800	Bank overdraft	1,400
Drawings	35,000	Capital, 1 July 2016	89,600
Electricity	2,400	GST payable	5,000
Freight outwards	1,700	Mortgage	
Insurance	3,000	(due 30 June 2035)	60,000
Interest	6,000	Purchases returns	3,900
Inventory, 1 July 2016	29,500	Sales	270,000
Land and buildings (cost)	140,000		
Purchases	146,600		
Rates	2,800		
Sales returns	7,000		
Salaries (office)	22,400		
Shop fittings (cost)	11,000		
Telephone expense	1,400		
Wages (shop)	18,000		
	$432,400		$432,400

Inventory on hand at 30 June 2017, $30,000.

Additional information:

- A new cellphone costing $920 (including GST) was purchased on credit during March and the invoice remains unpaid
- Depreciation of $600 is to be charged on the cellphones
- Depreciation is to be charged on shop fittings using the straight line method, based on an expected economic life of 10 years and residual value of $1,000
- Rates paid in advance, $750
- Wages of $600 and salaries of $800 are due but unpaid
- Interest of $1,200 is due but unpaid on the mortgage
- Customers have been invoiced for sales of $11,960 (including GST)
- Invoices owing for purchases amount to $13,800 (including GST).

Accounting – A Beginning

ISBN: 9780170211055

DO THIS!

a Prepare the adjusted trial balance.
b Prepare the fully classified income statement for *Barry's Bargain Basement*.
c Prepare the following extracts from statement of financial position:
i Current assets
ii Current liabilities
iii Non-current assets (including a note for property, plant and equipment).

5 The trial balance below was taken from the accounting records of *Corrosive Chemicals* as at 31 March 2019.

Corrosive Chemicals Trial Balance as at 31 March 2019			
Advertising	$ 3,300	*Accumulated depreciation*	
Buildings (cost)	120,000	– Delivery van	$ 5,000
Commission	4,600	– Fixtures and fittings	1,600
Delivery van (cost)	25,000	Bank overdraft	600
Delivery van expenses	6,400	Capital, 1 April 2018	150,000
Drawings	35,000	GST payable	3,300
Electricity	2,300	Mortgage	
Fixtures and fittings (cost)	8,000	(due 31 December 2027)	80,000
General expenses	300	Sales	426,500
Insurance	1,300		
Interest	6,200		
Inventory, 1 April 2018	47,300		
Land (cost)	100,000		
Petty cash	100		
Purchases	254,000		
Rates	2,100		
Salaries – office	20,700		
Wages – shop	30,400		
	$667,000		$667,000

Inventory on hand at 31 March 2019, $44,800.

Additional information:
- Invoices outstanding for sales totalled $55,200 (including GST)
- Unpaid invoices on hand for purchases totalled $29,440 (including GST)
- Insurance of $400 has been paid in advance
- Wages of $500 and salaries of $200 are due but have not been paid
- Interest of $2,000 is due on the mortgage but has not been paid
- Depreciation is to be charged on the delivery van at $5,000 per annum and on fixtures and fittings using the straight line basis with an economic life of 10 years and no residual value.

DO THIS!

a Prepare the adjusted trial balance.
b Prepare the fully classified income statement for *Corrosive Chemicals*.
c Prepare the following extracts from statement of financial position:
i Current assets
ii Current liabilities
iii Non-current assets (including a note for property, plant and equipment).

Cash Budgets

The income statement and statement of financial position are prepared to show the financial performance and position of a business at the end of a period of time. They are thus prepared on an historical basis – they report *past* events.

A budget, on the other hand, is a plan for the *future*. It is not a financial statement in itself, but a prediction of future financial statements. It is possible to prepare budgeted income statements and statements of financial position based on future expectations. In this course, however, we will be concerned only with the **cash budget**.

DEFINITION

Cash Budget

A cash budget shows the expected receipts and payments of cash and the closing bank balance for some period in the future.

Preparing a cash budget has a number of advantages:

- It forces the business to plan for the future.
- It helps predict periods when the business will have excess cash that could be used to earn interest and periods when there will be a shortage of cash so that extra borrowing can be arranged in advance.
- It enables the business to monitor income by comparing actual cash received with the budget.
- It enables the business to keep control over cash expenses by comparing the actual cash paid with the budget.
- It enables the business to respond quickly if actual cash receipts and payments are different from the budget. This may mean the difference between being able to meet business commitments and being forced to close down.

Cash budgets may be prepared for any length of time in the future. The most useful form is a budget for the full year, broken down into monthly periods. This enables actual cash receipts and payments to be compared regularly against the budget.

Sometimes it is necessary to adjust a cash budget if unexpected events take place. For example, there may be an increase in rent. If this happens, the budget for the rest of the year would need adjusting so that it reflects the new level of cash payments. Then the business owner can make arrangements for the extra expense in advance. Without a budget, an increase in expenses such as this could cause real difficulty in meeting cash outgoings on time.

Preparing the cash budget

For a cash budget to be useful, the information it contains must be as accurate as possible. The first information that is useful comes from the statement of financial position prepared at 30 June 2016. Here we find details of cash in the bank at the beginning of July, accounts receivable who are due to pay cash during July and the accounts payable and GST balances which will have to be paid in July. Quite often it is helpful to examine the cash receipts and payments journals for the same month in the previous reporting period. The owner can then estimate how these might change in the next period.

At 30 June 2016, *Trendy Tourz* had the following balances of current assets and liabilities that would affect the cash balance at the end of July:

Current assets		Current liabilities	
Cash	$9,100	Accounts payable	5,750
Accounts receivable	6,210	GST payable	6,460
Accrued income	200	Accrued expenses	150
Available cash	$15,510	Cash required	$12,360

Important!

- Prepayments are not included in the current assets listed above because they will not be received in cash.

- Income received in advance is not listed in the current liabilities listed above because it will not be paid in cash.

The information below has been taken from the cash records of *Trendy Tourz* for July 2015:

Cash receipts

- Cash received from customers $6,100
- Sale of outdoor equipment $500
- Contribution by owner $5,000

Cash payments

- Expenses paid $2,200
- Purchase of outdoor equipment $4,000
- Purchase of computer $3,000
- Loan repaid $200
- Cash drawings $500

This summary, together with the figures for current assets and liabilities, forms a useful starting point for preparing the cash budget for July 2016, the first month of the following reporting period.

The cash budget that Aroha prepared for *Trendy Tourz* for the month of July is shown below.

Trendy Tourz
Cash Budget for the month ending 31 July 2016

	$	$
Estimated cash receipts		
Cash from accounts receivable (June)	6,210	
Cash from accrued income (June)	200	
Cash fees (July)	18,300	
Total cash receipts		24,710
Less: Estimated cash payments		
Accounts payable (June)	5,750	
GST payable (June)	6,460	
Accrued expenses (June)	150	
Cash expenses	3,500	
Loan repayment	200	
Cash drawings	3,000	
New gear	15,000	
Total cash payments		34,060
Deficit of cash		(9,350)
Plus: Opening bank balance		9,100
Closing bank balance		$(250)

This cash budget shows that the bank account will be overdrawn by $250 at the end of July if Brad purchases new gear for $15,000.

 Accounting – A Beginning

ISBN: 9780170211055

Important!

- The cash budget shows **cash** receipts and payments only. Non-cash items such as depreciation do **not** appear in a cash budget because they are not paid in cash.

- The amount shown for expenses in the cash budget does not include the $2,000 of food expenses that Brad said would be payable in August. He will therefore need to make sure he has enough cash on hand to meet this payment when it is due.

Another Example

Aroha has decided to prepare a cash budget for the following year because she is thinking about opening another shop on the other side of town. She needs to accumulate sufficient cash for a deposit on the lease. She has predicted the following transactions for the year ending 30 June 2017:

- Sales for the year will be $180,000. Of these, $175,000 is expected to be received in cash with the balance of $5,000 outstanding at the end of the reporting period.

- Purchases will amount to $75,000 of which $3,000 will be outstanding accounts payable at the end of the year.

- Other cash income from commission is expected to be $8,500.

- Cash expenses paid will be wages of $30,000 and other expenses of $2,600.

- Depreciation for the year will total $5,600.

- Drawings totalling $45,000 are expected, with $400 of this being inventory for family gifts.

- Aroha expects to replace some of her shop fittings at a cost of $1,800. The old ones will be sold for $400, incurring a loss on sale of $250.

- Loan repayments for the year will total $2,200.

The statement of financial position on page 239 shows the following balances that will affect the cash budget:

Current assets		Current liabilities	
Cash	$8,195	Accounts payable	3,450
Accounts receivable	5,750	GST payable	3,000
Accrued income	25	Accrued expenses	200
Available cash	$13,970	Cash required	$6,650

Unfortunately Aroha has discovered that one of the debtors has recently died owing $250 and she does not want to ask his family to pay the debt.

The cash budget Aroha has prepared for *Kiwi Krafts* is shown below.

Kiwi Krafts
Cash Budget for the year ending 30 June 2017

	$	$
Estimated cash receipts		
Cash from accounts receivable (June 2016)	5,500	
Cash from accrued income (June 2016)	25	
Cash sales	175,000	
Sale of shop fittings	400	
Total cash receipts		180,925
Less: Estimated cash payments		
Accounts payable (June 2016)	3,450	
GST payable (June 2016)	3,000	
Accrued expenses (June 2016)	200	
Cash purchases	72,000	
Cash expenses	32,600	
Loan repayments	2,200	
Cash drawings	44,600	
Shop fittings	1,800	
Total cash payments		159,850
Surplus of cash		21,075
Plus: Opening bank balance		8,195
Closing bank balance		$29,270

Remember!

Depreciation is a *non-cash* expense so does not appear in the cash budget.

Important!

- Cash from 2016 accounts receivable will be $5,750, less the bad debt of $250, giving $5,500.
- Cash from sales is $180,000, less $5,000 unpaid at the end of the period, giving $175,000.
- Cash paid for purchases will be $75,000, less $3,000 owing at the end of the period, giving $72,000.
- Drawings in cash will be total drawings of $45,000, less the $400 of inventory, giving $44,600.

ISBN: 9780170211055

Activities

1 The following is a summary of the transactions expected for *Super Surveyors* for the month ended 31 December 2019:

Cash received from customers on account	$25,000
Cash fees received at the time of consultation	2,000
Cash paid for office wages	3,000
Cash paid for other expenses	6,900
Cash received from the sale of an old computer	300
Cash drawings by the owner	4,500

The bank balance at 1 December 2019 was $1,300 Dr.

DO THIS! Prepare the cash budget of *Super Surveyors* for December 2019.

2 *Viaduct* is a sole proprietor business that sells boating equipment. The business is owned and operated by Captain Chris. Chris estimated the following events for the month of July 2016:

Cash sales received	$45,000
Cash drawings	4,500
Cash purchases paid	18,000
Other expenses paid	8,000
Salaries paid	7,000

The bank balance at 1 July 2016 was $12,500 Dr.

DO THIS! Prepare the cash budget of *Viaduct* for July 2016.

3 Natasha owns and operates a small business, *Country Cooking*, baking specialty cakes and biscuits that are sold at local farmers' markets. She has estimated the following events for December 2016:

Cash sales received	$5,500
Cash drawings	750
Cash paid for purchases	2,350
Advertising paid	300
Other expenses paid	400
Wages paid	800
Fees paid to hire stalls	500
Cash paid to purchase new oven	2,000

The bank balance at 1 December 2016 was $6,250 Dr.

DO THIS! Prepare the cash budget of *Country Cooking* for December 2016.

4 Dr I Cureall commenced business on 1 September 2017 when he had $20,000 cash in his business bank account. The following are his estimates of transactions for the month of September:

Cash fees received	$ 4,200
Cash expenses paid	4,050
Cash paid for computer system	4,500
Loan received from bank	5,000
Other expenses paid	400
Wages paid	2,500
Contribution from Dr Cureall	5,000
Cash paid to purchase new car	15,000
Purchase of medical supplies on credit	2,700

DO THIS! Prepare the cash budget of *Dr Cureall* for September 2017.

5 Below are the estimated transactions of *Petz Hospital*, veterinarians, for the month of November 2018. The bank balance at 1 November was $1,100 Dr.

Cash fees received	$ 5,760
Cash expenses paid	5,490
Cash paid for new equipment	9,315
Cash sales of pet supplies	675
Loan received from bank	18,000
Other expenses paid	400
Wages paid	2,400
Sale of old equipment (loss on sale $200)	450
Contribution from owner	20,000
Cash paid to purchase new car	15,000
Outstanding customer invoices at 30 November	1,000
Interest received	15
Depreciation on equipment	150

DO THIS! Prepare the cash budget of *Petz Hospital* for November 2018.

6 Ann owns and operates *Tree Doctors*, a sole proprietor business that provides tree trimming and maintenance services. Ann's accounts manager estimated the following events for April 2019:

Cash drawings	$ 8,800
Bank loan received	10,000
Cash fees received	40,000
Depreciation on equipment	200
Employee salaries paid	12,500
Interest paid	300
Interest received	60
Other expenses paid	16,100
Vehicle expenses paid	1,500

Tree Doctors

The bank balance at 1 April was $8,000 Cr.

ISBN: 9780170211055

At 31 March, the statement of financial position showed the following balances:

Accounts receivable $6,000
Accounts payable   1,200
GST payable   1,300

Ann has a policy of paying all accounts due in the following month. She estimates that 80% of debtors will pay their outstanding accounts in April.

 Prepare the cash budget of *Tree Doctors* for April 2019.

7   *Safer Financial Services* is a sole proprietor business owned and operated by I M Lender. The business provides investment advice to retirees. The following events are expected to occur in May 2019:

Cash fees received	$1,700
Cash drawings	500
Wages paid	1,300
Commission earned but not yet charged	800
Depreciation on equipment	400
Purchase of new computer for cash	1,000
Unpaid invoice for new printer	400
Other expenses paid	1,700
Cash received from sale of old computer (gain on sale $200)	250

At 30 April, the statement of financial position showed the following balances:

Accounts receivable $1,200
Accounts payable   700
Cash   3,200   (in funds)

I M Lender has a policy of paying all accounts due in the following month. She estimates that 90% of debtors will pay their outstanding accounts in May.

 Prepare the cash budget of *Safer Financial Services* for May 2019.

8   *Sports Rewards* is a sole proprietor business owned and operated by Wiremu Woods. The business manufactures and sells trophies and plaques for sports teams. Wiremu has estimated the following events for October 2020:

Cash sales received	$28,000
Cash drawings	3,000
Cash paid for purchases	6,500
Commission owed to sales representatives	300
Depreciation on vehicles	500
Interest paid	420
Unpaid invoices for purchases	400
Unpaid invoices for sales	1,400
Other expenses paid	3,500
Sales expenses paid	1,200
Wages paid	6,000
Loan received	25,000
Vehicle purchased for cash	35,000

At 30 September, the statement of financial position showed the following balances:

Accounts receivable $1,200
Accounts payable   250
GST receivable   2,000
Cash   4,000   (in funds)

Wiremu has a policy of paying all accounts due in the following month. He estimates that 75% of debtors will pay their outstanding accounts in October.

DO THIS!   Prepare the cash budget of *Sports Rewards* for October 2020.

9   Stuart operates a business, *Perfect Play*, that provides services coaching retirees at lawn bowls. He is keen to ensure his business has sufficient cash to meet its obligations and has provided the estimates below relating to June 2018.

Cash fees received	$10,400
Bad debts written off	100
Cash drawings	4,500
Depreciation on vehicle	200
Drawings of sports equipment	380
Interest paid	25
Advertising expenses paid	2,800
Other expenses paid	1,440
Repayment on vehicle loan	800
Unpaid invoices for fees	1,260
Vehicle expenses paid	800

At 1 June, the statement of financial position showed the following balances:

Bank $1,800 overdrawn
Accounts receivable   1,600
Accounts payable   350
GST payable   900

Stuart has a policy of paying all accounts due in the following month. He estimates that 80% of debtors will pay their outstanding accounts in June.

DO THIS!   Prepare the cash budget of *Perfect Play* for June 2018.

ISBN: 9780170211055

CHAPTER 9

Analysing Financial Performance

- Percentage Change
- Looking at Sales
- The Gross Profit Percentage and Markup
- Looking at Expenses
- Looking at Profit

In previous chapters we have prepared the financial statements for sole proprietors. We will now analyse and interpret those financial statements to obtain a better picture of the financial performance of an accounting entity over a period of time. The next chapter will focus on interpreting the financial position at the end of the reporting period.

We have previously prepared the income statement, which shows the income, expenses and profit for the reporting period. This chapter will use a case study to show how we can calculate ratios and percentages that help us gain a better idea of the **profitability** of the business and how this has changed over time.

The income statement is the key financial statement that is used to assess the firm's profitability. Steve produced the income statement which had been given to him by the accountant. This is shown on the next page.

Surf's Up!
Income Statement for the year ended 31 March 2017

2016 $		$	$
	Revenue		
180,000	Sales		240,000
120,000	*Less:* Cost of goods sold		180,000
60,000	Gross profit		60,000
	Less: **Expenses**		
9,000	Distribution costs	14,400	
7,200	Administrative expenses	8,400	
5,400	Finance costs	7,200	
21,600	Total expenses		30,000
$38,400	Profit for the year		$30,000

Percentage Change

A useful guide to business performance may be found by looking at the percentage change in the various parts of the income statement between two reporting periods. For example, sales increased from $180,000 in 2016 to $240,000 in 2017, which is an increase of $240,000 – 180,000 = $60,000. To calculate the percentage change, we express this difference as a percentage of the first year's sales:

$$\text{Percentage change in sales} = \frac{\$60,000}{\$180,000} \times \frac{100}{1}$$
$$= 33.3\%$$

This looks to be a favourable trend – the level of sales has increased in dollar terms. We would hope that this would lead to an increase in profit.

We can calculate the percentage change for all sections of the income statement. These calculations give us an indication of the trends in operating performance over the two-year period. We use the general formula:

$$\text{Percentage Change} = \frac{\text{This year's figure} - \text{Last year's figure}}{\text{Last year's figure}} \times \frac{100}{1}$$

For the cost of goods sold:

$$\text{Percentage change} = \frac{\$180,000 - 120,000}{\$120,000} \times \frac{100}{1}$$
$$= 50.0\%$$

Accounting – A Beginning   ISBN: 9780170211055

This is an unfavourable trend because the cost of goods sold has increased by a greater percentage than sales.

If sales increased by 33.3% we would hope that the cost of goods sold would increase by the same percentage (or less). The income statement shows that the gross profit was the same ($60,000) in both 2016 and 2017. This means that, although the firm managed to increase the dollar amount of sales in 2017, there was no increase in the gross profit because the cost of goods sold increased by the same dollar amount.

The percentage changes for all of the sections of the income statement are shown in the following table:

Item	2016 $	2017 $	Change $	% change	Favourable/ Unfavourable
Sales	180,000	240,000	60,000	33.3	F
Cost of goods sold	120,000	180,000	60,000	50.0	U
Gross profit	60,000	60,000	Nil	Nil	—
Distribution costs	9,000	14,400	5,400	60.0	U
Administrative expenses	7,200	8,400	1,200	16.6	F
Finance costs	5,400	7,200	1,800	33.3	F
Total expenses	21,600	30,000	8,400	38.9	U
Profit for the year	38,400	30,000	− 8,400	− 21.9	U

When deciding whether or not a trend is *favourable* or *unfavourable*, it is helpful to use the percentage change in sales as a benchmark. Remember that sales increased by 33.3%. If all the expenses also increased by 33.3%, then profit would increase by the same proportion and the outcome would be favourable.

We have already established that the percentage change in cost of goods sold is *unfavourable* because it is more than 33.3%. If we examine the rest of the table, we find the following:

- **Distribution costs** have increased by 60%. This is an *unfavourable* trend because the increase is greater than the 33.3% increase in sales.

- **Administrative expenses** have increased by 16.6%. Since this only half the percentage increase in sales, the trend is *favourable*.

- **Finance costs** have increased by 33.3%. This is the same percentage increase as sales, so the trend is also *favourable*. It means that more sales have been achieved without a higher increase in the level of these expenses.

- **Total expenses** have increased by 38.9%. This is an *unfavourable* trend because the increase is greater than the 33.3% increase in sales. The poor control over distribution costs has more than offset the extra efficiencies in both administrative expenses and finance costs.

- **Profit** shows a decrease of 21.9%. This is an *unfavourable* trend, especially since sales have increased.

What can we conclude?
The negative percentage change in profit is due to poor control over both cost of goods sold and distribution costs.

ISBN: 9780170211055

Activities

1 Examine the cartoon on page 253. What two things is Steve complaining about?

2 The figures in the table below have been extracted from the income statement for *Surf's Up* on page 254.

Item	2016 $	2017 $	Change $	% change	Favourable/ Unfavourable
Sales	180,000	240,000			
Cost of goods sold	120,000	180,000			
Gross profit	60,000	60,000			
Distribution costs	9,000	14,400			
Administrative expenses	7,200	8,400			
Finance costs	5,400	7,200			
Total expenses	21,600	30,000			
Profit for the year	38,400	30,000			

DO THIS! Calculate the percentage change in each of the items and check your calculations against the figures in the table on page 254.

3 The table below shows a summary of the income statements of *Shoddy Shoes* for the years 2018 and 2019.

Item	2018 $	2019 $	Change $	% change	Favourable/ Unfavourable
Sales	100,000	120,000			
Cost of goods sold	50,000	56,000			
Gross profit	50,000	64,000			
Distribution costs	10,000	12,000			
Administrative expenses	7,000	9,800			
Finance costs	5,000	7,500			
Total expenses	22,000	29,300			
Profit for the year	28,000	34,700			

DO THIS!

a Complete the table, following the example on page 254.
b Choose **one** *favourable* trend and
   i fully explain why you consider that the trend is favourable; and
   ii suggest a possible reason for the trend.
c Choose **one** *unfavourable* trend and
   i fully explain why you consider that the trend is unfavourable; and
   ii suggest a possible reason for the trend.

Accounting – A Beginning ISBN: 9780170211055

Looking at Sales

In the previous section Yu Ting found that sales had increased by $60,000 in 2017. This looked like a good trend. However, if the selling price of surfboards had increased, it is possible that Steve could have sold fewer surfboards than he did last year.

In 2016:

Sales	= $180,000
Selling price	= $600
Number sold	$= \dfrac{\$180,000}{\$600}$
	= 300 surfboards

In 2017:

Sales	= $240,000
Selling price	= $800
Number sold	$= \dfrac{\$240,000}{\$800}$
	= 300 surfboards

The Gross Profit Percentage and Markup

The gross profit of a trading organisation is extremely important. Earlier we learnt that a business must earn sufficient gross profit to cover its expenses and thus provide a return to the owner.

One measure that can be calculated from the income statement is the gross profit percentage. This is calculated according to the formula:

$$\text{Gross profit percentage} = \frac{\text{Gross profit}}{\text{Net sales}} \times \frac{100}{1}$$

	2016	2017

Gross profit percentage $= \dfrac{\$60{,}000}{\$180{,}000} \times \dfrac{100}{1}$ $= \dfrac{\$60{,}000}{\$240{,}000} \times \dfrac{100}{1}$

$= 33.3\%$ $= 25.0\%$

This means that, in 2016, the gross profit represented 33.3% of net sales. In other words, for every $1.00 of sales, 33.3 cents remained after deducting the 66.7 cents for the cost of goods sold. This may be represented by the following diagram:

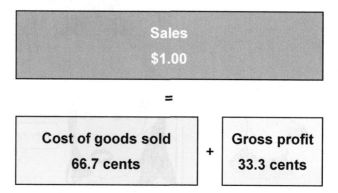

In 2017, the gross profit fell from 33.3% to 25.0%. This means that from each dollar of sales, there is now only 25 cents rather than 33.3 cents to both cover expenses and provide a return to the owner. This situation can be represented in a pie chart as follows:

Components of each $1 of sales

It is impossible to say whether or not any particular gross profit percentage is satisfactory. It should be compared with the gross profit percentage of other reporting periods, and also with the gross profit percentages of other firms in the same industry. The most satisfactory situation is if the gross profit percentage remains stable or increases. In the case of *Surf's Up!*, there has been a significant decrease in the gross profit percentage. This is an *unfavourable* trend and therefore needs close investigation.

Accounting – A Beginning

ISBN: 9780170211055

Activities

1 Steve thought that his business, *Surf's Up!*, had done a lot better this year (2017).

a Calculate the amount Steve paid for each surfboard that he sold in
  i 2016? **ii** 2017.
b Explain whether or not you agree with Steve's opinion and why.

2 The selling price of widgets in 2018 was $3.00 and in 2019 it had risen to $3.50. Total sales in 2018 were $6,000 and in 2019 sales were $8,400.

Calculate the number of widgets sold each year.

3 Harold Harvey sells squishes. In 2014 he sold 10,000 squishes at $2.70 each. In 2015 his sales were 12,000 squishes at $2.50.

Calculate the total sales for each year.

4 The table below shows the relationship between the selling price per unit, the number of items sold and total sales.

	Number of units	Selling price per unit $	Total sales $
Example:	100	20	2,000
a	5,000	2	
b	600		2,400
c		300	120,000
d	7,500	15	
e	250		50,000
f		5	15,000

Calculate the missing figures and complete the table.

5 A business paid $120 per unit for knick knacks which it sold for $150 each. During the year ended 30 June 2019, 2,500 units were sold.

a Calculate the gross profit per unit.
b Calculate the total cost of units sold during the year.
c Calculate the total sales for the year.

Looking at Markup

The gross profit for *Surf's Up!* was $60,000 in 2016 and has stayed the same in 2017. This means that, although the selling price of surfboards has increased, the dollar markup on each surfboard has stayed the same.

The gross profit is very important because it must cover the expenses of the business. If the gross profit is too low, it may not be enough to meet those expenses and the business could run at a loss instead of a profit. A loss *reduces* equity, so it erodes the owner's investment in the business.

Another name for gross profit is markup. This is the amount added to the cost of the goods to calculate their selling price.

In the previous chapter, we used the following formula to calculate gross profit:

Gross profit = Sales − Cost of goods sold

This can be rearranged to read:

Sales = Gross profit + Cost of goods sold

OR

Selling price = Cost price + Markup

Note!

We will ignore GST when we discuss the selling price in this chapter.

The diagram below shows this more clearly.

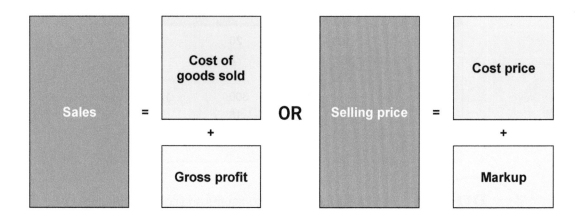

The markup percentage is given by the following formula:

$$\text{Markup percentage} = \frac{\text{Gross profit}}{\text{Cost of goods sold}} \times \frac{100}{1}$$

	2016		2017	
Markup percentage	$= \dfrac{\$60{,}000}{\$120{,}000} \times \dfrac{100}{1}$		$= \dfrac{\$60{,}000}{\$180{,}000} \times \dfrac{100}{1}$	
	$= 50.0\%$		$= 33.3\%$	

These calculations mean that in 2016, 50% of the cost of the surfboards was added to determine the selling price. In 2017 this decreased to 33.3% of the cost.

If we examine the income statement for *Surf's Up!* on page 254, we can see that the sales for the year ended 31 March 2017 had increased by $60,000 from the previous year. However, the gross profit remained the same for both years.

As well as looking at the dollar figures for sales and gross profit, it is important to look at both the gross profit percentage and markup percentage. This will tell us whether or not Steve's prices have kept up with the extra he has had to pay to buy the surfboards this year.

Yu Ting's calculations show that the gross profit percentage has fallen from 33.3% in 2016 to 25% in 2017. There could be several reasons for this:

- Steve could be selling a different type of surfboard which has a lower markup percentage even though it has a higher selling price. This means that the sales mix (types of items sold) has changed.

- Some of Steve's stock might have been stolen during the year.

- There could have been some surfboards omitted from the end of year stocktaking.

- Steve may have sold some old stock at a reduced price.

ISBN: 9780170211055

We can see that the reason for the reduced gross profit and markup percentages in this case was that Steve had added the same dollar markup per surfboard as he had last year. We worked out earlier that he sold 300 surfboards each year. He added $200 to the cost of each surfboard to work out the selling price as follows:

2016

Cost price　　= $400

Selling price　= $400 + 200　= $600

Markup %　　$= \dfrac{\$200}{\$400} \times \dfrac{100}{1} = 50.0\%$

Gross profit % $= \dfrac{\$200}{\$600} \times \dfrac{100}{1} = 33.3\%$

2017

Cost price　　= $600

Selling price　= $600 + 200　= $800

Markup %　　$= \dfrac{\$200}{\$600} \times \dfrac{100}{1} = 33.3\%$

Gross profit % $= \dfrac{\$200}{\$800} \times \dfrac{100}{1} = 25.0\%$

These markup and gross profit percentages are the same as we calculated earlier in the chapter.

When a business sells only one product we can use the cost price and selling price of one unit to calculate the gross profit and markup percentages as we have done here. However, most businesses sell more than one product. Each product will have a different markup percentage. Thus we use the *total* figures for sales, cost of goods sold and gross profit to calculate the *average* percentages for the firm.

What is an acceptable markup percentage?

We must be very careful when we make judgements about gross profit and markup percentages. If the percentages decrease, it may be a sign of business inefficiency. Stock may have been stolen or the stock-taking may have been done carelessly. However, sometimes a business will decide to reduce its markup in the hope of selling more goods. If this strategy is successful, the turnover (quantity of goods sold) will increase. More items are sold at slightly less profit per item. The result may be a higher figure for the gross profit in dollar terms, even though the percentage has fallen.

There is no 'ideal' gross profit or markup percentage. The rates depend on the type of business involved. What is important is the *trend* for the same business from year to year. Some businesses rely on selling a large quantity of items at a low markup. A supermarket is a good example of this type of operation. Others, for example jewellers, rely on selling fewer items at a higher markup.

> **Remember!**
>
> There is no ideal gross profit or markup percentage. It is the *trend* that is important.

Consider the following example:

	Supermarket	Jeweller
Sales	$1,000,000	$40,000
Gross profit %	2%	50%
Gross profit $	$20,000	$20,000

Accounting – A Beginning

ISBN: 9780170211055

Both of these businesses have made the same gross profit in dollar terms, i.e. $20,000. The supermarket must sell a large quantity of goods at a low markup percentage to produce a gross profit of $20,000. The jeweller, however, sells fewer items at a higher markup percentage to produce the same dollar result.

If we prepare a simple trading statement, we can use this to calculate the markup percentage:

	Supermarket	Jeweller
Sales	$1,000,000	$40,000
Less: Cost of goods sold	980,000	20,000
Gross profit	$20,000	$20,000

The markup percentage is calculated as follows:

Supermarket

$$\text{Markup \%} = \frac{\$20,000}{\$980,000} \times \frac{100}{1}$$

$$= 2.0\%$$

Jeweller

$$\text{Markup \%} = \frac{\$20,000}{= \$20,000} \times \frac{100}{1}$$

$$= 100.0\%$$

On an item which cost $1.00, the markup would be:

Supermarket

Markup	=	2% of $1.00
	=	2 cents

Jeweller

Markup	=	100% of $1.00
	=	$1.00

The selling price would be:

Supermarket

Selling price	=	Cost price + Markup
	=	$1.00 + 0.02
	=	$1.02

Jeweller

Selling price	=	Cost price + Markup
	=	$1.00 + 1.00
	=	$2.00

Thus the supermarket would need to sell 50 times as many items as the jeweller to produce the same dollar amount of gross profit.

The table below summarises possible reasons for a change in the gross profit percentage.

	Gross profit %	
	Increasing	**Decreasing**
Sales mix	More higher markup items sold	More lower markup items sold
Change in markup	Markup increased	Markup decreased
Stocktaking errors	Some stock counted twice	Some stock omitted from stocktake

1   A toy shop has a gross profit of 40% of sales. Sales for the year are $16,000.

DO THIS!

a   Calculate the
   i   gross profit
   ii   cost of goods sold
   iii   markup percentage.
b   Calculate the gross profit on
   i   a doll that sells for $30
   ii   a jigsaw puzzle that sells for $7.50.
c   Calculate the total gross profit on the sale of four dolls and three jigsaw puzzles.
d   Calculate the number of jigsaw puzzles that must be sold to produce the same amount of gross profit as one doll.

2   Harold Harvey sells squishes that cost $2.00 each for $2.50. Last year he sold 4,500 squishes. He is investigating selling squashes as well. Squashes cost $3.00 each.
   Harold estimates that sales of squishes will fall to 3,000 units if he starts selling squashes too. He expects to sell 1,500 squashes. The markup percentage will be the same as for squishes.

DO THIS!

a   Calculate the percentage markup on each squish.
b   Calculate the selling price of a squash if the markup is
   i   20%   ii   25%   iii   30%   iv   10%.
c   Calculate the difference in the gross profit if Harold goes ahead with the plan to sell squashes.
d   Make a *fully justified* recommendation to Harold as to whether he should sell squashes as well as squishes.

3   The table below shows the relationship between sales, cost of goods sold and gross profit with some of the percentages that can be calculated from these.

	Sales $	Cost of goods sold $	Gross profit $	Gross profit %	Markup %
a	100,000	80,000			
b		90,000	30,000		
c	50,000			25.0	
d		100,000			30.0
e			50,000		25.0
f	90,000	30,000			
g	40,000		10,000		
h	120,000			50.0	
i		150,000			20.0
j			20,000	10.0	

DO THIS!

Calculate the missing figures and complete the table.

ISBN: 9780170211055

Relationship between Gross Profit and Markup

The gross profit percentage and markup percentage are closely related. If we know the gross profit percentage, we can calculate the markup percentage. This can be done without knowing the actual figures for sales, cost of goods sold or the gross profit. The percentage is all we need, as shown below.

Calculating Markup Percentage from Gross Profit Percentage

Consider a gross profit percentage of 20%. This means that for every $100 of sales, there will be a gross profit of $20.

$$\text{i.e.} \quad \frac{\text{Gross profit}}{\text{Net sales}} \times \frac{100}{1} = \frac{\$20}{\$100} \times \frac{100}{1} = 20\%$$

If we rearrange these figures as a trading statement, we can calculate the cost of goods sold:

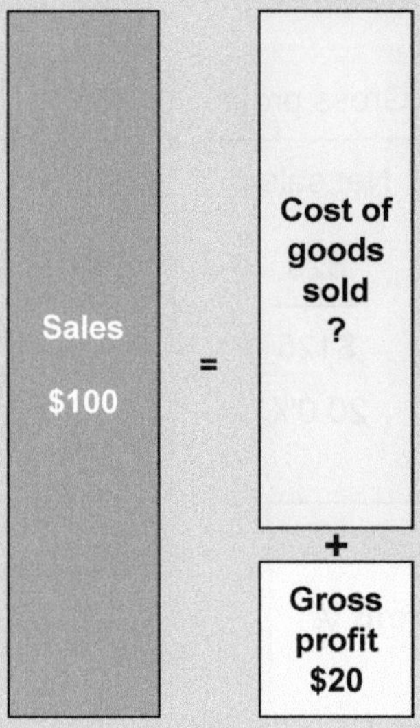

Sales	$100
Less: Cost of goods sold	80
Gross profit	$20

$$\begin{aligned} \text{Cost of goods sold} \quad &= \quad \$100 - 20 \\ &= \quad \$80 \end{aligned}$$

$$\begin{aligned} \text{Markup \%} \quad &= \quad \frac{\text{Gross profit}}{\text{Cost of goods sold}} \times \frac{100}{1} \\ &= \quad \frac{\$20}{\$80} \times \frac{100}{1} \\ &= \quad 25.0\% \end{aligned}$$

Sales $100 = Cost of goods sold ? + Gross profit $20

TRY THESE:

Gross profit %	Markup %
25%	?
50%	?
10%	?
33.3%	?

We can also carry out this process in reverse. If we know the markup percentage we can calculate the gross profit percentage. This process is shown on the next page.

ISBN: 9780170211055

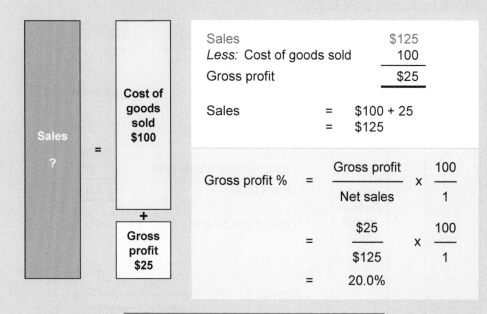

Calculating Gross Profit Percentage from Markup Percentage

Consider a markup percentage of 25%. This means that for goods costing $100, there will be a gross profit or markup of $25 added to the cost to determine the selling price.

i.e. $$\frac{\text{Gross profit}}{\text{Cost of goods sold}} \times \frac{100}{1} = \frac{\$25}{\$100} \times \frac{100}{1} = 25\%$$

If we rearrange these figures as a trading statement, we can calculate the sales:

Sales	$125
Less: Cost of goods sold	100
Gross profit	$25

$$\text{Sales} = \$100 + 25$$
$$= \$125$$

$$\text{Gross profit \%} = \frac{\text{Gross profit}}{\text{Net sales}} \times \frac{100}{1}$$

$$= \frac{\$25}{\$125} \times \frac{100}{1}$$

$$= 20.0\%$$

Sales ? = **Cost of goods sold $100** + **Gross profit $25**

TRY THESE:

Markup %	Gross profit %
50%	?
10%	?
33.3%	?
20%	?

Looking at Expenses

Control over expenses is very important because the higher the expenses, the lower the profit will be. This means that if expenses increase, the owner will receive a smaller return on the capital he or she has invested in the business.

For a trading organisation, we can calculate the total expenses as a percentage of sales using the following formula:

$$\text{Total expense percentage} = \frac{\text{Total expenses}}{\text{Net sales}} \times \frac{100}{1}$$

	2016		2017	
Total expense %	$= \dfrac{\$21{,}600}{\$180{,}000} \times \dfrac{100}{1}$		$= \dfrac{\$30{,}000}{\$240{,}000} \times \dfrac{100}{1}$	
	$= 12.0\%$		$= 12.5\%$	

This means that, in 2017, 12.5 cents of every sales dollar was used to meet expenses. We can also calculate the individual expense groups as a percentage of sales:

$$\textbf{Distribution cost percentage} \ = \ \frac{\textbf{Distribution costs}}{\textbf{Net sales}} \ \times \ \frac{\textbf{100}}{\textbf{1}}$$

	2016		2017	
Distribution cost %	$= \dfrac{\$9{,}000}{\$180{,}000} \times \dfrac{100}{1}$		$= \dfrac{\$14{,}400}{\$240{,}000} \times \dfrac{100}{1}$	
	$= 5.0\%$		$= 6.0\%$	

This means that, in 2017, 6.0 cents of every sales dollar was used to meet distribution costs.

$$\textbf{Administrative expense percentage} \ = \ \frac{\textbf{Administrative expenses}}{\textbf{Net sales}} \ \times \ \frac{\textbf{100}}{\textbf{1}}$$

	2016		2017	
Administrative expense %	$= \dfrac{\$7{,}200}{\$180{,}000} \times \dfrac{100}{1}$		$= \dfrac{\$8{,}400}{\$240{,}000} \times \dfrac{100}{1}$	
	$= 4.0\%$		$= 3.5\%$	

This means that, in 2017, 3.5 cents of every sales dollar was used to meet administrative expenses.

ISBN: 9780170211055

$$\text{Finance cost percentage} = \frac{\text{Finance costs}}{\text{Net sales}} \times \frac{100}{1}$$

	2016	2017
Finance cost %	$= \dfrac{\$5{,}400}{\$180{,}000} \times \dfrac{100}{1}$	$= \dfrac{\$7{,}200}{\$240{,}000} \times \dfrac{100}{1}$
	= 3.0%	= 3.0%

This means that, in 2017, 3.0 cents of every sales dollar was used to meet finance costs.

A summary of expense percentage calculations is shown in the table below.

		2016	2017
	Total expense %	**12.0%**	**12.5%**
comprising:	Distribution cost %	5.0%	6.0%
	Administrative expense %	4.0%	3.5%
	Finance cost %	3.0%	3.0%

ISBN: 9780170211055

Expenses – A Summary

- The **distribution cost percentage** has increased from 5.0% to 6.0% of sales. This is an unfavourable trend because distribution costs have increased in proportion to sales. However, we have seen that Steve deliberately increased his advertising expenditure to sell the new range of surfboards. It is just unfortunate that this increased expense did not produce the level of increase in sales that he had wanted.

- The **administrative expense percentage** has decreased from 4.0% to 3.5% of sales. This is a favourable trend because Steve has managed to increased sales without a corresponding increase in items such as rent.

- The **finance cost percentage** has remained at 3.0% of sales for both years. This is also a favourable trend because, although the dollar amount of these expenses has increased, the increase is in direct proportion to sales which means that the expenses have been controlled.

Looking at Profit

Profit is calculated from the formula:

> **Profit = Gross profit − Expenses**

The only ways to increase profit are to either:

- increase the gross profit; or
- decrease expenses.

Some trends are the result of voluntary business decisions. For example:

- Steve added the same dollar markup of $200 to each *Piha* surfboard this year as he had added to the *Takapuna* surfboards he sold last year. He may have been able to add a higher markup and still sell the same number of units. However, when deciding on a markup percentage it is important to check the prices that other businesses are charging to make sure that your price is competitive. If the price is too high, customers will buy from somewhere else.

- Steve decided to spend more on advertising because he was selling the new *Piha* surfboards this year. He really had no choice about doing this if he was to try and attract a different type of customer. The increased distribution costs were therefore a direct result of his decision to change the type of surfboard he was selling.

Other trends may be forced on a business by the market-place. For example:

- Increased competition may force a business to reduce its markup and thus lower the selling price.

- Sometimes suppliers may charge more for their goods, but the business may not be able to pass on these increases to customers without losing trade.

- Increased charges for expenses such as interest on borrowings, rent, telephone calls and electricity are also outside the control of the business.

ISBN: 9780170211055

Most business owners are interested in the profit more than anything else in their financial statements. This is because profit represents the return on their investment in the business.

The profit percentage is calculated from the following formula:

$$\text{Profit percentage} = \frac{\text{Profit}}{\text{Net sales}} \times \frac{100}{1}$$

	2016	2017
Profit %	$= \dfrac{\$38,400}{\$180,000} \times \dfrac{100}{1}$	$= \dfrac{\$30,000}{\$240,000} \times \dfrac{100}{1}$
	$= 21.3\%$	$= 12.5\%$

This means that, in 2017, 12.5 cents of every sales dollar was left after meeting all expenses. This amount represents the return to Brad, the owner.

Consider this example:

	2018	2019
Sales	$100,000	$150,000
Profit	$20,000	$22,500
Profit %	20.0%	15.0%

The profit percentage has fallen from 20.0% in 2018 to 15.0% in 2019. If we looked at the percentages on their own, we would conclude that the trend was unfavourable. However, the actual profit has increased from $20,000 to $22,500. This is a favourable trend. Which trend is more important – the dollar figure or the percentage?

The profit in dollar terms is higher in 2019. Even though the profit percentage has fallen, the owner is better off than in 2018. We must be very careful not to jump to conclusions when we are looking at percentages. The dollar figures are actually more important.

Warning!

Do not draw conclusions from trends in the *percentages* without looking at the *dollar figures* as well.

ISBN: 9780170211055

Summary of Profitability Measures

A summary of the percentages we have calculated for *Surf's Up!* is shown below.

	2016		2017	
	$	% sales	$	% sales
Sales	$180,000	100.0	$240,000	100.0
Cost of goods sold	120,000	66.7	180,000	75.0
Gross profit	60,000	33.3	60,000	25.0
Distribution costs	9,000	5.0	14,400	6.0
Administrative expenses	7,200	4.0	8,400	3.5
Finance costs	5,400	3.0	7,200	3.0
Total expenses	21,600	12.0	30,000	12.5
Profit	$38,400	21.3	$30,000	12.5

Examining the table leads us to the following conclusions:

- The profit decreased from $38,400 in 2016 to $30,000 in 2017. The profit percentage also decreased – from 21.3% of sales in 2016 to 12.5% in 2017. Both of these trends are *unfavourable*.

- Steve decided to sell a new type of surfboard this year. Although the total sales increased in dollar terms, the total gross profit stayed at $60,000 each year. Steve has reduced the markup percentage and thus the gross profit percentage. These trends are *unfavourable*.

- The total dollar figure for expenses increased from $21,600 in 2016 to $30,000 in 2017. This was an increase of $8,400 in total expenses, without a corresponding increase in the dollar amount of the gross profit. This is an *unfavourable* trend overall.

- Distribution costs increased from $9,000 in 2016 to $14,400 in 2017. The distribution cost percentage increased from 5.0% to 6.0%. This trend is *unfavourable* because the distribution costs increased by a greater proportion than sales.

- Administrative expenses increased from $7,200 in 2016 to $8,400 in 2017. The administrative expense percentage decreased from 4.0% to 3.5% of sales. This is a *favourable* trend because the expenses increased by a smaller proportion than sales.

- Finance costs increased from 5,400 in 2016 to $7,200 in 2017. However the finance cost percentage remained the same. This is a *favourable* trend because the expenses increased in the same proportion as sales.

ISBN: 9780170211055

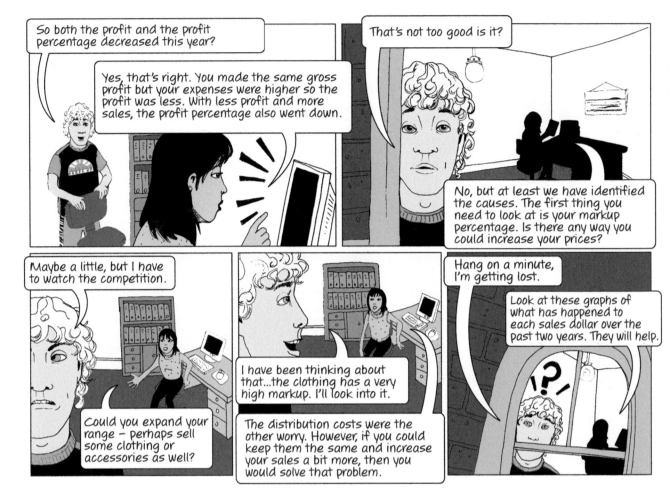

The operating results per dollar of sales for *Surf's Up!* are shown in the pie charts below.

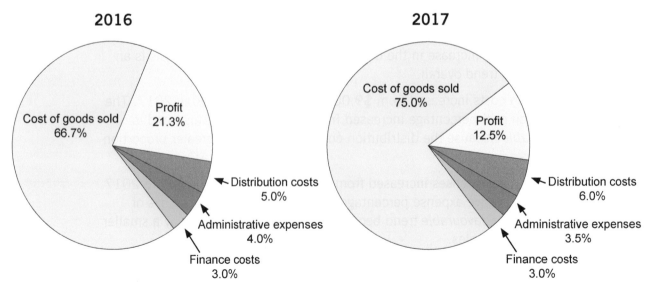

There is no 'ideal' profit percentage for any particular business. Just like the gross profit percentage, it is the *trend* which is important. We must take care to examine the dollar figures as well as the percentages. Any changes in the trends should always be investigated.

Accounting – A Beginning

ISBN: 9780170211055

Activities

1

This chapter has examined the financial performance and profitability of *Surf's Up!*. The questions below relate to this case study.

DO THIS!

Answer the following questions:
a State **one** reason for the trend in the gross profit percentage.
b Fully explain why the distribution cost percentage increased.
c The administrative expense percentage in 2017 was 3.5%. Explain what this means.
d The finance cost percentage was 3.0% in both 2016 and 2017. Explain why this is a *favourable* trend.
e Explain why is it important for Brad to keep strict control over business expenses.
f Identify **two** factors which affect the profit for any business.
g State **one** reason for the decrease in the profit percentage in 2017.
h Explain what would happen to Brad's equity if the current trend in profit continued into the future.

2 *Greater Garden Supplies* adds a markup of 25% on cost to all the goods it sells. In the year ended 30 June 2018, the cost of goods sold was $250,000. As a percentage of sales, the various classes of expenses were:

Distribution costs	5%
Administrative expenses	8%
Finance costs	3%.

DO THIS!

a Calculate the gross profit for the year.
b Prepare the income statement for the year ended 30 June 2018.
c Calculate the
  i gross profit percentage   ii profit percentage.

3 This table shows the operating results of *Kerry's Komputers* for the past three years:

	2016	2017	2018
Sales	$100,000	$120,000	$120,000
Gross profit	60,000	75,000	60,000
Profit for the year	20,000	25,000	10,000

ISBN: 9780170211055

DO THIS!

a Calculate the total expenses for each year.
b Calculate the percentage change from 2017 to 2018 for the
  i gross profit   **ii** profit.
c Calculate the following percentages for each year:
  i gross profit percentage
  ii total expense percentage
  iii profit percentage.
d Suggest **one** reason for the trend in the gross profit percentage from 2017 to 2018.

 4 The diagram below represents each sales dollar of *Dave's Dive Shop* for the year ended 31 March 2016. The total sales for the year were $400,000.

In the year to 31 March 2017 the markup percentage was 100% and profit was 30% of sales. Sales were $300,000 and the gross profit percentage was 50%.

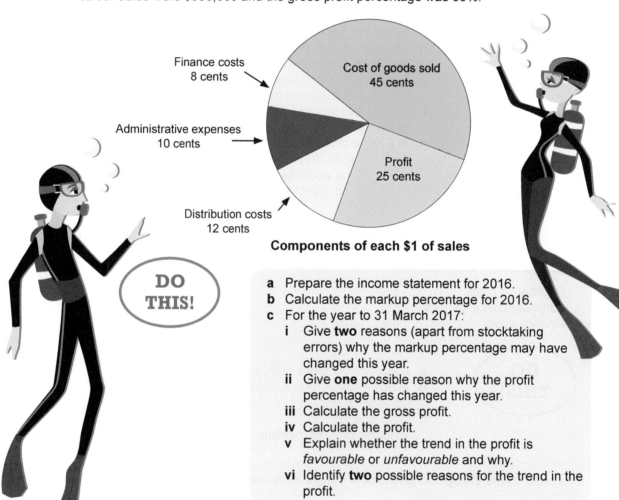

Finance costs
8 cents

Cost of goods sold
45 cents

Administrative expenses
10 cents

Profit
25 cents

Distribution costs
12 cents

Components of each $1 of sales

DO THIS!

a Prepare the income statement for 2016.
b Calculate the markup percentage for 2016.
c For the year to 31 March 2017:
  i Give **two** reasons (apart from stocktaking errors) why the markup percentage may have changed this year.
  ii Give **one** possible reason why the profit percentage has changed this year.
  iii Calculate the gross profit.
  iv Calculate the profit.
  v Explain whether the trend in the profit is *favourable* or *unfavourable* and why.
  vi Identify **two** possible reasons for the trend in the profit.

 5 The income statement on the next page was prepared for *Modern Designz Furniture* for the year ended 31 December 2019. The owner of the business, Terry Able, has given you the following information relating to the business accounts for the year ended 31 December 2020:

- Sales increased by 15%
- Cost of goods sold increased by 20%
- Administrative expenses increased by $3,500.
- Finance costs decreased by 25%.
- Distribution costs increased by 20%

ISBN: 9780170211055

Modern Designz Furniture Income Statement for the year ended 31 December 2019		
Revenue	$	$
Sales		210,000
Less: Cost of goods sold		140,000
Gross profit		70,000
Less: **Expenses**		
Distribution costs	10,500	
Administrative expenses	21,000	
Finance costs	2,800	
Total expenses		34,300
Profit for the year		$35,700

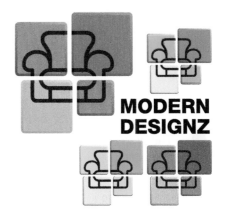

MODERN
DESIGNZ

DO THIS!

Answer the following questions:
a Prepare the income statement for *Modern Designz Furniture* for the year ended 31 December 2020.
b Calculate the following percentages for each year:
 i markup percentage
 ii gross profit percentage
 iii distribution cost percentage
 iv administrative expense percentage
 v finance cost percentage
 vi total expense percentage
 vii profit percentage.
c Explain the meaning of the result you have calculated for the administrative expense percentage in 2019.
d Identify **one** *satisfactory* trend and explain why it is satisfactory.
e Identify **one** *unsatisfactory* trend and explain why it is unsatisfactory.
f Suggest a possible explanation for the trend in the gross profit percentage.
g Suggest a possible explanation for the trend in the finance cost percentage.

 6

The table below shows the income statements of *Lyn's Luxury Lingerie* for the years 2017 and 2018, together with some percentage information. Some of the information in the table is missing.

	2017 $	2018 $	Percentage change 2017 to 2018
Sales	120,000	150,000	(i)
Less: Cost of goods sold	48,000	(ii)	12.5%
Gross profit	(iii)	(iv)	(v)
Less: Expenses			
Distribution costs	18,000	24,000	(vi)
Administrative expenses	20,000	(vii)	Nil
Finance costs	4,000	2,500	(viii)
Total expenses	42,000	(ix)	(x)
Profit for the year	(xi)	(xii)	65.0%

a Calculate the missing information **i** to **xii** in the table.
b For each of the following, suggest one reason for the trend between 2017 and 2018:
   i   gross profit   iii administrative expenses
   ii distribution costs   iv finance costs.
c Comment on Lyn's control over total expenses during the year. *Fully justify* your opinion by referring to the figures in the table.

 The graph below shows the sales, gross profit and profit of *Andrews Appliances* for the past five years.

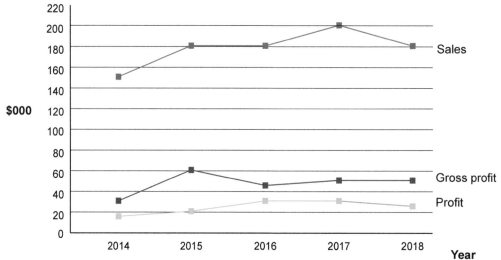

You had prepared the graph from an Excel® spreadsheet that was set out as follows:

	A	B	C	D	E	F
1		**2014**	**2015**	**2016**	**2017**	**2018**
2	Sales					
3	Cost of goods sold					
4	Gross profit					
5	Expenses					
6	Profit					

Unfortunately, after you had printed the graph, you accidentally closed the file without saving the data. You had wanted to change the graph to a column graph but now you have to reconstruct the spreadsheet before you can continue. You remember that all the figures were multiples of 5.

a Use the graph to enter the missing information in the spreadsheet.
b Describe the trends in the dollar amounts of the following over the five-year period:
   i   sales   iii total expenses
   ii gross profit   iv profit
c Calculate the following percentages for each year:
   i   gross profit percentage   iii total expense percentage
   ii markup percentage   iv profit percentage.
d Identify **one** *favourable* trend and give a possible reason for this trend.
e Identify **one** *unfavourable* trend and give a possible reason for this trend.

Accounting – A Beginning   ISBN: 9780170211055

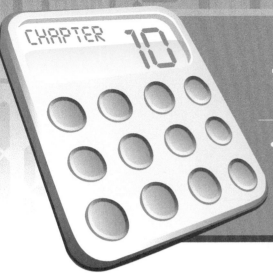

Analysing Financial Position

- Looking at Liquidity
- Financial Structure
- Service Organisations

The statement of financial position is like a snapshot which shows the financial structure of a business on one particular day. Some firms may 'window-dress' their statements of financial position to make the business appear to have a better financial structure than it really has. For example, a sale just before the end of the reporting period will improve the cash level and reduce inventory. However, we usually have to rely on the information given in the statement of financial position since we may have no other information to use for analysis.

Having analysed the income statement of *Surf's Up!*, Yu Ting turned to the statement of financial position. This statement is shown on the next page.

Looking at Liquidity

A business which is short of cash and cannot meet its short term obligations is said to have a *liquidity* problem. If it cannot pay its long term debts it is said to be *insolvent*. The business assets may have to be sold to pay the business debts. If the situation is serious enough, the owner may have to sell his or her personal assets as well and put the cash raised into the business.

ISBN: 9780170211055

Surf's Up!
Statement of Financial Position as at 31 March 2017

2016 $		$	$	$
	ASSETS			
	Non-current assets			
	Property, plant and equipment			
115,000	Total carrying amount (Note 1)			112,000
	Current assets			
22,500	Cash		—	
2,500	Accounts receivable		4,000	
30,000	Inventory		45,000	
55,000	Total current assets			49,000
$170,000	Total assets			$161,000
	EQUITY AND LIABILITIES			
	Equity			
91,600	Capital at beginning of the year		100,000	
38,400	Profit for the year		30,000	
(30,000)	Drawings for the year		(40,000)	
100,000	Capital at end of the year			90,000
	Non-current liabilities			
50,000	Mortgage (due 30 June 2026)		45,000	
	Current liabilities			
—	Bank overdraft (secured)	1,500		
18,500	Accounts payable	24,000		
1,500	GST payable	500		
20,000	Total current liabilities		26,000	
70,000	Total liabilities			71,000
$170,000	Total equity and liabilities			$161,000

Notes to the Statement of Financial Position

	1 *Property, plant and equipment*	
10,000	Shop fittings (net)	12,000
25,000	Van (net)	20,000
80,000	Premises (cost)	80,000
$115,000		$112,000

ISBN: 9780170211055

Working Capital and the Current Ratio

Working capital is one measure of business liquidity. Working capital is given by the formula:

$$\text{Working capital} = \text{Current assets} - \text{Current liabilities}$$

The working capital of *Surf's Up!* at 31 March 2017 is $23,000. This means that the business should have $23,000 in current assets left over after all current liabilities have been met in the next reporting period.

The liquidity of the business may also be measured by the **current ratio** which is given by the formula:

$$\text{Current ratio} = \frac{\text{Current assets}}{\text{Current liabilities}}$$

We can calculate the current ratio of *Surf's Up!* for 2016 and 2017 as follows:

		2016		2017
Current ratio	=	$\dfrac{\$55,000}{\$20,000}$	=	$\dfrac{\$49,000}{\$26,000}$
	=	2.75:1	=	1.88:1

In 2016, *Surf's Up!* had $2.75 of current assets with which to meet each dollar of current liabilities by the end of the reporting period, 31 March 2017. In 2017, this had fallen to $1.88 of current assets with which to meet each dollar of current liabilities due by 31 March 2018. Although the ratio has fallen, it would still appear to be satisfactory.

We must remember that, although the current ratio can be a useful measure of liquidity, we should also examine the individual current assets and current liabilities in the statement of financial position before drawing any definite conclusions. In the statement of financial position of *Surf's Up!*, we can see that although the firm has a satisfactory working capital and current ratio, it has no cash. The bank balance has fallen from $22,500 in 2016 to an overdraft of $1,500 in 2017.

Increasing or Decreasing Working Capital

We can **increase** working capital in two ways:

> *Either:* increase current assets
> *or:* decrease current liabilities.

Similarly, we can **decrease** working capital in two ways:

> *Either:* decrease current assets
> *or:* increase current liabilities.

Consider the following examples (ignore GST):

1   Received $300 in cash from accounts receivable

Current assets		Current liabilities		Working capital
Cash	+ $300	No change		No change
Accounts receivable	– $300			

In this case, one current asset is exchanged for another of equal amount. This means that there is no effect on working capital.

2   Sold inventory which had cost $80 for $100 cash

Current assets		Current liabilities		Working capital
Cash	+ $100	No change		+ $20
Inventory	– $80			

Working capital increases because a current asset which had cost $80 was exchanged for one of $100. Current assets have increased by $20.

3   Sold inventory which had cost $50 for $75 on credit

Current assets		Current liabilities		Working capital
Accounts receivable	+ $75	No change		+ $25
Inventory	– $50			

As in the previous example, one current asset (inventory of $50) was exchanged for another (accounts receivable of $75). Working capital increased by $25.

4   Paid accounts payable due, $150

Current assets		Current liabilities		Working capital
Cash	– $150	Accounts payable	– $150	No change

There is no effect on working capital because current assets and current liabilities both decreased by $150.

5   Bought inventory costing $250 on credit

Current assets		Current liabilities		Working capital
Inventory	+ $250	Accounts payable	+ $250	No change

Again there is no effect on working capital because current assets and current liabilities both increased by $250.

6   Owner contributes $5,000 cash to the business

Current assets		Current liabilities		Working capital
Cash	+ $5,000	No change		+ $5,000

In this case there is an increase in current assets of $5,000 and no effect on current liabilities. Working capital increases by $5,000.

Accounting – A Beginning

ISBN: 9780170211055

7 Borrowed $10,000 on mortgage

	Current assets	Current liabilities	Working capital
Cash	+ $10,000	No change	+ $10,000

Current assets have increased by $10,000. Since the mortgage is a non-current liability, it does not affect working capital. Working capital increases by $10,000.

8 Sold property, plant and equipment for $1,000 cash

	Current assets	Current liabilities	Working capital
Cash	+ $1,000	No change	+ $1,000

Current assets have increased by $1,000. Since property, plant and equipment are non-current assets that do not form part of working capital, the working capital increases by $1,000.

9 Owner takes inventory costing $50 for personal use

	Current assets	Current liabilities	Working capital
Inventory	– $50	No change	– $50

Working capital decreases by $50 because current assets have been withdrawn from the business. Current liabilities are unaffected.

10 Purchase of property, plant and equipment for $2,000 cash

	Current assets	Current liabilities	Working capital
Cash	– $2,000	No change	– $2,000

Working capital decreases by $2,000 because current assets have been exchanged for property, plant and equipment which are non-current assets. Non-current assets do not affect working capital.

11 Repayment of non-current liability, $500

	Current assets	Current liabilities	Working capital
Cash	– $500	No change	– $500

Working capital decreases because current assets have been used to reduce non-current liabilities. Non-current liabilities do not affect working capital.

Summary

The examples above show that the working capital of a firm can be increased by any of the following:

- selling inventory at a profit
- the owner investing cash in the business
- borrowing long term
- selling non-current assets.

Any one of these may not necessarily be a wise decision for a particular firm. The choice of how to increase working capital depends on the business concerned. For example, selling property, plant and equipment would increase cash but could also leave no means of carrying on business operations. Borrowing long term (increasing non-current liabilities) could cause cash flow problems in the future when repayments have to be made.

Activities

1 The table below shows the relationship between current assets, current liabilities and working capital. Some of the information is missing.

	Current assets $	Current liabilities $	Working capital $	Current ratio
a	100,000	80,000		
b	75,000		25,000	
c	6,000		2,000	
d		15,000	30,000	
e		2,000	8,000	
f	14,400	3,600		
g		10,000	(2,000)	
h	12,000	16,000		
i	10,000		(1,000)	

DO THIS!   Calculate the missing figures and complete the table.

2 The table below shows some transactions and their effect on working capital.

	Transaction	Current assets $	Current liabilities $	Working capital $
a	Paid wages, $500	– $500	No change	– $500
b	Owner contributed $3,000 cash to the business			
c	Paid suppliers $800 on account			
d	Received $1,200 on account from accounts receivable			
e	Bought new computer costing $3,500 for cash			
f	Repaid $1,000 off the mortgage			
g	Received invoice for electricity of $200			
h	Received long term loan of $10,000 from the bank			
i	Sold old furniture for $600 cash			
j	Paid suppliers $750 on account from personal bank account			
k	Owner took goods which had cost $50 for personal use			
l	Charged depreciation of $1,000			

DO THIS!   Complete the table. The first one has been done for you. (Ignore GST.)

ISBN: 9780170211055

The Liquid Ratio

As we have learnt earlier, the current ratio provides a measure of the *short term* liquidity of the business. By *short term*, we mean the next reporting period (usually one year). However, for a business to survive, it must be able to meet its debts on a month-to-month basis. The **liquid ratio** provides a measure of *immediate* liquidity. In other words, it tells us whether or not a business will be able to meet its debts *within the next month or so*.

If we wish to calculate immediate liquidity, we must consider only those current assets which we expect to turn into cash in the next month. We call these **quick assets**. We include any cash already on hand, accounts receivable (because we would expect to collect these within the next month and accrued revenue (as long as we expect to collect it within a month). We would **not** include inventory because, even if we sell it within a month it is likely to turn into accounts receivable (for a credit sale) and it will be about two months before we collect the cash. We would **not** include any supplies on hand, for example cleaning supplies or stationery, because we intend to use those and they are not going to turn into cash at all. Nor would we include prepayments because these are expenses which have been paid in advance and will be used up by the business, not refunded.

In a similar fashion, we would consider only those current liabilities which *must be paid within the next month*. We call these **quick liabilities**. If a bank overdraft was secured against the firm's assets, we would normally not be expected to repay it in the next month and could exclude it from our calculations. Income received in advance is not repaid in cash, so is not a quick liability. Many small businesses pay their GST every six months, so GST is not always a quick liability. However, in this chapter we will assume that the GST is payable within a month of the end of the reporting period.

There are two ways of calculating the liquid ratio. The first method involves identifying the quick assets and quick liabilities. For *Surf's Up!*, these are as follows (refer to the statement of financial position on page 278):

	2016	2017
Quick Assets		
Cash	$22,500	$ —
Accounts receivable	2,500	4,000
	$25,000	$4,000

	2016	2017
Quick Liabilities		
Accounts payable	$18,500	$24,000
GST payable	1,500	500
	$20,000	$24,500

The liquid ratio is given by the formula:

$$\text{Liquid ratio} = \frac{\text{Quick assets}}{\text{Quick liabilities}}$$

ISBN: 9780170211055

		2016		2017
Liquid ratio	=	$\dfrac{\$25{,}000}{\$20{,}000}$	=	$\dfrac{\$4{,}000}{\$24{,}500}$
	=	1.25:1	=	0.16:1

These calculations show that, in 2016, the firm had $1.25 in cash or equivalents to pay each dollar of current liabilities that were due in the next month or so, by 30 April 2016. In 2017, it had only 16 cents to meet each dollar of immediate debt, due by 30 April 2017. This is a very serious situation indeed. Depending on the overdraft limit allowed by the bank, the firm may quite possibly have to sell some property, plant and equipment to meet these debts.

Another formula

The liquid ratio is sometimes calculated using the following formula:

$$\text{Liquid ratio} = \frac{\text{Current assets} - (\text{inventory} + \text{prepayments})}{\text{Current liabilities} - \text{secured bank overdraft}}$$

This formula gives the same result as the earlier formula, *provided that* the firm has no income received in advance. The calculations for *Surf's Up!* using this formula are:

		2016		2017
Liquid ratio	=	$\dfrac{\$55{,}000 - 30{,}000}{\$20{,}000}$	=	$\dfrac{\$49{,}000 - 45{,}000}{\$26{,}000 - 1{,}500}$
	=	1.25:1	=	0.16:1

Where did the cash go?

If we look at the statement of financial position, it is clear that the bank balance went from $22,500 in 2016 to an overdraft of $1,500 in 2017. This means that *Surf's Up!* has spent $24,000 more cash than it received during the year. A closer look at the statement of financial position shows the following:

- Inventory has increased by $15,000, from $30,000 in 2016 to $45,000 in 2017. However accounts payable has increased by only $5,500 (from $18,500 to $24,000). This means that $9,500 of the inventory has been bought with cash.

ISBN: 9780170211055

- Shop fittings have increased from $10,000 in 2016 to $12,000 in 2017. This has used $2,000 additional cash.

- The mortgage has been reduced by $5,000, from $50,000 in 2016 to $45,000 in 2017.

- Steve has taken drawings of $40,000.

Comparing the statements of financial position for the two years gives us some idea as to where the extra cash has gone. It is also possible to prepare another financial statement, the **statement of cash flows**, that shows all the sources and uses of cash for the period. (Note: We do not learn to prepare this statement in this course.)

Whilst the financial statements can provide a picture of business events during the reporting period, it is necessary to interview the owner to establish the reasons behind those events. When a business is in financial difficulty, as is the case for *Surf's Up!*, a discussion with the owner will usually establish exactly what happened to cause the problem and enable potential solutions to be worked out.

- When we calculated the current ratio, it was 2.75:1 in 2016 and 1.88:1 in 2017. These ratios both appeared to be satisfactory.

- When we calculated the liquid ratio, we found that the ratio in 2017 was most unsatisfactory. The firm has only 16 cents to pay each dollar of liabilities that are due in the next month or so. This was because of the high level of inventory on hand which would not be turned into cash immediately.

- This shows that we must always look at the current and liquid ratios together. We cannot draw conclusions from the current ratio on its own.

Why is *Surf's Up!* short of cash?

The current ratio shows that *Surf's Up!* should have $1.88 of current assets to pay each $1 of current liabilities by the end of the next reporting period. However, the liquid ratio shows that only 16 cents is available to meet each dollar of debts that are due immediately.

Previously, we used the financial statements to establish some potential reasons for the cash shortage. Then we interviewed Steve to find out exactly what reasoning lay behind the decisions he had made. The shortage of cash has arisen because:

Warning!

Do not draw conclusions from trends in the *current ratio* without looking at the *liquid ratio* as well.

- Steve increased the levels of inventory on hand by $15,000, from $30,000 in 2016 to $45,000 in 2017. He bought more surfboards than he needed because they were more expensive than the old ones and by buying more he received a discount.

- Steve also has cash tied up in old models of surfboard that are not selling because the store down the road is selling them at a lower price.

- Accounts receivable have also increased by $1,500.

- Steve's drawings increased by $10,000 even though the profit decreased. He bought a new car and took a holiday this year.

- The business purchased more shop fittings for $2,000 to display the new boards and paid $5,000 off the mortgage.

What could Steve do now?

Steve needs to find $24,500 in cash to pay his accounts payable and GST within the next month. How can he do this? Yu Ting has suggested that he reduce the price of the old surfboards and clear them from the shelves. However, this is unlikely to raise enough cash to pay all the debts. Other things Steve could do are:

- Collect all the accounts receivable

- Sell off the old shop fittings that won't be needed when he sells excess stock

- Ask the bank manager for an increase in the bank overdraft or mortgage

- Discuss the situation with the suppliers and ask for more time to pay

- Invest more personal cash in the business by, for example, selling the new car.

Activities

1 The following information has been extracted from the statement of financial position of *Gardening Supplies*:

Accounts receivable	$30,000
Accounts payable	40,000
Prepayments	2,000
Inventory	80,000
GST payable	5,000
Bank overdraft (secured)	20,000

The creditors of *Gardening Supplies* are beginning to bring pressure for payment of their accounts.

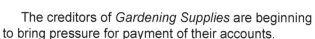

DO THIS!

a Calculate the following:
  i Working capital
  ii Current ratio
  iii Liquid ratio.
b For each of **i** to **iii** in **a** above, write a sentence explaining the meaning of your calculation.
c State **two** actions that the owner could take to improve the liquidity position of the business.

2 The following information has been extracted from the statements of financial position of four different businesses at 30 June 2017:

Business	a	b	c	d
	$	$	$	$
Current Assets				
Bank	13,000	55,000	—	—
Accounts receivable	8,000	120,000	8,000	16,000
Inventory	13,500	123,000	12,000	5,000
Prepayments	500	2,000	1,000	500
	$35,000	$300,000	$21,000	$21,500
Current Liabilities				
Bank overdraft	—	—	5,000	2,000
GST payable	500	20,000	1,500	750
Accounts payable	12,000	98,000	11,000	8,000
Accrued expenses	1,500	2,000	—	—
	$14,000	$120,000	$17,500	$10,750

The bank overdrafts are unsecured.

DO THIS!

For each of the businesses **a** to **d** above
  i Calculate the working capital.
  ii Calculate the current ratio.
  iii Calculate the liquid ratio.
  iv Write one or two sentences giving your opinion of the liquidity position of the business, based on the information you have been given and your calculations.

3 The following balances have been extracted from the ledger of a local garage:

Accounts receivable	$4,500	Accounts payable	$2,000
Inventory of parts	3,600	Prepayments	300
Tools and equipment	7,500	Bank overdraft (secured)	1,500
GST payable	500	Bank loan (5 years)	10,000

DO THIS!

a Calculate the working capital.
b Calculate the current ratio and explain the meaning of this calculation.
c State whether or not the current ratio is satisfactory and explain why.
d Calculate the liquid ratio and explain the meaning of this calculation.
e State whether or not the liquid ratio is satisfactory and explain why.

4 A business has a current ratio of 4.5:1 and a liquid ratio of 3.0:1.

DO THIS!

a Explain the meaning of the current ratio.
b Explain the meaning of the liquid ratio.
c Give **one** reason why these ratios would be considered *satisfactory*.
d Give **one** reason why these ratios would be considered *unsatisfactory*.
e Suggest **one** piece of advice to the business owner about managing the liquidity of this business.

5 Copy and complete the following sentences:

a If current assets are greater than current liabilities, then working capital will be
.... and the current ratio will be .... 1:1.
(positive/negative/zero)   (greater than/equal to/less than)

b If current assets equal current liabilities, then working capital will be
.... and the current ratio will be .... 1:1.
(positive/negative/zero)   (greater than/equal to/less than)

c If current assets are less than current liabilities, then working capital will be
.... and the current ratio will be .... 1:1.
(positive/negative/zero)   (greater than/equal to/less than)

6 The following are the assets and liabilities of *Video Wholesalers*:

ASSETS		LIABILITIES	
Accounts receivable	$25,000	Bank overdraft (secured)	5,000
Inventory	14,000	Accounts payable	13,500
Prepayments	1,000	GST payable	1,500
Property, plant and equipment	60,000	Non-current liabilities	20,000

DO THIS!

a Calculate the equity.
b Calculate the current ratio and explain the meaning of this calculation.
c State whether or not the current ratio is satisfactory and explain why.
d Calculate the liquid ratio and explain the meaning of this calculation.
e State whether or not the liquid ratio is satisfactory and explain why.

ISBN: 9780170211055

Financial Structure

In Chapter 2 we met the equity ratio, which shows the proportion of the business assets financed by the proprietor or owner of the business. The equity ratio is given by the formula:

$$\text{Equity ratio} = \frac{\text{Equity}}{\text{Total assets}}$$

The equity ratio is very important because it indicates the extent of the proprietor's equity or share of the business. If the ratio is less than 0.5:1 it means that the creditors have more of a financial interest in the business than the owner has. This is not a good state of affairs because, if the business became unable to meet its debts on time, the creditors could attempt to take over its assets.

Consider the following examples:

1

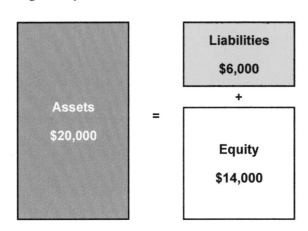

For this firm, the equity ratio is

$$\text{Equity ratio} = \frac{\$14,000}{\$20,000} = 0.70:1$$

This means that 70% of the business assets have been financed by the owner and 30% have been financed by external creditors. The business is in a secure position.

2

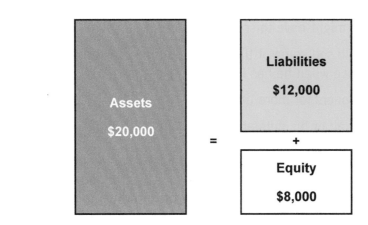

ISBN: 9780170211055

For this firm, the equity ratio is

$$\text{Equity ratio} \quad = \quad \frac{\$8,000}{\$20,000} \quad = \quad 0.40{:}1$$

This business is at risk. The liabilities represent 60% of the business assets and the equity is only 40%. If the business cannot meet its debts on time, creditors may bring pressure for payment and the owner may have to sell some of the business assets to meet their demands. If this were to happen, the business may not be able to continue operating.

		2016		2017
Equity ratio	=	$\dfrac{\$100,000}{\$170,000}$	=	$\dfrac{\$90,000}{\$161,000}$
	=	0.59:1	=	0.56:1

The equity ratio of *Surf's Up!* has fallen slightly from 0.59:1 in 2016 to 0.56:1 in 2017. This is not a very good trend as it is now becoming marginal. It would not be a good idea for Steve to try to borrow much more because he would be increasing the exposure of his business to creditors.

What are Steve's options?

We established in the previous section that *Surf's Up!* requires $24,000 more cash urgently and explored some possible options for raising the cash. However, we have now established that Steve is unlikely to be able to borrow any more from the bank because his equity ratio is marginal at 0.56:1. This illustrates the importance of looking at **all** the ratios before drawing conclusions or making recommendations. It is still possible for Steve to do one or all of the following:

- He could sell some of his out-of-date inventory (last year's surfboards) at a cheaper price. Although he may have to take a loss on these boards, he would at least convert them into cash which he could use to pay some of his debts.

- He could invest more of his own cash into the business. This would depend on whether or not he had personal sources of cash and was willing to increase his business risk. He might have to sell the new car if he has no other cash.

- The business could sell some of the old shop fittings since he may not need as much storage space when he has less stock.

- He could ask suppliers for more time to pay.

- He should collect all of his outstanding accounts receivable.

What, then, should Steve do? Probably the best answer is a combination of all of the above. No single one of these suggestions will solve the immediate problem on its own. In the medium term, he should reduce his drawings to a level less than profit so that his equity in the business is not eroded.

Accounting – A Beginning

ISBN: 9780170211055

Activities

1 The following ratios have been calculated from the statement of financial position of a local business:

Current ratio   2.0:1
Liquid ratio   0.9:1
Equity ratio   0.4:1.

DO THIS!

a Write a sentence for each ratio explaining what it means.
b State whether or not each ratio is satisfactory and explain why.
c State **one** problem that this business is likely to be experiencing.
d Suggest **one** way in which the owner might overcome this problem.

2 The following information has been extracted from the statement of financial position of Dr Ina Mill:

	2017	2018
Current assets	$ 4,500	$ 1,500
Current liabilities	3,000	1,500
Non-current assets	20,000	37,500
Non-current liabilities	7,500	20,000

DO THIS!

a For each year, calculate the following:
  i Equity   **ii** Equity ratio   **iii** Current ratio.
b Explain the meaning of the equity ratio you have calculated for 2018.
c Give **one** possible explanation for the change in the equity ratio.
d Explain the meaning of the current ratio you have calculated for 2018.
e Identify **one** problem that Dr Mill may experience in the next year and explain your reasoning.

3 The following information has been extracted from the statement of financial position of *Organic Biofoods*:

Total assets $200,000
Non-current assets   170,000
Non-current liabilities 70,000
Equity ratio   0.6:1

DO THIS!

a Calculate the following:
  i equity
  ii total liabilities
  iii total current assets
  iv total current liabilities
  v working capital.
  vi current ratio.
b State whether or not the current ratio is satisfactory and explain your reasoning.

PART A

Sailaway Surfboards had the following assets at 31 March 2018:

Cash at bank	$3,000	Inventory	$32,000
Accounts receivable	15,000	Equipment (cost)	50,000

The total liabilities and equity of the business are shown in the graph below.

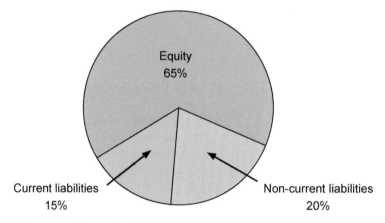

The only current liabilities of the business are accounts payable. The non-current liability is a bank loan which is due for repayment on 31 March 2022.

DO THIS!

a Prepare a statement of financial position for the firm as at 31 March 2018.
b Calculate the following ratios:
  i Current ratio
  ii Liquid ratio
  iii Equity ratio.
c Explain the meaning of **each** of the ratios you calculated in **b** above.
d State whether or not you consider **each** of the ratios you have calculated in **b** above is satisfactory or not and why.

PART B

The following analysis measures had been calculated for *Sailaway Surfboards* at 31 March 2017:

Current ratio	1.75:1
Liquid ratio	1.50:1
Equity ratio	0.60:1

The store's owner is pleased with the trend in the current ratio but concerned that the liquid ratio might become too low if the trend continues.

DO THIS!

a Suggest a likely explanation for the change in the current ratio from 2017 to 2018. You should also refer to the liquid ratio in your answer.
b Explain the meaning of a liquid ratio of 1.5:1.
c Explain why the owner would be concerned that the liquid ratio may become too low. You should explain the consequences of a low liquid ratio in your answer.
d Suggest a likely explanation for the change in the equity ratio from 2017 to 2018.
e Explain whether or not you consider the equity ratio of 0.60:1 is satisfactory and why.

Accounting – A Beginning

ISBN: 9780170211055

Service Organisations

In this chapter so far we have examined the accounts for *Surf's Up!*, which is a trading organisation. The analysis and interpretation of the financial statements for service organisations is almost the same. There are two exceptions:

- Service organisations have no cost of goods sold, so there is no gross profit percentage or markup percentage.

- Service organisations have no inventory. This often means that there is only a small difference between the values calculated for the current and liquid ratios.

Service organisations tend to have a higher profit percentage than trading organisations.

Consider the following example:

Greener Gardens is a lawnmowing and landscaping service. The financial statements for the year to 31 March 2018 are shown below.

Greener Gardens
Income Statement for the year ended 31 March 2018

2017 $		$	$	$
	Revenue			
45,000	Fees			50,000
	Less: **Expenses**			
	Gardening expenses			
800	Advertising	1,200		
900	Depreciation on equipment	1,500		
4,000	Depreciation on van	4,000		
9,000	Petrol and oil	10,800		
2,700	Repairs and maintenance	3,000		
17,400			20,500	
	Administrative expenses			
600	Accountancy fees	750		
1,400	Cellphone expenses	1,750		
2,000			2,500	
19,400	Total expenses			23,000
$25,600	Profit for the year			$27,000

Greener Gardens
Statement of Financial Position as at 31 March 2018

2017 $		$	$	$
	ASSETS			
	Non-current assets			
	Property, plant and equipment			
13,000	Total carrying amount (Note 1)		11,500	
	Investment			
5,000	Term deposit (3 years, 6%)		5,000	
18,000	Total non-current assets			16,500
	Current assets			
1,000	Cash		4,000	
2,500	Accounts receivable		3,000	
3,500	Total current assets			7,000
$21,500	Total assets			$23,500
	EQUITY AND LIABILITIES			
	Equity			
12,400	Capital at beginning of the year		18,000	
25,600	Profit for the year		27,000	
(20,000)	Drawings for the year		(25,000)	
18,000	Capital at end of the year			20,000
	Current liabilities			
1,800	Accounts payable	2,000		
1,700	GST payable	1,500		
3,500	Total liabilities			3,500
$21,500	Total equity and liabilities			$23,500
	Notes to the Statement of Financial Position			
	1 *Property, plant and equipment*			
1,000	Mowers and equipment (net)			3,500
12,000	Van (net)			8,000
$13,000				$11,500

Analysing the Income Statement

If we measure the profit from services as a percentage of the total income earned from providing those services, we can get an idea of the amount of service income which must be earned in order to produce a certain level of profit. We will call this calculation the profit percentage. It is calculated from the formula:

$$\text{Profit percentage} = \frac{\text{Profit}}{\text{Service revenue}} \times \frac{100}{1}$$

Accounting – A Beginning   ISBN: 9780170211055

We are interested in this profit from services percentage because we wish to compare the results from providing services from one reporting period to the next.

Greener Gardens

Profit %

	2017		2018
$= \dfrac{\$25,600}{\$45,000} \times \dfrac{100}{1}$		$= \dfrac{\$27,000}{\$50,000} \times \dfrac{100}{1}$	
$= 56.9\%$		$= 54.0\%$	

This percentage means that for every $1 of service revenue earned in 2018, 54.0 cents is left as a return to the owner after meeting the expenses of earning that revenue.

The profit percentage has fallen marginally in 2018. However fees have increased and the dollar amount of profit has also increased so we should not be too concerned about the small decrease in the profit percentage.

It is also useful to calculate total service expenses as a percentage of service revenue. We can calculate the total expense percentage from the following formula:

$$\text{Total expense percentage} = \frac{\text{Total expenses}}{\text{Service revenue}} \times \frac{100}{1}$$

Greener Gardens

Total expense %

	2017		2018
$= \dfrac{\$19,400}{\$45,000} \times \dfrac{100}{1}$		$= \dfrac{\$23,000}{\$50,000} \times \dfrac{100}{1}$	
$= 43.1\%$		$= 46.0\%$	

This percentage means that for every $1 of service revenue earned in 2018, 46.0 cents will be used to meet the expenses of earning that revenue.

The total expense percentage has increased marginally in 2018. This explains the decrease in the profit percentage. However, while it is an unfavourable trend we should not be too concerned about it unless it continues into the future. We must remember that the dollar amount of the profit has increased.

It is also possible to calculate each type of expense as a percentage of service revenue. For *Greener Gardens*, the service expenses were subdivided into *Gardening expenses* and *Administrative expenses*. Each of these expenses can be represented as a percentage of service revenue by using the following formulae:

ISBN: 9780170211055

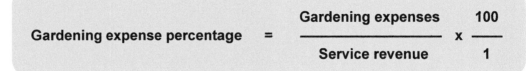

$$\text{Gardening expense percentage} = \frac{\text{Gardening expenses}}{\text{Service revenue}} \times \frac{100}{1}$$

Greener Gardens

		2017				2018	
Gardening expense %	$=$	$\dfrac{\$17{,}400}{\$45{,}000}$	$\times \dfrac{100}{1}$	$=$	$\dfrac{\$20{,}500}{\$50{,}000}$	$\times \dfrac{100}{1}$
	$= 38.7\%$			$= 41.0\%$		

This means that, in 2018, 41.0 cents in every dollar of service revenue was used to meet gardening and vehicle expenses. This is an increase of 2.3 cents since 2017. If we examine the income statement, we can see that there were increases in advertising, petrol and oil expense and depreciation on equipment.

Advertising has increased by 50% – from $800 in 2017 to $1,200 in 2018. A possible explanation for this trend is that advertising expenses were increased to try and improve income. While this has worked to some extent, (gardening fees increased from $45,000 to $50,000), the amount of the increase is not in proportion to the increase in advertising expenses.

The increase in petrol and oil may either be due to a price increase or to the increased level of activity (more lawns mowed). If we calculate the percentage change for petrol and oil, we may be able to identify a reason. Petrol and oil increased from $9,000 in 2017 to $10,800 in 2018. This is a 20% increase. Gardening fees increased from $45,000 to $50,000, which is an increase of 11.1%. It would seem that a price increase could be the reason for the increased petrol and oil expense.

The depreciation on equipment has increased because the firm has purchased a new mower. The statement of financial position shows an increase in equipment of $4,000 in 2018. (If the new mower uses more petrol than the old ones, this could also explain the reason for the increase in the petrol and oil expense.)

$$\text{Administrative expense percentage} = \frac{\text{Administrative expenses}}{\text{Service revenue}} \times \frac{100}{1}$$

		2017				2018	
Administrative expense %	$=$	$\dfrac{\$2{,}000}{\$45{,}000}$	$\times \dfrac{100}{1}$	$=$	$\dfrac{\$2{,}500}{\$50{,}000}$	$\times \dfrac{100}{1}$
	$= 4.4\%$			$= 5.0\%$		

ISBN: 9780170211055

This means that, in 2018, 5.0 cents in every dollar of service revenue was used to meet administrative expenses. This is an increase of 0.6 cents since 2017. This is a very small increase and should not cause too much concern.

Profitability – A Summary

The percentages we have calculated for *Greener Gardens* are summarised in the table below.

	2017		2018	
	$	% fees	$	% fees
Gardening fees	$45,000	100.0	$50,000	100.0
Gardening expenses	17,400	38.7	20,500	41.0
Administrative expenses	2,000	4.4	2,500	5.0
Total expenses	19,400	43.1	23,000	46.0
Profit	$25,600	56.9	$27,000	54.0

Remember!

Do not draw conclusions from trends in the *percentages* without looking at the *dollar figures* as well.

- There has been a small decrease in the profit percentage due to increases in both of the expense percentages.

- The main increases were in the gardening expenses. Advertising increase by 50%, probably due to an attempt to increase business. The petrol and oil expense increased by 20%, possibly due to increased prices. Depreciation on equipment increased because another mower has been purchased.

- There was a higher level of dollar profit this year. The $1,400 increase in profit is positive, even though the profitability percentages have decreased.

- The financial performance of this business is quite satisfactory although the owner should monitor expenses to make sure they do not increase too much. If this happened, he would have to consider increasing his fees.

Analysing the Statement of Financial Position

The statement of financial position allows us to measure the liquidity and the financial structure of the business. The formulae for service firms are the same as for the trading firm that was covered earlier in the chapter.

Liquidity

There were two measures of liquidity: the current ratio and the liquid ratio. The formulae for the these ratios are:

Remember!

The current ratio shows how many $ of current assets will be available to meet each $ of current liabilities in the *next reporting period*.

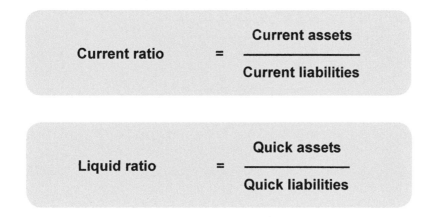

$$\text{Current ratio} = \frac{\text{Current assets}}{\text{Current liabilities}}$$

$$\text{Liquid ratio} = \frac{\text{Quick assets}}{\text{Quick liabilities}}$$

Remember!

The liquid ratio shows how many $ of cash or equivalents will be available to meet each $ of current liabilities in the *next month or so*.

The current ratio for *Greener Gardens* is calculated as follows:

		2017		2018
Current ratio	=	$\dfrac{\$3,500}{\$3,500}$	=	$\dfrac{\$7,000}{\$3,500}$
	=	1.0:1	=	2.0:1

This means that, in 2018, there will be $2.00 of current assets to cover each $1 of current liabilities due in the next reporting period. If we examine the statement of financial position of *Greener Gardens*, we see that the only current assets are cash and accounts receivable. The current liabilities are accounts payable and GST payable. The firm is a service organisation and therefore has no inventories. Since there is no bank overdraft either in this case, the liquid ratio is the same as the current ratio. This is quite common in service businesses.

Both ratios have increased from 1.0:1 to 2.0:1 between 2017 and 2018. This is a *favourable* trend. In 2017 the ratios were marginal at 1.00:1, meaning that if all the cash had not been collected from accounts receivable, the business may have had difficulty in meeting its debts on time. The ratio in 2018 means that the business has double the current assets needed to cover its current liabilities.

It is pleasing to see that the business is holding more cash and therefore has more liquidity. However, accounts receivable have increased by 20% ($2,500 in 2017 to $3,000 in 2018). This compares to an increase of only 11.1% in gardening fees. The owner will need to monitor his credit customers carefully and make sure that he collects the cash they owe.

Financial Stability

The financial stability of the business is measured by the **equity ratio**:

$$\textbf{Equity ratio} \ = \ \frac{\textbf{Equity}}{\textbf{Total assets}}$$

For *Greater Gardens*,

		2017		2018
Equity ratio	=	$\dfrac{\$18,000}{\$21,500}$	=	$\dfrac{\$20,000}{\$23,500}$
	=	0.84:1	=	0.85:1

The equity ratio in 2018 means that 85% of the business assets have been financed by the owner. This is a satisfactory position because there is little risk that creditors will demand repayment of their debts. The good liquidity ratios indicate that the business can easily pay its debts on time. The financial position of this business is very strong.

ISBN: 9780170211055

Activities

1 The following percentages have been calculated for *Independent Internet Solutions* which is an internet service provider:

	2012	2013	2014
Revenue from subscribers	$180,000	$200,000	$190,000
Profit %	40	35	40
Total expense %	60	65	60
Administrative expense %	15	15	20
Communication expense %	35	42	33
Finance cost %	10	8	7

a State which year the business earned the greatest profit.

b Suggest **one** possible reason for the trends in *each* of the following percentages:
  i Administrative expense percentage
  ii Communication expense percentage
  iii Finance cost percentage.

2 The following income statements were prepared for *Advanced Advertising* for the years ended 30 June 2017 and 2018:

Advanced Advertising
Income Statement for the year ended 30 June 2018

2017 $		$	$	$
	Revenue			
200,000	Fees			250,000
	Less: **Expenses**			
	Advertising expenses			
11,200	Advertising	30,000		
100,000	Salaries	119,500		
111,200			149,500	
	Administrative expenses			
2,200	Accountancy fees	2,500		
10,000	Depreciation on computers	12,000		
1,400	Electricity	1,500		
3,800	Insurance	4,000		
2,200	Rates	2,400		
5,200	Telephone and internet	5,600		
24,800			28,000	
	Finance costs			
10,000	Interest		12,500	
146,000	Total expenses			190,000
$54,000	Profit for the year			$60,000

ISBN: 9780170211055

The table below shows some percentages that can be calculated from this income statement.

	2017	2018	Satisfactory/ Unsatisfactory
Profit %	27.0%		
Total expense %	73.0%		
Advertising expense %	55.6%		
Administrative expense %	12.4%		
Finance cost %	5.0%		

DO THIS!

a Complete the table above.
b Choose **one** *satisfactory* trend from the table and explain why it is satisfactory.
c Choose **one** *unsatisfactory* trend from the table and explain why it is unsatisfactory.
d Suggest **one** reason for the trend in the finance cost percentage.
e State whether the profitability of the business is satisfactory or unsatisfactory. Explain your reasoning using the figures that you have calculated in the table.

3 The following information has been derived from the statements of financial position of *Supreme Surveyors* at 31 March 2018 and 2019:

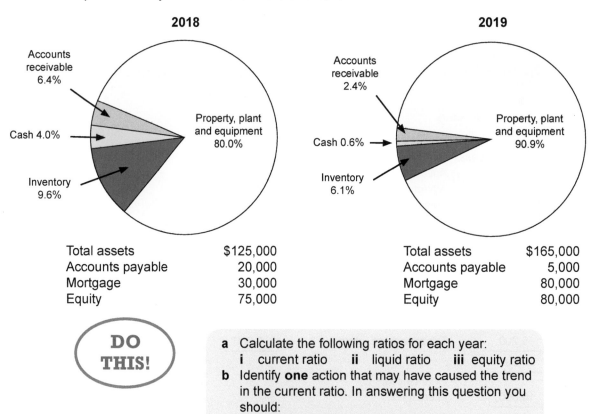

2018	
Total assets	$125,000
Accounts payable	20,000
Mortgage	30,000
Equity	75,000

2019	
Total assets	$165,000
Accounts payable	5,000
Mortgage	80,000
Equity	80,000

DO THIS!

a Calculate the following ratios for each year:
   i current ratio   **ii** liquid ratio   **iii** equity ratio
b Identify **one** action that may have caused the trend in the current ratio. In answering this question you should:
   i discuss the trend in the liquid ratio
   ii explain why the action was taken.
c Identify **one** action that may have caused the trend in the equity ratio.
d Fully justify whether or not you consider the action you identified in **c** was wise or not.

Accounting – A Beginning

ISBN: 9780170211055

Index

ISBN: 9780170211055

ISBN: 9780170211055